CONCEPT DEVELOPMENT IN THE
Secondary School

PETER LANGFORD

CROOM HELM
London • New York • Sydney

© 1987 Peter Langford
Croom Helm Ltd, Provident House, Burrell Row,
Beckenham, Kent, BR3 1AT

Croom Helm Australia, 44-50 Waterloo Road,
North Ryde, 2113, New South Wales

Published in the USA by
Croom Helm
in association with Methuen, Inc.
29 West 35th Street
New York, NY 10001

British Library Cataloguing in Publication Data

Langford, Peter
    Concept development in the secondary school.
    1. Educational psychology 2. Cognition
    in children 3. Education, Secondary
    I. Title
    370.15′2   LB1051
    ISBN 0-7099-4163-3

Library of Congress Cataloging-in-Publication Data
Langford, Peter.
    Concept development in the secondary school.

    "Published in the USA by Croom Helm in association
with Methuen, Inc." — T.p. verso.
    Bibliography: p.
    Includes index.
    1. Learning, Psychology of. 2. Concept learning.
3. Adolescent psychology. I. Title.
LB1062.L35   1987   370.15′2   87-15681
ISBN 0-7099-4163-3

Laser printing by Dead Set Publishing and Information Services Ltd,
169 Bourke Street, Melbourne, Australia
Printed and bound in Great Britain
by Billing & Sons Limited, Worcester.

CONTENTS

Chapter 1

INTRODUCTION

GENERAL ORIENTATION

The aim of this book is to introduce the secondary teacher to recent work in the area of cognitive development that is relevant to the interests of the classroom practitioner. The field of cognitive development is one that has changed quite considerably in recent years and it is as well to be aware of the general nature of these changes.

For many years the best-known work in the area was that of the Swiss psychologist Jean Piaget (1896-1980). From the publication of his first book, *The Language and Thought of the Child* in 1926, until his death in 1980, Piaget published over forty books and innumerable journal articles on cognitive development in children. His leading idea was that the child's thinking moves through stages of increasingly abstract concepts until it reaches adulthood. He outlined three main stages in development: the sensorimotor stage from 0 to about 2 years, during which the child's thinking is closely tied to practical activity; the stage of concrete operations, from about 2-11 years of age, during which children think about what is physically possible, such as adding together collections of objects or altering the world by moving things around, lifting them up, stretching them or otherwise subjecting them to transformation; and finally, the stage of formal operations from about 11 years onward, in which the adolescent learns to think about purely abstract entities like geometrical points and lines, to understand mathematical functions and how to control factors in an experimental situation.

Piaget also believed that children's thinking develops primarily as a result of their activity in the world: in making things, altering situations and transforming objects. It was partly as a result of this Piagetian emphasis on learning through doing that primary schools in the UK began to adopt 'activity methods' of teaching in the 1930s in which children were encouraged to explore the natural environment in a practical way, to undertake projects and to learn mathematics by using practical apparatus enabling them to count collections of objects and observe relationships between objects. In the 1950s and 1960s, this adoption of activity methods became widespread and also migrated into secondary schools, although even in the 1970s, surveys showed that many primary schools continued to emphasise paper-and-pencil activities rather than practical work and projects.[1]

Piaget's ideas were never without their critics within psychology and education. In the 1930s many of the criticisms aired in more recent years received publicity.[2] However, Piaget persisted with the main elements of his theory, though continually breaking new ground in his study of specific topics and the details of their treatment. In the 1960s his ideas received new popularity in both the UK and the USA. In academic psychology the 1950s produced the 'cognitive revolution'. Behaviouristic psychology's emphasis on 'rats and stats', the formation of habits and its neglect of thinking and higher mental processes began to be challenged. A professional joke of the time was 'First psychology lost its soul, then it lost its mind.' In this new climate, Piaget came to be seen as a kind of hero of the cognitive revolution, who had held out against behaviourism and accumulated a vast store of observations on children's thinking in real-life situations. This was at a time when American psychologists of the 1930s had sometimes appeared lost in the mazes along with their rats.

In education the 1960s saw two changes that helped Piaget's cause in that field as well. American education became concerned with the apparent technological lead held by the Russians in space research. It was felt that the education system should devote more of its time to developing the thinking, conceptual understanding and problem-solving skills needed by the scientist and engineer. At the same time the youth revolution and 'flower power' of the 1960s led many educators to search for a less rigid and formal view of learning than that which had hitherto dominated educational thinking. Again, Piaget seemed to have something to offer.

The three best known alternatives to Piaget within educational psychology in the 1960s, and still to some extent even today, were all Americans. During the 1950s and 1960s, Bruner, Gagné and Ausubel all proposed alternative views of how children learn. Of these, Bruner's views have declined in popularity in recent years, while considerable publicity has been given to both Gagné and Ausubel as promising alternatives to Piaget. For the present I will only comment on the relation between Piaget and Gagné. Ausubel's work will resurface continually throughout the book.

The idea of a hierarchy of skills is crucial to recent discussions of cognitive development. There are two kinds of hierarchy of skills, which we can call expression hierarchies and logical hierarchies. Reading, writing and drawing are examples of expression hierarchies as they involve low-level skills like handwriting, word recognition and skill with a pencil in the service of expressing high-level concepts or ideas. Logical hierarchies occur when there is a logical sequence of concepts within a curriculum area. We find, for instance, that in geometry, where the concept of a straight line logically precedes those of angles or triangles, we need the concept of straight line to define angles and triangles.

It is typical of the Piagetian approach to think that in expression hierarchies learning is top-down. If the child or adolescent gets their high-level general concepts sorted out, then the lower-level skills will automatically fall into place. The way to get the student to understand broad and general concepts is to encourage discovery of basic principles by exposing the learner to situations and materials that will allow them to discover such principles without much assistance from the teacher.

Piaget's contention in regard to logical hierarchies was that such orderings are an illusion produced by taking a logical rather than a psychological approach to development. In his view, the various concepts involved in a topic like arithmetic or geometry develop alongside one another rather than in a logical sequence, finally achieving logical rigour more or less simultaneously as a new intellectual structure is formed.

Gagné says that for both expression and logical hierarchies the child must begin at the bottom of the hierarchy with low-level skills and work up to more general levels of understanding. The way to do this is to place the child in a highly structured learning programme that teaches the skills to be acquired with a minimum of errors.

To give examples, in the area of writing the Piagetian educator will tend to say that we should concentrate on the topic of writing, say, pigs. Once the child knows all about pigs, their habits, intelligence, usefulness to human beings, food, etc., then an ability to write well about pigs will quickly follow. The Gagnéan teacher will say that we should first begin with the skill of letter formation, then practise writing in words, then sentences, and finally look at information about pigs to help us to write stories about them.

In a curriculum area like geometry, the Piagetian teacher will delay instruction until the structure of geometrical thinking has matured, which in the case of Euclidean geometry is not held to occur until early adolescence. The Gagnéan teacher will begin teaching simple concepts like straight line and angle much earlier and use these to gradually develop more advanced geometrical instruction.

The main message of more recent work and classroom experience has been as follows. Firstly, for expression hierarchies, there is no general prescription as to whether learning should be top-down or bottom-up. What the child needs to learn in order to develop a given cognitive skill will depend mainly on the levels at which they are weakest. This may differ from child to child and from area to area. In some areas it may be that most children need more help with low-level skills, in others they may need more help with high-level conceptual understanding.

3

For logical hierarchies we find that it tends to be true, as alleged by Gagné, that a strictly logical understanding of a topic does require an orderly development from basic concepts to those that are defined with them. However, it is both possible and desirable to provide intuitive and pictorial insights into a topic as a whole before proceeding with detailed logical development. In geometry, for instance, we might want to begin by showing examples of how relatively advanced Euclidean geometry can be used in such things as calculating the distance of the sun from the earth or the height of an unclimbable mountain before proceeding to detailed definitions and methods of proof.

Another finding is that there is no single prescription as to how best to learn a given cognitive skill. Children may benefit from exploration, discovery, hands-on experience or from being told, from a demonstration or a tightly sequenced programme to develop a specific skill. Most children seem to benefit most from a mixture of these methods. Some generalisations about learning are, however, possible. It is usually better to practise an expression skill like reading or writing as a meaningful whole, even though the student may initially be very weak in all aspects of the skill, than to break up the task into component subskills like handwriting or word recognition and practise these in isolation. However, a moderate amount of practice with component skills will be accepted by the student once they have realised where these skills fit into the overall skill of reading or writing. It is, on the other hand, desirable to sequence the curriculum in accordance with the logical sequence of concepts, particularly in science and mathematics.

It is always important to keep the student interested and mentally involved in the activity in question. It is important to ensure that the activity does actually practise the skills it claims to practise. Teachers should look very carefully at claims that practice in one area benefits skill in an apparently unrelated area. Direct practice of a skill is always better than transfer from another area.

DESCRIPTIVE CHANGES IN COGNITIVE ABILITIES

Piagetian theory was in some respects rather successful in suggesting the kinds of topics appropriate for primary-age children. Piaget called the period from roughly 7-11 years of age the 'substage of concrete operations', which is to say that it is a substage of the broader stage of concrete operations extending from about 2-11 years.

By this he meant that in the age range 7-11, children successfully understand the world in terms of operations they can actually perform on it. It is important here to avoid a misunderstanding that beginners often make in approaching Piagetian ideas. 'Concrete operations' does not mean simply understanding what does happen in the world. Even 4-5-year-old children enjoy stories about dwarfs and giants that they have never seen. They have seen things getting larger and smaller and they can imagine what people would be like if they got larger or smaller. Concrete operations means possible extensions of concrete experiences.

In some ways it would be more realistic to think of concrete operations in this sense as the period from 4-9 years. From 4 years children begin to understand things like arithmetic and logic from a concrete point of view. By 9 years there is already evidence that children can in some circumstances break away from physical reality in their mathematical thinking. Thus, Langford (1974) asked children to imagine the number 1, to add 1, then another 1 and so on. When asked, 'Would we ever have to stop?', a majority of 9-year-olds said 'No', showing that, unlike younger children, they can imagine going on forever, which is physically impossible, but is a concept used by mathematicians. Younger children tend to say 'You would have to stop for lunch', or even 'You would die'!

Given this slight downward revision in the age range, Piaget's idea that children in middle childhood conceive only physically possible operations on the world remains valid. His serious mistakes began when he tried to say (a) that there is a sudden overall shift in patterns of thinking at around age 7; and (b) that these patterns can be described by logically coherent systems called 'grouping structures'. These claims are not widely accepted today.

In addition to this general description of children's thinking from 4-9, we can also add three rather well-established principles that, other things being equal, will determine the difficulty of a concept for a child in this period. Rather than finding the sudden emergence of a whole bundle of concepts what we find instead is the gradual emergence of concepts in a fashion indicated by these principles. The first is that any problem or statement that involves a difficult constituent concept will be difficult.[3] Two examples of difficult constituent concepts are 'not', as in 'Ducks are not mammals', and 'includes', as in 'The class of herbivores includes the class of horses'. A statement involving both concepts, such as 'Cats are not herbivores', will be doubly difficult.

The second principle is that the more complex a statement is, the more difficult it will be to grasp or operate with.[4] Thus an arithmetical statement like $(2 + 3) \times (6 + 4)$ is more complex than 2×6. No one has ever satisfactorily defined this kind of complexity, but in an intuitive sense we know it when we see it.

The third principle is that any problem or statement that places a greater load on memory will be more difficult to deal with.

The upshot of these three principles acting together is that the development of thinking from 4-9 shows a gradual increase in the complexity and memory-taxing powers of the problems and ideas mastered and in the difficulty of constituent concepts that can be tackled. Even after 9 years, although the first truly 'abstract' ideas appear, many of the more complex and difficult principles governing the logic and mathematics of physically possible situations are still not grasped. The process of learning these goes on right through adolescence.

We also find that concrete statements like $2 + 3 = 3 + 2$ are understood before rules that apply to such statements, such as the commutative law of addition which says that for any numbers A and B, $A + B = B + A$.

In adolescence a number of logical and scientific abilities appear that are similar to those that have emerged in the primary years in that they refer to things that can exist or can be done. What separates this group of abilities from earlier ones is that they are more complex and they build on earlier achievements. In general logic it is not possible to separate out any one ability as a 'landmark' achievement; new forms of argument are continually being mastered all through early and middle adolescence (Ennis, 1976, 1982). In the area of scientific thinking one kind of ability does, however, stand out as it has such widespread application. This is the rule of 'all other things being equal', used to investigate situations where we want to know which of a number of different factors are involved in producing an effect (first studied by Inhelder and Piaget (1955)). An example of this would be to find out which factors influence petrol consumption in a car: size of engine, load, streamlining, state of tyres, average speed, etc. In using the rule of all other things being equal we assume that each factor will, if it has an influence, exert this influence alone or in combination with other influences (it acts 'independently'). To operate the rule we hold all factors but one constant and vary that one. If it influences the effect (e.g. change in size of engine influencing fuel consumption) then we know there is an influence that is due to that factor alone.

Apart from these logical abilities that seem to reflect mainly an increase in complexity, there are three aspects of adolescent thinking that can be said to represent something new. These three aspects are not known to be closely linked into anything resembling a Piagetian stage, but an awareness of them helps teachers form an overall idea of what to expect from their students.

The first aspect is the acceptance of ideal entities like geometrical points with no size, geometrical lines with no width, and ideal gases composed of particles with no size and a given mass. These ideas go beyond the limits of anything that is possible in the everyday world. As such their status is extremely problematic for young children, who think of lines as pencil lines and points as dots made with the pencil. There are three aspects of breaking away from this everyday notion. One is the recognition that processes like 'getting smaller' or 'halving' can go on forever. The idea that things can go on getting larger or doubling forever emerges around 9 years, but it is not until around 13 that halving is seen as a potentially indefinite process. The second aspect is to conceive of a 'something' with zero size or width. Finally, we have the even more difficult process of linking up the idea of indefinite halving with its mathematical limit, zero.

The second novel aspect of mathematical thinking that appears in adolescence is the idea of a function. If we have a variable y (e.g. a person's annual income) and another one x that is related to it (e.g. a person's taxable income, which is that income above the amount c which is the taxation threshold) then y = x + c for every taxpayer. In this situation, y is said to be a function of x because for every value of x, we can find out what y is by adding c. Very simple functions of this kind can be understood from 7 or 8 years of age and in this sense the origins of the function concept lie well before adolescence. However, even such an elementary function as y = x x c is not grasped by most children until around 11 years of age; thus instruction in any depth in functions must be delayed until adolescence. As functions get more and more complex they get more and more difficult to understand right up to undergraduate level and beyond. Gradual understanding of more complex functions is fundamental not only in secondary mathematics and physical sciences but also in economics and social sciences.

The third novelty about thinking in adolescence is that it becomes more systematic. Piaget thought that thinking was systematic right from the start, in the sense that all the implications of a logical or mathematical system were worked out by the child. Actually, in logic and mathematics, few adolescents, saving those exceptionally interested in mathematics, are interested in working out the implications of mathematical systems, although in late adolescence many do begin at least to understand that there are implications to be worked out. It is rather in the area of schematic organisation of knowledge that thinking becomes more systematic. Unfortunately there is very little research on this, but on an intuitive level, we know that young children's curiosity tends to be of the shotgun variety. They ask a myriad of unconnected questions and seem to have difficulty in relating the answers to one another. As children go up through primary school and on into secondary school they start to ask questions because 'something doesn't fit'. By the early secondary years teachers know that the brighter children will often keep them on their toes with searching questions about how new items of information or ideas relate to things they aleady know. An example of this from my own experience came when watching a student teacher introduce the topic of measurement in fractions to a junior secondary school class. 'Why do we have to do this when you can measure in decimals?', some students asked. When told that you can't express two-thirds of a centimetre in millimetres, one replied that you could use a micrometer (an instrument used by engineers for measuring thousandths of a centimetre). Here existing knowledge about measurement in decimals was being compared to knowledge about measurement in fractions.

The finding that cognitive development does not proceed in sudden leaps also has implications for the teacher. It means that we need in most cases to use methods that allow a student to find their own level rather than allotting them to a level of work on the basis of some rather general label like 'late concrete operations' or 'early formal operations'. Two ways of achieving this are to use an individualised programme in which the student works through workbooks and activities that are sequenced in order of difficulty and allow each student to find their own level; or by allowing for self-directed learning, as when students choose their own books to read or their own topics to write about.

THE PROBLEM OF WORKING MEMORY

We have already seen that one of the difficulties that children must overcome is that imposed by limited memory. All cognitive tasks require the child to hold a certain number of ideas or mental 'items' for a short time in 'working memory' while they are acted upon. This has caused a number of theorists to think that the main thing holding up the development of children's thinking is the limitations of this working memory. Examples of this can be found in Pascual-Leone (1971), Case (1979) and Halford and Wilson (1980). These three groups of authors have actually suggested that the working memory capacity of children could be used to provide a new kind of definition for stages in intellectual development to replace those of Piaget. Thus children at one stage would have a working memory capacity of two items, at the next stage of three items, and so forth.

There are, however, serious limitations to such approaches. To begin with, the general idea that working memory limitations are the chief thing holding up development is not inherently obvious; it is at the outset just as plausible to think that the problem of learning new ways of processing information—new recognition of concepts, new routines and new strategies—is just as great a source of difficulty for the child. Thus we would need some kind of empirical proof that it is actually the case that working memory problems are what holds the child up. While the authors mentioned above do try to provide such evidence, their critics have been less than totally convinced by the evidence offered.[5]

The difficulties are threefold. It is hard to arrange an independent assessment of the working memory capacity of a child as we never really know how long information must be stored in the child's mind during processing. We know that both adults and children can remember a lot more for only half a second than they can for, say, three seconds. Secondly, it is hard to know just how children chunk information while performing a task. If the child needs to remember the number 12, for instance, this might normally be two items; on the other hand, it might be the child's age or their birthday, in which case 12 will be chunked as 'my age' or 'my birthday'. As working memory load has to be defined in terms of number of chunks stored, this creates a further difficulty. Thirdly, there has been dispute about the actual strategies children use to perform the particular tasks studied when testing the models. It is, of course, likely that limitations on working memory play a partial role in restricting the abilities that young children can acquire, as suggested in the model of solving arithmetical problems proposed by Brainerd (1983). It seems, however, quite premature to conclude that this is the main difficulty restricting performance. If it is not the main difficulty then there is little point in trying to define stages of development using assessments of working memory.

HOW CHILDREN LEARN CONCEPTS

It is rather easy to see how children come by much of what they know: either they have seen it themselves, they have seen a picture of it, or they have heard about it. A child may know from its own experience that 'James is a friend of John's'; they may have seen a cartoon on TV and know that 'Tom is not a friend of Jerry's'; they may have heard the stories about Pooh Bear and know that 'Pooh is a friend of Piglet'.

Even this kind of knowing is not as simple as it appears. It would be much easier to judge that 'James is taller than John' than to judge that 'James is a friend of John's'. To judge that James is taller than John you just have to get them to stand next to one another. But simply seeing James in some kind of friendly social situation with John does not show they are really friends. The idea of friendship contains a notion of 'is regularly friendly with'. Even quite young children manage to make this kind of judgement. If we ask them 'Who is friends with whom?', they may say things like 'Mary is not friends with Jill today' or 'Peter is sort of friends with Dianne'. Similarly they know what it means to be a robber or a witch, to be grateful or careless, to be wobbly or in a hurry.

How do children pick up these rather subtle meanings without being told? Most psychologists now explain this as being through a kind of 'hypothesis evaluation'. On hearing mother tell them 'Now you are friends with Bill', the child automatically begins to think of some guess or hypothesis that will explain what this means. Suppose that the two children have just had a fight and made it up. This may lead to the idea that 'friends' means just having had a fight and being friendly again. But the next time the word 'friends' is used may be in the question 'Would you like to have your friends around today?'. This example will tell against the association with fights and perhaps encourage the child to think of friends as children who regularly come to play.

At one time it was popular to think that children are very efficient at evaluating hypotheses of this kind. Most recent research shows, however, that children of less than 11 years are generally rather inefficient in evaluating hypotheses.[6] In particular, if they come upon examples that disprove hypotheses they have formed to explain a situation, they often ignore these counterexamples and retain the original hypothesis. After enough counterexamples they abandon the hypothesis and move on to a better one, but they may need several experiences of disconfirmation to do this. For this reason we can explain much conceptual learning in primary age children as being due to the fact that correct guesses will, in the long run, usually be those that are most often called forth by a given situation. So in the case of learning the concept 'friends', the majority of situations in which this is used will be cases where friendly relations over a period of time are suggested. Situations where friends fight and make it up or where two friends happen to be wearing the same kind of jumper may appear occasionally and lead to temporary misconceptions. But in the long run, such ideas will drop out in favour of those suggested more frequently.

To give another example of this kind of learning more closely related to school work, we know that by about 7 years of age, most children know that for any two numbers A and B, the commutative law of addition holds such that $A + B$ is always equal to $B + A$. If a child sees that $2 + 3 = 3 + 2$ it may hazard a guess that 'It doesn't matter which order you add them in'. Alternatively, it may think 'If one lot of numbers begins with A and the other lot ends with A, then the two totals are the same.' The first idea will always be true, while the second will often be false and so will drop out. If, of course, a situation regularly suggests a misleading idea then this will also become firmly rooted. An example of this is that most children and adults will predict that if a stone is placed in a bath of mercury it will sink, though many stones will actually float. We have always experienced stones sinking in liquids and think this is always so.

After 11 years of age, adolescents are able to evaluate hypotheses more systematically, and once a counterexample comes up they can discard their incorrect hypothesis permanently.[7] However, both adolescents and adults operate for much of the time in a 'semi-automatic' state in which they generate hypotheses about situations but don't bother much about implementing strictly logical strategies for eliminating incorrect hypotheses. Thus, even as adults, many of our ideas continue to be those that have most frequently been suggested by a situation and the occasional counterexample is simply forgotten.

LEARNING IN THE SECONDARY CLASSROOM

In most areas of the secondary curriculum there are new high-level concepts that need to be developed. Some of the most important of these have already been described in the section on descriptive changes in thinking. One of the main dilemmas faced by the secondary teacher is that while many students do not spontaneously develop such concepts by the time they are needed, these have proved rather difficult to teach. Thus the temptation is always present either to delay teaching any topics involving difficult concepts or to teach students how to get the right answer or to function effectively in limited situations even though they don't understand what they are doing. It is idle to minimise the difficulty of tackling new concepts, but on occasions this is necessary and some general principles can assist.

Piagetian theory tended to make learning in adolescence rather different from that in primary school. Thus students who had reached 'formal operations' could, to some extent, dispense with practical activity as an aid to learning. Once practical operations had been internalised in the earlier period of concrete operations, further development consisted in 'reflective abstraction'; that is to say, thinking about thinking. At the same time it was fairly evident that such important aspects of 'formal operations' as the rule of 'all other things being equal' were essentially practical. In order to apply the rule of 'all other things being equal' you have to perform experiments. Certainly most 'Piagetian' secondary science programmes recommended undertaking actual experiments as the means for learning this and other rules about experimental design. On the other hand, when we deal with the various factors influencing an historical event like the French Revolution or World War I, we cannot rerun history with different weights attached to the factors operating. We have to be content with the mental experiment of asking what would happen if concessions had been given to the middle classes, or if Germany had successfully developed African colonies. Being 'practical' here may mean asking students to actively consider such possibilities and project their outcomes.

Another difficulty of applying Piagetian theory was that he was chiefly interested in the learning of abstract rules and a rather limited range of strategies. It would be misleading to apply ideas from these areas in a mechanical way to the learning of,for example, mental models or subject content.

The view of adolescent thinking taken by more recent work suggests that there is less fundamental difference between learning rules and strategies in adolescence and earlier learning. Even though in many cases we find that later rules incorporate entities established by earlier ones (e.g. algebraic letters refer to numbers), the more complex rules refer to aspects of the world that are simply not captured by the simpler rules. This necessitates a return to practical activity as an aid to learning. Thus the function $y = x + c$ as applied to taxable income (x) and total income (y) tells us something about the relation between all possible taxable incomes and all possible total incomes. Children begin to appreciate this kind of relation when they see a large number of examples demonstrating the relationship. In younger children we can relate the practical activity of counting to a single example of addition by counting all the pennies or cents they have, taking away, say, five and counting those remaining. Here the practical activity of counting is used to establish the numbers and subtraction is used to arrive at an answer. With adolescents we can usually dispense with the counting part and begin our practical activities with information already expressed in numbers or by means of other symbols.

When introducing a new principle or concept it often helps to bear in mind the cycle of learning activities developed by the American educationist Karplus. This involves the three phases 'exploration', 'concept introduction' and 'concept application'.[8] Thus 'exploration' might consist in a laboratory session where students are asked to investigate some phenomenon (e.g. weight of objects or types of flowers) using various measuring devices (if necessary) and some specimens they have collected. Hopefully this initial phase will stimulate interest and allow some conjectures to form in the child's mind. During 'concept introduction', a film or teacher demonstration is given in which, say, the concept of weight or a simple way of classifying flowers is given and explained. Finally, during 'concept application', the students are given a session in which they actually apply the concept or method to do something, such as measuring density or classifying some flowers. While it would be wrong to apply this learning cycle too rigidly it provides a good example of the application of learning theory in practice. While some commentators have seen Piagetian influences in the Karplus cycle, it is, like other activity methods, just as easily understood in terms of the hypothesis-formation view of learning.

Having now dealt with learning rules and principles, we can turn briefly to looking at strategies and mental models (or schemas). One course that probably contributes a lot to strategy learning is simply success rate. If a certain way of attacking a problem has been successful in the past, children will choose it again in the future. Seeing analogies between a familiar situation and an unknown one is also an important source of successful lines of attack.

A further source of strategies is obviously instruction; someone tells you the best way to approach a problem. As with other kinds of rules, practice in activities that involve use of a strategy is likely to be the most effective way to learn it. Also, because initial guesses about likely strategies are liable to be inaccurate and lead to inefficient learning, explicit instruction in good strategies is likely to yield dividends in students of all ages. Everyone knows that learning to solve mathematical problems, do crossword puzzles or play chess is made much easier if, instead of just jumping into the activity and relying on native wit, we try out a few problems (or a few games or puzzles) and then look at a book that gives instruction in strategy. Once again, Karplus's learning cycle is relevant here: exploration without instruction, followed by an enunciation of principles, followed by activities where the principles can be applied.

Finally, we can turn to learning schemas or mental models. In physics and chemistry we encourage students to form a mental picture of what various kinds of atoms and molecules 'look like' or to form a mental picture of magnetic lines of force or the direction of an electric current. In English we may hope that students will form a mental picture of the layout of the eponymous house in *Wuthering Heights* or of London at the time of Dickens. In history we may hope for a mental map of the Peninsula War or of a German battleship at the time of World War I.

Learning in such cases may proceed simply by the learner gradually receiving assorted pieces of information about the topic (e.g. visits to different places in a town or reading a book with pictures of battleships) and then at a certain point organising these into an overall picture (e.g. a mental map of the town or a mental picture of the ship). As these two examples illustrate, the items of information may come from direct experience or from reading or other ways of gathering information. A second style of learning involves helping the learner to form an overall picture by presenting a verbal or pictorial summary at the start of, or during, more detailed presentation of information or experience. Ausubel *et al.* (1978) argue that such 'organisers' of knowledge should generally precede instruction and a number of studies have reported that this is more successful than learning without organisers or learning when they are presented at the end of instruction. When a picture such as a map or diagram is used as an organiser it is usual to either keep the picture up during the whole presentation or to keep bringing it out at various points during the session.[9]

Another useful general principle is that schemas are more readily learned when they are actively used to direct practical activities and problem-solving. Such active use of the schema may take several forms. The first is simply its use to recall information from memory. Thus, having formed a mental picture of voyages of discovery, we might ask students to redescribe the voyages in their own words. A second use would be to set problems that require information that can be derived from the schema. Here we might ask the students to say what kinds of food they think the explorers could have obtained in the places at which they called, or how long each leg of the voyage took. A third way of manipulating the schema is rather more literal. Here we actually have students build a physical model of the schema, take one to pieces or redesign one that is made in modules. Examples of this are molecular models, drawing a map or picture, or building a working model.

Teachers and students make use of a variety of methods for picturing how knowledge is organised. Two common ones are flow diagrams that tell us 'what leads on to what', and hierarchical charts that tell us 'what belongs with what'. In considering the organisation of an industrial process or food chains in nature, a flow diagram will tell us such things as that the output of a coking furnace (coke) provides one of the inputs to a blast furnace, or that the nutrients synthesised by plants are incorporated into the animals that live on them. In attempting to organise the properties of objects or materials, a hierarchical or cross-classifying chart is often more useful. A well-known example of such a chart is the periodic table of the chemical elements, which groups together such elements as 'rare earth metals' or 'inert gases' and gives some explanation of why they have their own peculiar properties.

Novak and Gowin (1984) point out that students will often become more involved in organising schemas if they are encouraged to construct them for themselves. This can be done by either giving a presentation on a topic or having students read a passage about the topic and then asking them to identify the ten or twelve most basic concepts that they have encountered. Students then arrange their concepts into a hierarchy with the most general concepts at the top and the less general lower down. In a map of concepts related to 'feudalism', we might find 'The Monarch', 'Guilds' and 'The Church' at the top of the hierarchy, with groups of important nobles listed under The Monarch, different kinds of guilds under Guilds, and various church institutions listed under The Church. Relationships that do not follow a strictly hierarchical pattern can then be shown by diagonal lines with labels on them.

While concept 'mapping' of this kind is undoubtedly a helpful tool, it is only one way of encouraging students to actively organise their learning. Often specific subject areas have their own devices, such as making a model of an historical structure like a castle or a battle, simulation games, using apparatus to model the number system or model atoms to construct molecules. Anything that helps the learner to take an active part in constructing knowledge, and which also provides a memorable picture or model to help with memory, will be useful.

CONCLUSIONS

Piaget's descriptions of 'concrete operations' and 'formal operations' thinking are still of use for teachers provided we realise that development is not as neatly organised into stages as Piaget believed. On the other hand, his claim that development proceeds with sudden transitions between stages has been progressively eroded by more recent work.

There are two kinds of learning hierarchy: expression hierarchies used to express ideas and feelings, and logical hierarchies which structure the logical sequence of curriculum content. It has been common to counterpose the top-down view of learning expression hierarchies of Piaget with the bottom-up view of the construction of such hierarchies developed by Gagné. More recent thinking tends to emphasise that learning needs to concentrate on that level in the skill hierarchy that has been left the weakest by the child's previous experiences in a particular area. Thus it may be that for some students and topics more attention needs to be paid to high-level general concepts and principles, for others the problem may lie in the nitty gritty difficulties at the bottom of the hierarchy. The ordering imposed on the curriculum by the logical sequence of concepts is now believed to be of crucial importance in determining the sequence of instruction.

Piaget's view that 'real understanding' develops chiefly through practical activity, especially in the primary years, has given way to a more eclectic view of learning that emphasises a combination of practical activities, observation and instruction as the best route to effective learning.

FURTHER READING

On the deficiencies of Piaget's logic and his explanations of stages see Seltman and Seltman (1985). For alternative proposals about the development of logical competence, see Ennis (1976), Sternberg (1979), Langford (1981), Siegler (1981). On associationist views of learning, see Wilson (1980); on hypothesis evaluation in children see Ault (1977), Whiteley (1985). Expositions of Gagné's ideas and extensions of them appear in Gagné (1984), Fischer (1980) and Fischer and Pipp (1984). A convenient introduction to Ausubel is Ausubel *et al.* (1978). A useful survey of Piaget's ideas is still Piaget and Inhelder (1969). There are innumerable books explaining Piaget to the teacher, any of which can be useful.

NOTES

1. See Bennett (1977).
2. See later chapters this volume for details.
3. See Osherson (1974), Ennis (1976), Sternberg (1979), Langford (1981), Siegler (1981).
4. See 3 and Bullock *et al.* (1982), and Bullock (1985).
5. See, on Pascual-Leone, Trabasso and Foellinger (1978), Trabasso (1978), Kennedy (1983); on Halford and Wilson, Langford (1980, 1984); similar difficulties arise with the Case model. On the difficulty of equating short-term memory with working memory, see Brainerd and Kingma (1985).

6. The main exception to this is that on simplified tasks young children can be taught hypothesis testing in the laboratory (Spiker and Cantor, 1983); but it is doubtful that this occurs much in everyday life.

7. See Inhelder and Piaget (1955).

8. See Karplus (1980), pp. 161-9, Abraham and Renner (1986). Another approach to learning is that of Tennyson *et al.* (1981), McKinney *et al.* (1983) and Dunn (1983) which argues that presentation of a clear prototype (ideal example) is superior to either discovery or verbal explanation alone. It is unfortunate that they don't compare prototypes with discovery plus explanation, but the prototype method undoubtedly has its uses. Prototype learning should be clearly distinguished from schematic learning, something Norman (1980) fails to do.

9. For reviews see Lott (1983), Anderson and Armbruster (1984).

Chapter 2

ENGLISH

WRITING AND THE WRITING PROCESS

Process methods of teaching writing have become popular at all levels of schooling in recent years. The main features of such methods are to allow students to write rough drafts, to mull things over, to pick their own topics, to do a large portion of their own correction, to discuss their work in 'conferences' and to publish finished pieces to be read by other students. The chief rationale given for this is that it is the natural process of writing and follows the methods used by adult writers.[1]

Process writing has some clear advantages. It avoids the need for a lot of teacher correction, which is often discouraging for the student. It helps students to write about things they want to deal with and hence encourages them to feel there is some point in writing. On the other hand, the claim that process writing methods allow students to follow the methods of composition that are most 'natural' and are those used by adult writers, is often made in an exaggerated form. Adults tend to use first drafts and then redraft them when dealing with difficult and unfamiliar topics; in writing a letter or a journalistic article, many people write the piece straight out in finished form. In addition, some process writing approaches, particularly that of Elbow (1973), discourage the use of the method of starting with a plan.[2] Here again, on more familiar and easier topics many adults do begin with a written plan. On other occasions they will draw up a written plan to organise their piece before they begin the second draft. While we don't need to force students into beginning their first draft with a plan on every occasion, organising content is one of the major problems faced by writers at the secondary level. Writing out a plan at some point is a proven method of helping students organise their material.

Flower (1979) has pointed out that among adolescents and college students the most common form of inability to structure a piece is the tendency to produce a narrative of the writer's mental odyssey in encountering the topic at hand. The example she gives is of a student's account of a work experience project. The student begins the piece by describing in turn the first three meetings attended at Oskaloosa Brewing. The reader wades through the paragraphs on these meetings wondering what the problem is going to be and where the discussion is heading.

Narrative is one of the earliest forms of writing 'frame' and it remains one of the easiest to operate. Weak writers tend to give a narrative of their own mental processes. The main problem faced by such writers is to proceed from a first draft to an edited version in which organisation is in terms of ideas and argument. While Flower does not explicitly mention a written plan, she seems to imply that this will help in the first stage of editing. She says that the transformation to reader-based prose involves:

> selecting a focus of mutual interest to both reader and writer... moving from facts, scenarios and details to concepts ... transforming a narrative or textbook structure into a rhetorical structure built on the logical and hierarchical relationships between ideas and organized around the purpose of writing, rather than the writer's process. (p. 37)

Another aspect of the rationale given by both Wason (1970) and Elbow (1973) for separating initial drafts from later drafts in writing, is that this allows the writer to work out ideas before working out their expression. But like the rationale given earlier, this does not really justify that opposition to deliberate planning sometimes associated with process writing approaches. The occasions on which we really need to just write out an undigested 'stream of consciousness' as it occurs to us do, however, exist and can be divided into two. The first is when we have a 'writing block' and we just need to relax and get things flowing. Elbow in particular has specialised in this kind of problem. At the same time, we should beware of treating everyone as if they had writer's block; only a minority of students suffer from this to any serious extent.

The second kind of occasion students will need to begin with an unplanned outpouring is when they are quite unfamiliar with the topic or have not yet worked out their ideas about it. This is an experience we all have. We write out a first draft, leave it for a while, and on returning we see that it is a bit like a stew with a lot of unnecessary fluid (the 'padding') with a lot of things floating about in it (the 'good points'). The trick is to pour off the padding and to organise the floating lumps into some kind of whole. Often it is not until we can have a look at the individual good points that it occurs to us how to organise them. In our initial phase of thinking and research we were still too busy trying to distil information and experience into points. At this stage, we had no attention left over to organise the points into anything larger. In this sense, writing is a bit like doing a jigsaw; we need to fit several pieces of the same colour together before we see 'it's a shepherd', or 'it's a dog'. After that we think about where the shepherd and the dog belong in the overall picture.

This analysis shows that in a difficult piece of writing there are at least three phases.[3] At the start we try to establish the various points we want to make. Next we try to organise these into a whole and get rid of padding. Finally, we read the whole thing over for spelling, syntax and punctuation. In dealing with a topic we know well we can often short circuit the first phase as we already know what points we want to make and can get straight on to trying to organise them. However, in some cases, even when we already know the points, we need to get them down on paper and have a look at them before the organisation will occur to us.

A further suggestion made in some approaches to process writing is that students must always choose their own topics. Again, this derives little justification from adult writing as adults are often asked to write things at work with no choice of topic. Allowing choice of topic does often create greater student interest. However, the practice of leaving everything up to student choice has been repeatedly criticised in recent years as tending to erode general education in favour of fads and as tending to favour soft options at the expense of hard ones.

A final issue is whether something more specific than the advice 'find a plan' can be helpful in producing organisation. This topic can be conveniently approached in two parts: firstly, descriptive studies of children's reasoning abilities in English in secondary school; secondly, interventions to improve such abilities and organisation more generally.

One of the traditional aims of the English teacher has been to teach clearly written expression and argument. Two classic studies by Peel relate to this. Peel (1966) gave secondary students the following passage: 'Only brave pilots are allowed to fly over high mountains. This summer a fighter pilot flying over the Alps collided with an aerial cable railway, and cut a main cable causing some cars to fall to the glacier below. Several people were killed and many others had to spend the night suspended above the glacier.' The questions then asked were: 'Was the pilot a careful airman?' and 'Why do you think so?'

Peel analysed responses to these questions into three main categories:

a. Answers dominated by irrelevancy, tautology and inconsistency.
b. Answers based mainly on the main result of the action (cutting the cable).
c. Those in which extenuating circumstances were discussed (e.g. that the crash could have been due to mechanical failure or poor visibility).

He found that those responding at level (a) were on average about 10 years, those at level (b) about 12½ and those at level (c), about 13½ years. Two other passages dealing with the local impact of closure of a railway station and with damage to art treasures during a flood in Italy yielded similar results, though 11 and 12 year olds performed considerably better than in the earlier study (Peel, 1971).

Peel (1971, p. 34) points out that level (b) answers to the airman passage involve two distinct types of thinking. In (b)(i) the argument is, 'If he

19

crashed the plane, then he was not careful.' In (b)(ii), the argument is, 'If he had been careful he would not have crashed the plane.' In classical logic these arguments are called *modus ponens* and *modus tollens* respectively. Notice that if we accept the premise that (b)(i) is true, then it is quite proper to condemn the airman out of hand. The argument then runs: 'If he crashed the plane then he was not careful', 'He crashed the plane', therefore 'He was not careful'. This is impeccable logic; its weakness lies in accepting the fallacious initial premise. As adults, we realise that a plane crash could have several causes, only one of which is carelessness.[4]

These are two kinds of argument that students attempt to use; younger students failing in diverse ways. It would, however, be wrong to conclude from this that all we need to do is make sure students get clear in their minds about *modus ponens* and *modus tollens*. In reality there are a number of other commonly used forms of argument that students should be able to manage. Some of these are strictly logical, while others are what Aristotle called 'rhetorical' arguments, which make something plausible rather than certain. Most of the main forms of logical and rhetorical argument outlined by Aristotle are still in wide use (and abuse) in our everyday discussions. An interesting exercise, for instance, is to look at the forms of argument used by writers to the letters columns of newspapers. I have found that nearly all Aristotle's rhetorical forms of argument can be discovered both whole and mangled in this way.

To conclude, the forms of argument looked at in 'clear thinking' exercises by Peel (1966, 1971) are unnecessarily restricted and we need to both teach and research a fuller range of arguments for use by secondary students that differ widely in complexity and difficulty. This leads us to a fundamental problem. Do students learn more about correct forms of argument from solely engaging in argument and debate, or is there a role for the explicit teaching of forms of argument?

Traditional university education in Europe relied chiefly on Aristotle's correct forms of logical and rhetorical argument as methods for organising discourses. The rounded rhetorician would be a master of both areas, employing logic when the calibre of the audience and the difficulty of the topic permitted, sliding into the slightly suspect procedures of rhetoric when occasion demanded. Teaching of the Aristotelian forms of argument must have varied considerably over the years, but if students read Aristotle's *Logic* and *Rhetoric*, they were presented with general principles, usually but not always accompanied by examples. Thus in rhetoric the principle of argument by opposites says that 'The opposite of A is the opposite of B. Therefore A is B.' The example given is that 'Temperance is beneficial, because licentiousness is harmful.'

This kind of teaching of general principles of logic and rhetoric is exactly parallel to, if less common than, the teaching of explicit rules of grammar, which also come provided with examples. There seem to be no studies of its relative effectiveness as a means of promoting clear writing and thinking, which is a pity as it could be a very effective method, particularly in conjunction with plenty of opportunities for practice. Although there are no studies of how children cope with explicit presentations of logical principles at different ages, studies summarised in Ennis (1976) show that children in mid adolescence usually already know many of the figures of Aristotelian logic.

A second approach to rhetoric teaching, this time more in the mould of the empiricist school, is provided by Toulmin's widely read *The Uses of Argument* (1958). According to Toulmin, every correct argument has a layout that includes claims, data, warrants, backing, reservations and qualifiers. Here emphasis is not so much on particular logical moves as on the overall 'syntax' of the presentation of an argument. Again we are lacking convincing empirical studies on the effectiveness of such methods, but there is no reason to think that, if one accepts knowledge of this kind as valuable, adaptations of Toulmin's ideas such as that by D'Angelo (1975) would not teach it.

These examples illustrate quite well one kind of rhetoric teaching: the giving of principles, followed by examples and practice. The enterprising teacher could certainly vary this by allowing the students to first try to discover each principle from a number of examples before giving it. What distinguishes this kind of approach is that principles of clear thinking are made explicit at some point.

A third kind of rhetoric teaching, which includes both the Platonist and the New Rhetorical schools, is less concerned with making principles conscious and more concerned with trying to have students abide by them. The argument here, probably shared by many classroom teachers with no particular commitment to any formal rhetorical school, is that students learn by doing, not by talking about doing. Thus plenty of writing on self-chosen topics, classroom debates, specimen fallacious arguments to unravel, will put students on the right road.

Students in mid adolescence are becoming able to reflect on their own processes of logical thinking to a far greater degree than younger children. Thus it would be wrong to rule out the possibility that deliberate, explicit presentation of rules of argument can assist students. Students may waste a lot of time discovering in an unconscious manner principles that could be put under their noses for conscious inspection. Whether this method, implemented under good conditions of student motivation and interest, is in fact better, is a matter that is at present far from any empirical resolution.[5]

AUDIENCES AND CODING

While this topic is quite separate from that of organising structure in the primary school, by the secondary years the two things tend to merge. This is largely because most of the low-level problems about writing for an audience have been solved. Thus typical difficulties of the primary years such as saying 'the' for 'a' and not knowing when it is appropriate to use slang or begin a letter 'Dear Sir', have either disappeared or can be settled fairly quickly. As Flower (1979) has pointed out, the chief remaining difficulty is to shift from essays organised according to the mental processes of the writer, to those organised according to the requirements of the reader.[6] This usually means taking the various points made by the writer out of the order in which they occurred to the writer and putting them into some kind of logical organisation. It also means obeying such rhetorical injunctions as that which says you must first introduce your subject and orient the reader. Another common problem is to get away from purely narrative organisation towards logical organisation.

At the same time the ability to write for a particular kind of audience develops. Kroll (1985) found that when asked to rewrite a story for a young reader, students in grades 5 and 7 tend to just simplify the vocabulary, while older students try to simplify the underlying gist and story structure.[7]

Garner (1985) looked at undergraduates writing a piece designed to persuade a particular individual on a particular topic. The individual was a middle-aged man whom the students had seen interviewed on film. He was interviewed on the topic of the advisability of raising the minimum driving age from 18 to 21 and students were asked to write him a paper designed to help him make up his mind. Two examples of the productions of non-proficient and proficient writers were as follows:

Non-proficient writer:

> The law should not be changed for many reasons. One reason is if the age was raised it would be unfair for those who were 19 already. Another reason is in the constitution a person is an adult at 18. My final reason . . .

Proficient writer:

> I would certainly like to discuss some of the things you stated in your interview . . . In answering one of the questions you stated that it might be a feasible idea to keep the age lowered to give adults a chance to show their trust in youth. I agree with this, yet I realise that the young people might take advantage of this "gift".
>
> I couldn't agree with you more when you say that people grow up a lot from eighteen to twenty-one. I know it's true, but I also feel that some people are responsible enough to drink at eighteen and other people are too irresponsible to drink at twenty-one. Those three years make more of a difference for some people than for others, and raising the legal age to twenty-one would still leave too many irresponsible drunk drivers on the highways.

These pieces differ in at least two ways. In the first there is no mention of the opinions of the person who is being written to, although these were clearly stated in the interview and the student had a transcript of this in front of them. The second piece, on the other hand, mentions what the person being addressed has said and either agrees, disagrees or tries to qualify it. The other difference is that the first piece contains much shorter and simpler sentences. These two aspects are related: the second writer several times contrasts their own views with those of the audience in the same sentence.

Garner suggests that one important reason why the non-proficient writers failed to mention the opinions of the reader was that the non-proficient writer is too taken up with the mechanics of low-level skills like spelling and syntax to have enough attention left over to attend to the interests of the reader. Another likely reason is that the poor writer probably has more difficulty with the high-level problem of constructing an argument about the topic and this, too, may distract attention from problems connected with the audience. While in the two cases quoted both writers are having difficulty with their arguments, the second writer fails in developing more subtle and qualified arguments, while the first writer manages to be illogical even in developing a simple argument.

This suggests that the poor writer needs to try to separate out the tasks involved in writing into a number of distinct components, so that attention can be given to each component separately. A process writing approach that separates initial drafting designed to clarify the main argument from later drafts designed to package the argument for the reader and then still further drafts designed to fix up the syntax and spelling should help here, though unfortunately, poor writers often need the most encouragement to separate out their drafting processes.

Another topic that has been of interest is the intended audience of students' writing. Britton *et al.* (1975) found that in the first year of secondary schooling, writings were almost equally divided between 'teacher-learner dialogue' and 'pupil-examiner', with a slight preponderance of the former. Teacher-learner dialogue is a more informal style of writing, where the writer asks as well as gives information. By the sixth year of secondary schooling, less than one-quarter was teacher-learner dialogue, while nearly three-quarters was addressed to an examiner-type audience.[8] These authors also found a steady decline in writing designed to work through personal experience during the secondary school years. This was replaced by information-conveying and theoretical writing.

It has been common to decry these trends as showing the increasingly impersonal nature of the school and its expectations and its increasing emphasis on scientific training as opposed to personal development. However, whether this is really reprehensible depends very much on one's view of the function of education in industrial societies. In some ways these trends are inevitable within such societies and when 'too little' emphasis is given to the impersonal and the scientific, we find the schooling system being widely condemned as promoting self-indulgence and failing to meet the needs of a technological society. An example of this kind of problem has been that in schools where students do not face internal exams in the early secondary years they face an unpleasant shock and often failure when they encounter external exams in the senior forms. Abolishing external exams has its attractions but leads to difficulties in comparing standards and even in having standards at all.

METAPHOR AND SIMILE

Until the mid 1970s Piaget's (1926) study of metaphor in children exerted an overwhelming influence on thinking in this area. In this study he asked children to match proverbs with one of several statements as to their meaning. He concluded that it is not until about 11 years that children have much success with this. However, more recent studies have considerably modified this conclusion.

Even before recent experimental studies began to modify this conclusion, one piece of evidence in particular made it perplexing: preschool children often use vivid metaphors and similes in their speech. This raises the possibility that young children may understand metaphor but not be able to translate this understanding into an alternative or even recognise an alternative translation when they see one. Another difficulty with Piaget's (1926) study was that it used some rather complex proverbs in which the intended analogy seems remote, even to adults. An example of this was the proverb, 'White dust never comes out of a coal sack'.

Four different kinds of tests for metaphoric understanding can be considered: production (Does the child use metaphors in speech or writing?); preference (What kind of metaphors does the child prefer?); comprehension (Are metaphors understood?); and explanation (Can the child explain what they mean?).

A number of studies of children's production of metaphor in their written schoolwork as well as in experimental tasks showed a complex pattern of trends.[9] Although third graders (8 year olds) could often use metaphor correctly, in Pollio and Pollio's (1974) study, older children in high socio-economic area schools decreased their initially high use of figurative language with age, while those in low socio-economic area schools increased their initially low use with age. Pollio and Pollio noted that this effect was greatest for tasks similar to those given marks in school, while high socio-economic area children continued to increase their use of figurative language with age in a task not associated with the receipt of marks. From this they concluded that hesitancy about language that might receive an adverse grading was influencing them. On a slightly more optimistic note, Schonberg (1974) found that, even in high socio-economic area secondary schools, use of figurative language in school-like work increased again after 11, perhaps because students now felt more confident about the kind of figurative language likely to please the teacher.

In a study of children's preferences as to figurative language, Gardner *et al.* (1975) found preschoolers had little preference. Seven year olds preferred literal responses, 11 year olds conventional responses, and 14 and 19 year olds conventional and appropriate responses. Examples of these response types were illustrated by the following suggestions for completion of 'His voice was as quiet as . . .':

a. 'the quietest sound we've heard' (literal);
b. 'a mouse sitting in a room' (conventional because of the standard simile 'as quiet as a mouse');
c. 'dawn in a ghost town' (appropriate and, like all choices in this category, non-literal); and
d. 'a family going on a trip' (inappropriate).

It is a matter of common observation that preschool children often show a marvellously imaginative use of language that declines after they go to school. Gardner *et al.* (1975) believed they were measuring the effects of social expectation on children's preferences. The younger child was relatively uninhibited in choice of comparison, while the preference for literal comparisons in the 7 year old may well stem from a desire not to appear 'silly' by making a far-fetched comparison that could be ridiculed by peers or teachers. The taste for an appropriate but still imaginative category of comparison in the older children may reflect an increasing confidence in selecting comparisons that are impressive but not silly.

Turning to a study of comprehension, Pollio and Pollio (1979) asked children to match paraphrases to an original figurative example chosen from examples generated by children. They found that among primary school children understanding improved grade by grade, and that novel comparisons were harder than conventional ones that might already be known.[10]

Perhaps the most ambitious study of the growth of figurative language has been that of Pollio and Pickens (1980). These authors looked at all four kinds of ability using tests of production, preference, comprehension and explanation with children from grades 3-11. Results showed that some kind of crucial change in the pattern of results seemed to occur around grade 6 (about age 11 years). Production of conventional comparisons reached a low point here and then began to climb again; on the other hand, novel comparisons were preferred to routine ones below grade 6, but routine to novel after. In addition, correlations between tasks were much higher up to and including grade 6 than thereafter. That is to say, a primary age student who did well on one test tended to do well on others, but this was much less true of older students.

Pollio and Pickens (1980) suggest that it is forced to interpret this crucial change at grade 6 as the onset of Piagetian 'formal operations'. The change occurs at around the right time for this, but the nature of the changes tells against this explanation. It seems most likely, as the authors suggest, that the third of these changes originated from the general tendency, noted by earlier writers, for abilities to become more specific and less intercorrelated during adolescence.[11] The first two effects are disconcertingly difficult to relate to the changes in attitude described earlier. The production task involved something like written schoolwork and thus we might have expected the use of conventional comparisons to increase throughout the child's school career, or for conventional comparisons to drop off in secondary school as confidence with novel comparisons increased. Instead, novel comparisons show a slight but persistent decrease throughout the school years while conventional comparisons decline to grade 6 and revive thereafter. One explanation for this might be that between grades 3 and 6 children increasingly find that they are mishandling even conventional comparisons and thus drop them until a point is reached where they are more adept in their use. The switch in preference from novel to routine at around grade 6 would fit in with this suggestion. However, as the composition writing 'production' task may have been seen as either more or less like schoolwork than the preference test, this is a fairly ad hoc speculation.

The studies discussed in this section show that developmental trends in figurative language are too complex to be understood simply as the gradual acquisition of cognitive capacities. We find rather the interaction of the influence of social acceptability with the use of maturing cognitive abilities.[12]

READING STRATEGIES

A number of strategies are commonly suggested by teachers as likely to help students organise, understand and remember what they read. Four common ones are taking notes, summarising, underlining significant sentences or phrases, and asking questions about the passage. These strategies may be built into the textbook, which gives notes at the end of the chapter, gives a summary before or after a chapter, underlines or italicises important points or lists questions at the end of the chapter. On other occasions the teacher may offer sheets showing these things or, with the exception of the last (questioning), the students may be encouraged to do these themselves.

Although many of the studies of these activities have been on college students, the results are probably valid for the secondary years. As all these strategies encourage active organisation of a schema or knowledge core to represent and remember the information in the passage, we might expect all of them to improve learning. Cook and Mayer (1983) report that this is so.[13] While there are few direct comparisons of active, student-implemented strategies as opposed to ready-made notes or underlining in the text, it has generally been found that the former is superior to the latter. This is particularly true for underlining and reflects the fact that individual methods of approaching understanding and forming a schema for a passage vary widely. Actively generating summaries or notes also helps to activate a search for the underlying gist of the passage and to relate this to the individual's past experience.

Another way to encourage an active search for understanding among students is to try to teach them to implement such strategies for themselves while they read, either without or in addition to the methods described above. Survey, Question, Read, Recite, Review (SQ3R) is one such method originally reported by Robinson (1961). During the survey stage readers skim through the chapter title, subheadings and summaries to find out what the chapter is about before they start. They then restate major subheadings as questions. Thus 'Causes of the Revolutionary War' becomes 'What were the causes of the Revolutionary War?' In the third step students read minor subheadings (if any) and try to formulate answers to the questions produced in the previous phase. Thus, if the first subheading is 'Economic Conditions', students try to think what economic conditions might have been and how they might have produced the revolutionary war. In the rather misleadingly named recite phase, readers flesh out their answers to the questions by actually reading the relevant passage. During the review stage they try to recall the entire chapter, pausing at each subheading to recall as much as possible about that section.

SQ3R provides one way of attempting to get novice readers to do what expert readers do. Naturally, once novices have got used to the idea of using headings and posing questions they should be encouraged to realise that expert readers use this kind of strategy more frequently when they already know something about the topic. When the topic is quite novel it may be necessary to just plough through the passage. On the other hand, when expert readers read to extract information on topics they know well, they generally use the contents or index to target key passages and only read these thoroughly. Expert readers also often skim the first couple of pages to try to recognise the author's overall line or to assess the level of competence of the work. At the same time, if you are trying to read a novel for enjoyment, there isn't much point in targeting the crux of the plot or the pages where it tells you who dunnit. In reading novels many people read more slowly and try to build up an imaginary picture of the characters and the scenes as they go along, whereas in reading for information the abstract meaning is more important.

As Cook and Mayer (1983) point out, SQ3R is an appealing procedure and it encourages students to take an active attitude to reading. However, empirical support for its effectiveness is thin and some studies have reported student unwillingness to try it. Both these things may stem from the rigidity of the procedure, which fails to take account of the reader's particular needs at the time of reading.

Directed Reading and Thinking Activity (DRTA) is a somewhat more flexible method (Stauffer, 1975). In the first step students read the title and first paragraph of the passage and are then asked to predict what the passage is about. In the reading stage they read the passage to see if their predictions are right. In the final 'proving' stage they are asked to give reasons (out loud or on paper) as to why their predictions were right or wrong. Evaluations of this method show generally positive findings in terms of organisation, comprehension and recall and it can be applied as early as the upper grades of the primary school.

Re Quest also allows for considerable flexibility in approach (Manzo, 1969). Here, student and teacher read a passage silently and then take turns asking one another questions about it. While evaluations have yielded positive initial findings, this method would have to be considerably adapted for classroom use. Teachers often have students discuss passages in pairs or small groups that are asked to assemble their main conclusions or questions arising from the passage. This obviously allows for much more efficient use of the teacher's time.

In practice most teachers use a mixture of the various techniques described above, as well as such activities as showing a schematic diagram before or after the passage, showing a film, video or slides to stimulate interest in and provide an alternative organisation of the material and having students read two conflicting views of the same topic. While these latter techniques have not been investigated empirically, anything that stimulates an active effort to ask key questions, draw inferences and construct a schematic interpretation of a passage will almost undoubtedly help the reader.

CONCLUSIONS

Process writing approaches, while they have many advantages, have sometimes shown an exaggerated faith in spontaneity in writing. In particular, their occasional advice not to encourage the use of a plan either at the start of the first or of the second or subsequent draft, is questionable. More specific instruction in the construction and presentation of arguments has had a long history. Although this seems likely to improve written organisation on general theoretical grounds, there are as yet no empirical studies to demonstrate this.

Concern has sometimes been expressed about the tendency for students to increasingly address examiner-type audiences as they proceed through secondary school, but abolishing assessment (and thus the examiner role) remains a Utopian hope which could lead to undesirable side effects.

Use and understanding of various types of metaphors show a complex pattern of development throughout both the primary and secondary years. The most plausible means of explaining this pattern lies in assuming that metaphor use is strongly influenced by the expected reactions of teachers and other audiences, and in particular the desire not to make 'silly' comparisons. It is always galling for the secondary teacher to find that many students become more inhibited in the early secondary years and this can affect both the imaginative quality of their ideas as well as use of metaphors. Before we conclude that the answer to this is simply to allow more uninhibited expression, two important countervailing arguments should be noted. Firstly, the individual teacher will be relatively powerless to influence the desire to appear 'grown up' and to avoid ridicule that stems not only from other teachers, but also from parents, peer group and the media. Secondly, while imagination is an appealing quality in young children, if childishness persists into adolescence in other areas it can be less than appealing when manifested as dependence, intellectual immaturity or uncontrolled aggression. Only a small minority of adolescents will manage to retain the imaginativeness found in many (though not all) young children while becoming mature in other ways and we don't at present understand how this occurs.

A variety of techniques is available to encourage students to adopt active reading strategies, including taking notes, summarising, underlining significant sentences, asking questions, diagrams, audio-visual material, presentation of contradictory arguments on the same topic, group discussion. It is likely that all of these techniques can assist students in an active search for meaning.

FURTHER READING

On the writing process Elbow (1973, 1981) should be read critically; more satisfactory accounts are Flower (1979), Flower and Hayes (1981b), Flower *et al.* (1986), while Bereiter and Scardamalia (1982) is a useful additional source; on writing for audiences see Flower (1979) and Collins and Williamson (1981); on the use of metaphor see Pollio and Pickens (1980); on reading strategies see Cook and Mayer (1983) and Brown *et al.* (1984).

NOTES

1. For a useful contrast between 'romantic' versions of the process approach and classical rhetorical approaches, see Duffy (1982).
2. Bereiter and Scardamalia (1982) are also critical of process approaches for this reason, though their prescriptions for success are a little different from those suggested here. Murray (1978), often identified with 'process writing', is favourable to students beginning with a plan, while even Elbow (1981) admits its usefulness at second draft stage. Sommers (1980) found that proficient writers at college level were distinguished from poor writers by their tendency to revise at the overall plan level.
3. See Flower and Hayes (1981b).
4. Actually *modus tollens* was probably rather more difficult than claimed by Peel as he made the mistake of describing his (b) (ii) responses as involving correct use of this.
5. Some rhetorical approaches go further than just helping the student to organise known material and try to teach inquiry into the content of the discourse (Larson, 1968; Young *et al.*, 1970). Studies of the effectiveness of teaching heuristic inquiry principles have yielded somewhat equivocal results, though there is no reason to doubt the possibility of teaching such principles. See Odell (1974), Young and Koen (1973), Burns (1980), Dutch (1980), Ebbert (1980).
6. For other studies of writing for audiences see Moffatt (1968), Greenfield (1972), Shaughnessey (1977), Olson (1977), Hirsch (1977), Smith (1977), Kroll (1978), Collins (1979), and Collins and Williamson (1981).
7. See also Monahan (1984).
8. See also Tamburrini *et al.* (1984).
9. In addition to those mentioned below, see Pollio (1973).
10. See also Winner *et al.* (1976).
11. See Asch (1936), Anastasi (1958).
12. Studies by Billow (1975), Cometa and Eson (1978) and Smith (1976) have claimed support for Piagetian theory, but the indices of 'concrete operations' thinking used in the first two are so restricted that it is hard to interpret the results. Smith's (1976) findings are contradicted by those of Winner *et al.* (1976) and an easy resolution is not apparent. See also Ortony (1984).
13. See also Brown *et al.* (1984), Tierney and Cunningham (1984).

Chapter 3

SOCIAL SCIENCE SUBJECTS

SOCIAL COGNITION

The area of social cognition has become fashionable in developmental psychology in the past decade. Whereas in previous decades the study of the growth of concepts about the physical world tended to take the limelight, to some extent this imbalance has been redressed in recent years. In the process a number of issues have been raised about how children's understanding of other people and social institutions might differ from their understanding of the physical world.

Much of children's understanding of social institutions involves understanding the rules governing these institutions. From this point of view, understanding the social world is similar to understanding the physical world. The main problem is whether the mechanisms by which social rules are learned are parallel to or diverge from those by which physical rules are learned. There are a number of reasons to think that divergence might occur here. In interacting with other people, from quite an early age children are aware that other people have emotions like their own. Although objects in the physical world are often endowed with consciousness by very young children, by 5 years this has declined considerably. If we compare learning the conservation of number with learning the exchange of commodities of equal value, obvious differences appear. Assuming that one major source of information about numbers is counting, a child may believe two collections are unequal in number, count them and then find them to be equal. This information comes out 'coldly' from the result of a physical operation. On the other hand, once a child has reached the age at which some competence in handling shopping transactions is expected, say about 7 years, then the discovery that the child has not offered enough money for an intended purchase is likely to be corrected with an air of disappointment by the shopkeeper and possibly some explanation of why it is 'unfair' to offer less than the marked price for the item.

This illustrates two dimensions of difference between physical and social rules. People, unlike physical bodies, express their emotions on their faces and explain their reasons for obeying rules in words. It also suggests two further dimensions; social rules can be altered and they can be broken. It is unlikely that the conventional and mutable nature of social rules in the wider society is understood by children until adolescence (Piaget, 1972). Even young children, however, understand quite well that social rules can be broken, both by others and by themselves.

At first the breaking of social rules is thought of purely in terms of factual conformity. If a child breaks a cup accidentally, this is as bad as breaking one deliberately. At around 7 or 8 years of age children, however, come to view intent as the vital ingredient in social behaviour, as do most written systems of law (Piaget, 1965). If a cup is broken accidentally this is less serious than deliberate breaking. This notion of intent is closely connected to that feature of human activity which Kant considered separated the human social world from the physical world—freedom of choice. When human beings abide by social rules we often consider that a deliberate choice has been made, unlike a physical body, which is thought to have no choice in obeying physical laws.

A further area in which we might look for differences between physical and social cognition is in the logical structure of thought. Some Marxists have claimed that drawing close parallels between physical and social logic reflects the bourgeois tendency to interpret the social world as if people were things (Lenin, 1961; Trotsky, 1966). Their answer to this is to recommend the use of dialectical thinking in political thought in particular. There are several ways to construe this. One, which seems to have been the view of both Lenin and Trotsky, is to argue that dialectical thinking is a kind of superordinate thought that does not cancel out 'formal' logic and mathematics but provides a means of seeing their products as a whole and of applying them more effectively to the real world. To give an example, some traditional Marxists have argued that the falling rate of profit within capitalism will eventually lead to the collapse of the system. Capitalism as a system functions according to laws of economics that suggest a considerable area of similarity with the physical world; just as the adding up and subtraction of numbers is governed by the laws of arithmetic, so is the adding up and subtraction of amounts of money or the prices of goods. At a certain point, however, this order may break down, producing a dialectical leap. One does not have to be a Marxist to see the utility of this. In one of the few existing studies on the topic, I found that in thinking about development children can co-ordinate the idea of change in quantity leading to qualitative change from about 5 years (Langford, 1975). What remains much less clear is the age at which social systems can be viewed in this way, though common experience would suggest mid adolescence as the appropriate time.

A second way of thinking about dialectics in social life is to give more priority to human freedom, as for instance attempted by Sartre in his *Critique of Dialectical Reason*. Here it is not simply the rules of the system that change but also their inner meaning, which Sartre interprets chiefly in terms of their tendency to signal 'being' (existence as a physical object, at its height under passive obedience to rules and authority) or 'nothingness' (existence as a spontaneous consciousness).

Another related argument has been canvassed in relation to the relevance of dialectics for social thinking in children. This is that human subjectivity makes necessary the use of dialectical thinking in dealing with both the physical and the social world because all knowledge is inherently subjective (Riegel, 1973; Buck-Morss, 1975). While this is an interesting argument in general, its proponents have, in my view, so far failed to show what it means concretely in the study of children's thinking.

We could go on expanding this list of ways of looking at dialectics and the differences between human life and inanimate objects until we arrived at a complete textbook on social theory. This highlights one serious problem in dealing with children's thinking about society; they grow up to think about society in very different ways. In addition, many of us probably have a rather incoherent view of society that tacks together a variety of somewhat divergent models. Actually this does not clearly separate thinking about society from thinking about the physical world, as recent studies have shown that both adolescents and adults tend to think about physics in this way. The problem is, however, more acute in thinking about the social world as there is a wider variety of models accepted as valid by adult 'experts'. In addition, models of society may well express ideologies; that is social and personal interests justified by systems of ideas.

Recent work on the development of social thinking has taken these points into account and we are beginning to understand something about how divergent ideas about society emerge in adolescence. At the same time it is relevant to ask how the most fundamental underlying concepts about society develop, out of which we build our divergent views of society.

To summarise our discussion so far: five areas of difference between concepts of the social and concepts of the physical world have emerged.

1. Obedience to social rules as well as their violation are accompanied by various kinds of feelings and the belief that the rules have an inner meaning.
2. Obedience to social rules and their violation may be accompanied by intellectual explanations about their origins and purpose.
3. Social rules can be violated, either deliberately or by accident.
4. Social rules can be changed either by common agreement or by slower, less deliberate means.

5. Social rules might obey a different underlying logic to that of the physical world. I have already expressed skepticism about the last point, except insofar as social rules are subject to sudden changes.

I now propose to review the writings of five well-known writers on social cognition to see what light they shed on these and other areas of potential divergence. These writers are, in order of treatment, L. Kohlberg, E. Turiel, D. Elkind, R. Selman and H. Furth.

Kohlberg has reported a number of studies of how children respond to moral dilemmas.[1] One example of such a dilemma runs as follows:

> In Europe, a woman was near death from cancer. One drug might save her; a form of radium that a druggist in the same town had recently discovered. The druggist was charging £2,000, ten times what the drug cost him to make. The sick woman's husband, Heinz, went to everyone he knew to borrow the money, but he could only get together about half of what it cost . . . The husband got desperate and broke into the man's store to steal the drug for his wife. Should the husband have done that? Why?

Kohlberg divides children's answers to such dilemmas into three levels, which he believes represent sequential levels in development. Each level is divided into two stages, giving six stages in all. In his more recent writing he has recognised that it is misleading to speak of a child or adolescent being 'at' a single one of these stages. Rather, most children show responses at a number of different levels and stages, and we can obtain our overall picture of their moral thinking by looking at the percentages of answers at different stages.

Kohlberg (1984) describes each stage as containing three aspects: a view of what is right, a view of reasons for doing right, and a social perspective. At stage 1 (heteronomous morality) the child thinks it is right to avoid breaking rules backed by punishment because this avoids punishment and considers the point of view of only one social actor. At stage 2 (instrumental exchange) the child thinks it is right to follow rules that create a fair deal for those directly involved because this allows conflicts of interest to be resolved and is aware that conflicting interests exist. At stage 3 (mutual interpersonal expectations) it is right to act out one's social role (son, brother, friend, etc.) in a friendly and co-operative manner because it is desirable to be seen by others as a good son, brother or friend, and is aware of shared feelings and obligations as a result of the ability to imagine him or herself in another person's shoes. At stage 4 (social system and conscience) it is right to fulfil one's agreed obligations and to obey the law because this keeps society going as a whole, and the adolescent can now separate the welfare of society from that of groups and individuals within it. At stage 5 (social contract or utility) it is right to uphold contracts and laws because these ensure the welfare of all and it is realised that the individual has values and rights prior to social attachments and contracts, and that conflicts between the rights of the individual and the welfare of all can usually (but not always) be resolved by impartiality and due process. At stage 6 (universal ethical principles) it is right to follow ethical principles chosen by the individual because there is belief in personal commitment to moral principles and it is understood that just laws and contracts may be justified by such principles and believed that people are ends in themselves and must be treated as such.

We can illustrate these stages in the three areas of political, economic and legal thinking. In stages 3 and 4, predominant in the junior secondary school, politics is thought of primarily in terms of the need to play out one's role in the political system and to avoid social dislocation. There is, however, a realisation that the interests of different social groups may conflict, as for instance in the conflict between capital and labour, or between development interests and conservation groups. When it comes to resolving such political conflicts the younger adolescent will tend, particularly at stage 4, to appeal to the need to reach some kind of compromise so the system will work. Thus capitalists shouldn't drive down wages so far that workers will revolt; on the other hand, workers shouldn't ask for so much that they send enterprises bankrupt. How far the adolescent is able to explore more sophisticated versions of this argument will depend upon their background knowledge. In the senior secondary school we will find more adult-like versions of the social order argument appearing, such as the Keynesian argument that if capital drives down wages too far the wages of the workers will fail to create sufficient demand for goods and production will fall, more workers will be laid off and a vicious cycle will set in. On the other hand, the conservative argument that excessive wage increases lead to a fall in profits and thus a drop in investment also begins to be appreciated. Notice that in Kohlberg's scheme it is not the sophistication of the argument that counts but rather the underlying moral rationale behind it. Thus if the adolescent bases his or her argument on the idea of not disrupting social functioning, both the Keynesian and much simpler ideas about political compromise will be judged as belonging to stage 4. At stage 5, on the other hand, such arguments, whether naive or more sophisticated, will be backed by the idea that changes should be made in the political balance and the political system to promote various kinds of human rights, such as the right to work or the right to the means of subsistence or the greatest happiness of the greatest number. At the same time such stage 5 arguments lead on more easily to suggestions for radical social reform rather than the somewhat bland tinkering of stages 3 and 4.

In economic thinking ideas about the justice of existing economic arrangements exert considerable influence upon adolescents' thinking about economics. At stages 3 and 4 people like shopkeepers, workers and employers should live up to the obligations of their roles. At the same time, economic fairness still tends to be judged according to the standard of reciprocity previously established at stage 2. According to this, people should act in face-to-face exchanges so that everyone gets an equal share of resources; if people put something into the system they should get the same amount back. Of course these ideas will sometimes conflict with one another. Thinking based on reciprocity seems to emerge chiefly from the 'children's economy', where fair exchange during swaps is the rule, and when someone gives to their friends they expect to get something back. Economic thinking based on reciprocity leads to the ideas that prices added on by wholesalers and the payment of interest are immoral and should be abolished. Both these are examples where the middleman appears to do no directly productive work and is thus condemned. The more abstract idea that such local injustices must be tolerated for the sake of promoting the welfare of the social system as a whole is rejected, probably because of the difficulty of conceiving the many operations and effects that go to make up the economic system as a whole. In the senior secondary school more abstract arguments of this kind begin to be appreciated.

Legal thinking in the junior secondary school tends to assume that we should obey existing laws against theft and murder as well as more controversial laws against such things as euthanasia and smoking marijuana, simply because 'that is the law'. Accidental actions are, however, accepted as less worthy of punishment than deliberate flouting of the law and mitigating circumstances will sometimes be taken into account in considering an appropriate sentence for a crime. When laws conflict with social duty, as in the case of Heinz stealing the drug to save his wife, younger adolescents understand that there is a conflict to be resolved, but they will tend, particularly at stage 4, to do so by arguing that we ought not to disrupt the smooth running of society. This may either take the form of an argument that we should uphold the law in case it falls into disrepute and society breaks down through lawlessness, or the form of an argument that husbands must look after their wives to protect the family as an institution. At stage 5, on the other hand, the argument that we should act to benefit the greatest number comes into play. This may conclude that the benefit to Heinz's wife and to Heinz outweighs the injury to the owner of the store and the damage to the law. On the other hand, it may be argued that Heinz and his wife must be sacrificed because the injury that will follow a lessening of respect for the law is more widespread and in the long run will harm more people. There is also greater willingness to conclude that crimes without a victim, like homosexuality and smoking marijuana, should be decriminalised (though, of course, arguments that in some crimes of this type there really are victims will continue to play a large role).

Kohlberg thinks that the child learns about social rules chiefly through an interest in social roles. The child is, as a child, asked to behave in certain ways. One very large class of social rules sets out how people in a given role should behave rather than how people in general should behave. Kohlberg is not particularly interested in whether or not children understand a given rule, such as 'Children are not allowed to run in the corridor'. He assumes that they have already mastered this. What he wants to know is how they understand the wider significance of such rules, particularly when they come into conflict with one another, as when 'Husbands should care for their wives' conflicts with 'Thou shalt not steal'. His series of levels relates to the understanding of such conflicts, rather than to the rules themselves. As such, it is based on one of the five peculiarities of social rules discussed earlier, namely that social rules can be broken. When two physical principles interact, the net result can always ultimately be checked by observation. When two social rules conflict, different people will make different adjudications and do different things. Kohlberg (1969) argues that it is primarily through 'role-taking opportunities' that children come to develop points of view regarding the 'right' thing to do in cases of conflict. By, for instance, being allowed to consider what mother should do when something has been broken, the child learns that there is a wider question at issue than just staying out of trouble: that issue concerns the overall well-being of the family and the well-being of all its members. Such consideration will lead the child from Level 1 reasoning to Level 2 reasoning.

Rest (1979, Ch. 7) has summarised a variety of other factors that might promote moral development: discussion; exposure to higher-level thinking; internal contradictions in one's viewpoint; new real-life responsibilities; making decisions about one's life; experience of tragedy and of evil; meeting people with a very different viewpoint. In reviewing the many studies of attempts to produce changes in children's and adolescents' moral reasoning he concludes that there is some evidence for the influence of all these factors.[2] A number of studies have also shown that a certain level of conceptual development is often necessary for transition to a new level of moral thinking.

Three questions are worth pursuing in relation to Kohlberg's ideas. The first relates to the issue of explanations given by adults. While role-taking surely plays some part in this process, mustn't the type of explanation offered for social rules also play some part? While Kohlberg (1969, p. 400) is able to point to a number of studies showing that opportunities for role-taking within families are positively correlated with moral development, opportunities for role-taking are probably strongly confounded with amount of explanation.[3]

A related aspect of the influence of explanation is raised by the allegation that Kohlberg has tried to place some views of morality held by perfectly respectable philosophers on a lower level than his own Kantian belief in absolute moral principles. The widely-held theory of utilitarianism, which holds we should act to promote the greatest good for the greatest number, is for instance placed at Kohlberg's stage 5.[4]

Kohlberg (1984) has finally succumbed to criticism on this point and admits that none of the longitudinal studies of moral development into adulthood reported in the literature have identified individuals whose moral reasoning is primarily at this level. He also admits that the few case studies of individuals who do seem to have attained this stage were of people with considerable training in and commitment to particular systems of moral belief that emphasise moral principle (p. 270). Kohlberg now says that stage 6 is a purely theoretical construction and not a description of a final stage of moral development reached by an appreciable fraction of the population, as claimed earlier.

A second issue concerns the relation of Kohlberg's notions to the Freudian concept of identification and to notions of defence mechanism generally. While this issue lies rather beyond the scope of the present treatment, it is worth pointing out that Kohlberg (1969) puts emphasis on the purely cognitive side of moral development, explicitly rejecting the idea of neo-Freudian writers that the internalisation of sexual and power relations with the parents may decisively affect later political and social beliefs.[5]

A third issue, more directly relevant to our present concerns, is as to the stage-like qualities of Kohlberg's levels and sub-levels. Kohlberg (1969) calls each of the sub-levels a 'stage' and claims that children must pass through each stage in turn. This sequence of stages has been somewhat altered in more recent years; its most recent variant appearing in Kohlberg (1984). The broad description of stages has not, however, altered radically, although the details of the scoring procedures have been somewhat refined. Longitudinal studies attempting to investigate the sequential nature of the stages, as well as cross-sectional studies investigating their Guttman scalability (a statistical method of investigating stage-like sequences), have generally provided positive results.[6]

In the course of these investigations, particularly those of Kohlberg and Kramer (1969) and Kohlberg (1974), it was, however, discovered that among college students one often finds an apparent regression from predominantly stage 4 or stage 5 responding to stage 2 (maximising of personal pleasure). Kohlberg and Kramer (1969) argued that this might be due to the temporary release from social constraints and the 'psychosocial moratorium' provided by the college environment. In nearly all cases this was later followed by a return to stage 4 or 5 responding. Kohlberg (1974) decided to dub this 'outsider' and 'beyond society' viewpoint 'stage 4½', claiming it was not a true regression, but rather a step on the way to stage 5, resulting from the college students' initial inability to formulate general moral principles.

Turiel (1977, 1978) has argued that Kohlberg's work concentrates too exclusively on moral rules, neglecting that game rules and certain kinds of conventional social behaviour may be viewed in a different light. His terminology here is, in my view, a little confusing as he refers to laws against stealing as 'moral rules', while Kohlberg would call a 'moral principle' something designed to justify such a law, such as the view that laws against stealing benefit the majority. Perhaps the term 'legal rules' would cause less confusion here. Whatever the terminology, Turiel (1977) found that 6 year olds are able to distinguish legal, conventional and game rules and that they understandably regard conventional and game rules as more alterable than legal rules.[7] This is a significant setback for Kohlberg's view that moral development occurs in a strongly unified manner. Apparently the idea that social arrangements can be altered takes root initially in those areas where the child actually sees rules being altered, in games and social conventions, only later spreading to general legal rules. Turiel has distinguished seven levels of thinking about conventional- social issues, such as sex-appropriate behaviour or table manners, and these are claimed to form a developmental sequence.[8] There are approximate parallels with Kohlberg's levels of moral reasoning. Thus at level 4 (about 12-13 years) conventions are considered as nothing but social expectations (comparable to Kohlberg's stage 3); at level 6 (about 17-18 years) they are considered as expressions of the expectations of society (comparable to Kohlberg's stage 4). By this time it seems that conventional thinking is actually lagging behind the corresponding moral and legal ideas.

Elkind has proposed that adolescent social cognition rests chiefly on residual forms of egocentrism found at this stage of intellectual development.[9] Particularly notable are emphasis on an imaginary audience, personal uniqueness, indestructibility and the power of ideal social arrangements to right the wrongs of the world; the latter being a feature emphasised by Piaget (1967).

The imaginary audience is thought to pay great attention to the actions and personal appearance of the adolescent: adolescents often believe they are unique people, with a unique mission; they believe that car accidents, drug addiction, alcoholism or marriage break-up won't happen to them. Both common experience and a number of empirical studies can be cited in support of these characteristics.[10]

In comparing this tradition of research with that of Kohlberg, it appears that Elkind's imaginary audience would parallel Kohlberg's stage 3 'good boy-nice girl' orientation, while belief in the power of ideal social arrangements to right the wrongs of the world would be more typical of Kohlberg's stages 5 and 6 involving ideal moral principles.

Selman has proposed a series of stages in the development of social role-taking.[11] Such role-taking is considered by Kohlberg (1969) to lie behind the process of transition between stages in moral development, but

Kohlberg considers only its effects in the moral sphere rather than the process itself. By asking children about social dilemmas as opposed to moral dilemmas, Selman has been able to study role-taking directly. An example of such a dilemma is: 'Eight-year-old Tom is trying to decide what to buy his friend Mike for his birthday party . . . Mike is extremely upset because his dog Pepper has been lost for two weeks . . . He (Mike) tells Tom, "I miss Pepper so much I never want to look at another dog again".' The child is asked to express an opinion about Tom's dilemma. Selman concludes that there exists a sequence of five stages in the predominant type of response to such problems. At stage 0 the child is unable to adopt another person's social perspective (predominant from age 3-6). At stage 1 children can adopt another person's perspective, but are often unsuccessful in doing so. Conflict resolution is of an all-or-nothing variety. An aggrieved party should either 'go away' or 'go and hit him' (predominant from age 5-9). At stage 2 the pre-adolescent achieves greater facility in taking the social viewpoint of another. Conflict resolution is by co-operation (predominant from 9-12). At stage 3 the adolescent develops a conception of a 'generalised other person'. Previously the child considered the social viewpoints of others one at a time, placing himself or herself in the place of each participant sequentially. Now this leads on to considering what an average group member might think about things. Conflict resolution takes account of the long-term features of relationships (predominant age 10-15). At stage 4 the views of average group members are co-ordinated to produce the viewpoint of the overall social system. It is considered that others can and should also adopt this viewpoint. The idea of social arrangements being based on a social contract takes root. (This stage begins to emerge after age 15, but is not attained by all adults.)

Byrne (1974) has investigated the relation between stages in the development of logical thinking and those in the development of Selman's role-taking and Kohlberg's moral judgement. He found that individual children may reach a level in logical thinking without attaining the corresponding role-taking and moral judgement levels.[12] A similar relation between logical thinking and moral judgement has also been found by other investigators.[13]

Furth et al. (1976) and Furth (1980) have outlined a series of general 'stages' in the development of social thinking based on interviews with children from 5-11 years of age. The most complete account of their work appears in Furth (1980). Their interviews covered the concepts of community, roles, money, shops, change, school, government and local council, and personal relations at home. They outline a number of general criteria for their four stages as follows:

Stage I
'Children fail to recognize the basic functions of money and confuse personal and societal roles, neither of which they understand. In contact with societal events they either do not see a need for explanation of what they observe or, when they do, they associate personal experiences in playful elaborations, largely unconstrained by logical or functional exigencies. The dominant context in which they think about social events, personal or societal, is their own psychological reactions.'

Stage II
'Children understand the basic function of money as a special instrument of exchange in transactions they observe, but not much more beyond that. In familiar instances they distinguish realistically the acquisition of a societal from a personal role. Their images beyond the experienced social events, lacking an interpretive system, are playful and person-centered. The images engender in children's minds a static social order, thereby avoiding possible cognitive conflict that eventually leads to Stage III.'

Stage III
'Children construct functional part-systems, through which they interpret societal events beyond first-order observations. These differ from the playful images of Stage II in being "functional", i.e., adapted to the actual societal system. However, the systems are incomplete, hence, "part-systems" and thereby lead invariably to cognitive conflict of which the children may be more or less aware. This is another contrast with Stage II thinking where conflict is largely absent. They understand qualitatively—not quantitatively—the mechanism of buying and selling and of a paid job.'

Stage IV
'Children understand the basic mechanism of monetary transactions and can move from personal possession of money to its wider societal use. They recognise the money base of societal roles, including the function of the government. They take into account individual differences between people and differences in societal roles according to context and need of the community. Generally, they appreciate differences in scale between personal and societal events. The children have eliminated the major inconsistencies and conflicts found in Stage III and the playful images of earlier stages. Nevertheless, their understanding of the political system and governmental functions is still quite vague and their thinking about the general needs of a societal community, its historical traditions and cultural symbols is concrete and therefore unsystematic and principally on an affective-emotional level.'

Furth (1980) does not claim these stages are strictly sequential, but only that children are more likely to give answers classified as belonging to a higher stage as they get older (p. 51). Even this claim must, however, be qualified by his criteria for assigning answers to stages. For it was not these, rather vague, definitions that were chiefly used to assign children to stages, but much more specific aspects of children's economic thinking.

While the general stage descriptions given by Furth (1980) have some intuitive appeal, anyone who has tried to categorise interviews with children will recognise that the descriptions are really too vague for effective use. This, no doubt, was part of the reason he fell back on the money-related criteria, which were much sharper. Our appreciation of his work must therefore be tempered by this methodological qualification.

ECONOMIC CONCEPTS

Much of the research on the development of economic concepts relates to the elementary understanding of buying goods in shops and the payment of wages for work. Difficulty in understanding these ideas is largely overcome by the end of the primary years, but it will be of interest to begin with a summary of this work.

Strauss (1952) asked children a large number of questions related to the purchase of goods in shops, employment and investment. From scale analysis of the answers, nine stages in the development of understanding were distinguished. In the first two stages (up to about 6 years) children see purchase in shops as a ritual in which the customer gives coins and the shopkeeper offers both goods and change, but the quantitative relations between the amounts of these are not understood. At stages 3 and 4 (up to about 8 years) glimmerings of an understanding of these relations appear, as well as the realisation that shopkeepers are in business to make money. At stage 5 (up to about 8½ years) children understand that the amount paid by the customer less purchase price gives the amount of change, but do not yet understand how the shopkeeper makes money. At stage 6 (up to about 9 years) children understand that the shopkeeper can make money by paying shop assistants less than the total takings, but do not know of the difference between wholesale and retail price. Credit is beginning to be understood by some children, which is of importance as it represents a decline in the ritual understanding of trade, which concentrates on who does what when, and an increase in understanding that transactions are governed by arithmetical logic. At stages 7 and 8 (up to about 10 years) children come to realise that shopkeepers buy goods for less than they sell them, though initially this realisation is impeded by the idea that to do this would be morally wrong. At stage 9 (up to about 11 years) the existence of short changing by shopkeepers is admitted. Strauss comments that even at this age children tend to reject the role of middlemen, such as wholesalers, in the distribution process, on the grounds that it doesn't make any sense.

Danziger (1958) used a more flexible clinical interview approach and distinguished four stages in the development of early economic understanding, generally parallel to those found by Furth (1980) for general social understanding. Like Strauss (1952) he was struck by the fact that understanding of processes involved in production, such as investment and profit, lagged considerably behind the understanding of the exchange processes visible in shop transactions, presumably because children have little experience in the former.[14]

We now turn to studies involving older children. Jahoda (1981) interviewed children of 12, 14 and 16 years about shop transactions and the function of banks. He found a number of response types; the more advanced becoming more common in the older children. The most elementary was an absence of knowledge about interest evidenced by the claim that you always get back or pay back the original amount lent or borrowed without interest. In the next category interest is on deposits only. This of course potentially leads to the question of who provides the money for this interest as it is not paid by the borrower. In the next category interest is paid on both loan and deposit but more on deposit. In the next interest is the same on deposits and loans. Finally, it is appreciated that interest is greater for loans.

At age 16 over one-third of middle-class and one-half of working-class students had failed to reach this final level. However, Jahoda found that by presenting students with the contradictions inherent in their viewpoint, one-third of those who had not already achieved full understanding were in this way enabled to do so.

Since the early investigations of Strauss, students of economic understanding have been struck by the extent to which children's and adolescents' moral conceptions interact with economic understanding. Cummings and Taebel (1978) have interviewed American children and adolescents on three topics in the political and moral aspects of economic understanding: trade unions, private ownership and state intervention in the economy. In third grade (about 8 years) most reactions to trade unions were neutral or non-evaluative, while by twelfth grade (about 17 years) 60 per cent of replies were negative, crystallising around the idea that trade unions are too big, too powerful and jeopardise social stability. Most third graders (8 year olds) were neutral about private ownership of the means of production, while by twelfth grade (17 year olds) 64 per cent were positive. Sixth graders knew little about the differences between private enterprise, socialism and communism, while by ninth grade (about 14 years) explicit but stereotyped differences were perceived. It was realised that private enterprise means private ownership of the means of production and communism means state ownership of the means of production. There was also thought to be a lack of civil liberties and poor productivity under the latter. Under socialism and communism, according to a typical ninth grader, a person 'can't do what he wants to do, so they don't work so hard; if you can't do anything you want to do you aren't going to work much.' Twelfth grade respondents often appeared to confuse communism as state ownership of the means of production with egalitarian or equal sharing of resources.

Third graders viewed government in a remarkably positive light, with 67 per cent of respondents being favourable to a high level of government intervention in the economy, perhaps because the state is seen as a kind of glorified parent. 'The government has factories and machines that make money, and they keep it in a secret place' was one comment. By twelfth grade the percentage in favour of strong government involvement in the economy had declined to 31 per cent, though only 41 per cent were negative to this. The rationale given by ninth and twelfth graders for negative views was largely that state intervention stifles the incentive to produce.

Cummings and Taebel (1978) interpret their findings as showing the success of American schools, families and media in socialising children into beliefs and attitudes favourable to the prevailing economic arrangements in America. This was perhaps predictable, even though a sample spread across occupational groupings was used. Studies in other countries would no doubt reveal a different pattern of beliefs.

Leahy (1983a,b) found that there were some class differences in the social outlook of American adolescents and that beliefs sometimes followed a contradictory developmental course. Thus upper middle-class children and adolescents were more likely to explain inequalities in wealth as being due to lack of industry by the poor than those from other social strata. Between 6 and 11 years acquisition of wealth was increasingly explained as a joint product of education, intelligence and hard work. However, after 11 years, work was judged as of increasingly less importance as age increased, perhaps because those among their peers destined to do well in school now appeared a relatively fixed group. Ways of eliminating poverty in society suggested by adolescents increasingly relied on changes in the social structure designed to provide a fair reward for effort, though even at 17 years less than one-third of respondents thought complete elimination possible.

A study by Sosin and McConnell (1979) found that among American college students the negative attitudes to equality of income distribution reported among high school students was partially reversed by a first semester course in introductory economics. Although there was no control group and these results might partially reflect the generalised liberalism of undergraduate students, the magnitude of shift was positively related to course grade, implying that the course directly influenced conceptions of the unemployed and welfare recipients.

Perhaps the most relevant study for the secondary economics teacher has been that of Schug (1980, 1983). Basing himself on an influential American curriculum guide for economics teaching (Hansen *et al.*, 1977) he investigated understanding of seven basic economic concepts: economic wants, limited income, choice, opportunity cost, monetary value, and two items on the price mechanism. Replies to the interview questions were coded as unreflective (based on the physical characteristics of commodities and economic actors, consideration of the interests of only one actor or group, and confusion between cause and effect), transitional and reflective (use of abstract ideas, adjudication of conflicts of interest and correct analysis of cause and effect). Price mechanism, choice, opportunity cost and limited income were understood by a majority of students by grade 9 (about 14 years); the remaining concepts were only grasped by a minority by this level.

Four of the items deserve special consideration: the two on price mechanism and those on economic wants and monetary value. The two, easier, items on price mechanism involved the manufacture of a good (yoyos). One question asked what would happen to the price of yoyos if the factory made fewer yoyos due to shortage of yoyo string; another asked what would happen if competing factories were opened up. The harder economic wants questions asked the students to name several items they wanted to buy and then went on to ask questions attempting to elicit the notion that as economic wants are satisfied, new wants appear, leading to the infinite extension of wants. While ninth grade students tended to score poorly on this item, success at a 'reflective' level required an abstract exposition of the infinite nature of economic wants or some other indication of abstract thinking. The idea that we all desire particular goods and services that are delivered in exchange for money appeared to be present even at the 'unreflective' level. A similar point can be made about monetary value. Here 'transitional' responses usually involved the belief that 'money was valuable because it was functional and could be used to purchase desired goods and services' (Schug, 1980). A reflective score, on the other hand, mentioned either that 'the mint makes it', that tradition sanctioned it or there was a social contract to agree upon its use. Thus in most respects the transitional form of reasoning would suffice as a basis for an introductory economics course. In summary, Schug's study is notable for its investigation of the economic concepts taught in introductory economics, but he rather exaggerates the extent to which ninth grade students (14 year olds) have difficulty with basic ideas.

POLITICAL UNDERSTANDING

Like economic thinking, political understanding is strongly influenced by moral beliefs and emotional factors. Topics such as the influence of parental and peer beliefs and attitudes on later political stance and voting preference have been extensively studied under the rubric 'political socialisation'.[15] It would be impractical to cover this enormous literature here. It is, however, perhaps relevant to mention that both the political credos of parents and peers can be shown to have considerable influence on the professed sympathies of children and adolescents, but it is widely believed that the link between parental beliefs and later voting patterns has weakened in most Western countries in recent decades.

This section will concentrate on more narrowly conceptual understanding and capabilities. In this area, four large-scale studies are of particular importance and will be described in what follows.

Hess and Torney (1967) found that young American children in grade 2 (about 7 years) tend to think of political groups and doctrines such as nations, political parties and systems like democracy and communism, as good or bad, without any real understanding of what these groups or systems are or how they work. Only later do they gradually acquire greater conceptual understanding of such issues.

Hess and Torney distinguish three phases in the development of the understanding of nations. In the first stage there is a strongly emotional attachment to national symbols such as the American flag and the Statue of Liberty, accompanied by considerable denigration of other nations on the grounds that they are inferior in nearly every department of practical activity. In the second phase, beginning roughly from grade 5 (about 10 years), ideological superiority begins to be the basis for national pride; 'freedom' and 'the right to vote' are seen as making America superior to other countries, rather than the possession of better cars and toys. In the third phase, whose onset is not clearly defined by the authors, but which seems to follow rapidly on the second phase, children come to understand that their own country forms part of an international system of nations. Thus among younger children most think the United States does the most to preserve world peace, while among secondary school children most think it is the United Nations, rising to 87 per cent at grade 8 (13 years).

The second and third grade child's understanding of government is largely confined to knowing who is in government. The government is a man who lives in Washington (the President) and the Congress is a lot of men who help him. At this age such information is, in addition, often wrong. Insofar as young children know about the functions of government, they again tend to think of individuals as exercising these functions. Thus in second grade 76 per cent thought the President made laws and 5 per cent the Congress. By eighth grade 85 per cent chose Congress and only 5 per cent the President. When asked 'Who does the most to run the country?', 86 per cent of grade twos thought the President. By grade 8 (about 13 years) this has fallen to 58 per cent, while 35 per cent now think Congress. Among teachers 61 per cent think it is Congress. As children grow into adolescence they shift from a primarily person- and particularly President-centered view of government to understanding that government involves institutions with rules. Thus children now say 'The government is made up of representatives that the people elect', or 'The government is just an organisation that the people formed to rule themselves'.

Children's understanding of strategies for influencing government also improves with age. Children were asked to agree or disagree with various definitions of democracy. At grade 4 only 40 per cent agreed to 'All grown-ups can vote', while by grade 8 this rose to 75 per cent. Agreement with 'You can say things against the government' rose from 15 per cent to 55 per cent in this period, with 'The people rule' rising from 26 per cent to 76 per cent. Throughout this period the President was ranked as the most important person in deciding which laws were made, followed by labour unions. 'The average person', however, rose from least important (from eight possibilities) to third most important. As children grow older they think that the average voter should become informed about political issues so as to exercise their vote wisely, but they remain sceptical as to the level of interest the average voter has in becoming informed. More than half of the sample agreed that 'Politics are interesting, but not as interesting as sports or dancing for most people'. Scepticism about the personal qualities of candidates for election to government also increased from grade 4 to grade 8, with estimates of candidates' honesty, ability to keep promises, unselfishness and intelligence all declining!

Young children's view of election campaigns tends to minimise the element of conflict, with children in grade 3 largely thinking that the 1960 Presidential race between Kennedy and Nixon was free from personal abuse or even conflict. While this conflict is more readily admitted by older children, they also have a greater tendency to think that after an election campaign candidates should bury the hatchet and work together amicably, 75 per cent of grade 8 children favouring this outcome.

While an understanding of what political parties stand for develops later, attitudes towards them begin early. While many grade 3 children will already support a political party, it is not until grade 8 that the Republican Party begins to be seen as helping the rich and the Democratic Party as helping the unemployed and 'protecting citizens' rights'. Even at this age (about 13 years) the percentage who perceive such differences has not nearly approached the adult level for the first two issues (helping the rich versus helping the unemployed).

Connell (1971) agrees with Hess and Torney in finding that the earliest political conceptions among Australian children involve persons rather than institutions: in this case the people are the British Queen and the Australian Prime Minister. Around 7 or 8 years, Connell claims, children develop what he calls a 'task pool', which is a pool of ideas about the tasks involved in government that are then assigned rather haphazardly to governing figures. The tasks of government are modelled on schools and local government, including bossing people around, telling people to be quiet, building roads, organising garbage collections and helping the sick.

A further important step is taken, usually after the age of 7, when children realise that in politics there is a hierarchy of command. In

Australia in the 1960s this usually first took the form of realising that the Queen could command the Australian Prime Minister, an idea often associated with the knowledge that the Queen had command over a larger territory that included Australia.

Connell argues against Hess and Torney's finding that young children minimise conflict in politics. However, Hess and Torney were referring chiefly to personal attacks during election campaigns, whereas Connell's examples of recognition of conflict are drawn from war and party conflict. He agrees with Hess and Torney that understanding that such conflict is usually over a series of issues does not appear until early adolescence. Sigel (1979) showed that among 17 year olds in the United States and Germany, recognition that party conflict is indispensable to democracy is still ambivalent among the majority of students who would still rather there were no differences of opinion. It should perhaps be added that even the most fervent adult partisans of democratic party competition usually see many drawbacks to it, so this belief on the part of youth is not simply an 'immature' one, a point also acknowledged by Sigel.

On most other issues, Connell is also in agreement with Hess and Torney, though on some he provides more detail. He is particularly interesting on the role of television, finding it to be by far the most common source of political information cited by children and young adolescents. He also discusses the concentration of television on such things as fighting and disasters rather than administration or policy formation. He feels this reinforces children's natural inability to interpret the broader structure of political events, preventing most children from understanding this until later adolescence. Unlike many other radical critics of television, however, he does not see its impact as all for the bad. While the portrayal of global events is superficial, it is now introducing children to a global society that only a few generations ago would have been quite foreign to the majority of children and, a few more generations back, to a majority of adults.

Jennings and Niemi (1974) confined their study to American twelfth graders (about 17 years old). The questions focused on differences between the Democratic and Republican Parties. A slight majority saw no difference between the parties, while only one-third perceived such a difference. The types of difference perceived were categorised as 'broad philosophy' (47 per cent), 'group interests' (29 per cent), 'fiscal and monetary issues' (6 per cent), 'specific domestic policies' (9 per cent), 'foreign policy' (7 per cent). Included among broad philosophy were comments on such issues as 'attitude toward change', 'attitude to social welfare, socialism and free enterprise', 'power of Federal Government', 'relation of individual and government', and the use of such terms as 'liberal', 'progressive', 'conservative', 'reactionary', 'moderate'. There was a similar percentage breakdown among students to that found among a comparison group of parents matched for level of education.

Within the broad philosophy category of answer, students were more concerned than parents about the parties' attitudes towards change, new ideas and quick response to problems, and less concerned than parents about private enterprise, socialism and social welfare programmes. Jennings and Niemi point out that it is hard to know whether or not this reflects changes in conceptual approach to politics from late adolescence to adulthood. It might reflect a general shift in political thinking among younger sections of the adult population away from the traditional 'packages' of issues towards more specific approaches to problems.

Using prompting techniques it was found that only 47 per cent saw some meaning to the idea that Democrats and Republicans differed on a liberal-conservative dimension. Whether this was due to inability to conceptualise such a dimension or to lack of belief in its applicability in this instance is not clear.

Another finding was that the type of difference between Democrats and Republicans perceived by students bore almost no relation to the type of difference perceived by their parents. This indicates that while emotional identification with a party is influenced by parents, political understanding is something students develop either for themselves or from other sources.

Torney et al. (1975) describe a very large-scale study of 10 and 14 year olds and senior high school students in ten countries. Factor analysis showed that there were strong factors relating to discrimination on the basis of race and religion, treating different social groups equally, the rights to vote and criticise the government and support for the rights of women. Most students had fairly well-defined perceptions of these issues by age 14. The rights of women were more strongly supported by girls and by students in West Germany and Finland than by boys or American and Dutch students. In many countries there was a tendency for political attitudes to be more strongly shaped by home background at 14 and by attitudes of school and teachers in senior high school.

A number of American studies have also attempted to investigate the impact of civics and social studies courses on the political and social beliefs and attitudes of students. The majority of such studies show either insignificant or negative effects.[16] Two studies of experimental programmes have reported such effects as decrease in political chauvinism and increase in support for the democratic creed.[17] One has to suspect that the enthusiasm so often generated by experimental programmes contributed to these effects. However, there is evidence from studies in both the United States and Germany that imaginative civics teaching does have an impact on the ideas and ideals of students.[18] It may well be that in most studies the negligible effects of poor instruction have swamped those of provocative and intelligent teaching.

Moessinger (1981) investigated children's understanding of the distinction between static and shifting majorities in voting. In a static majority the majority is always made up of the same group of voters; in a shifting majority voting patterns alter. Seventy-six per cent of 13 year olds could distinguish these, while none of the 8 year olds mentioned could do so. Eight year olds wanted minorities to have occasional opportunities to enact their wishes under both fixed and shifting majorities. All 13 year olds who distinguished between the two ideas wanted the majority view always to be enacted for shifting majorities, with alternation of decisions for the fixed majority.[19]

Sigel (1979) asked 1000 American high school senior students to explain what they meant by democracy, followed by requests to amplify their explanations. Explanations were distinguished as 'simple', 'more complex' and 'sophisticated'. Forty-four per cent gave simple explanations which included mainly the answers 'individual freedom', 'equality' or 'the people get a voice in government', with only minimal elaboration. A further 25 per cent gave more complex explanations which consisted of some analysis of how the above characteristics related to one another and a more elaborate explanation of these basic characteristics. It was, however, only in 16 per cent of these 17 year olds that the interconnection of the various features of democracy within the political system was explained in any systematic fashion. Studies in Austria and West Germany show that both understanding of and positive evaluation of democracy are even lower among youth in those countries.[20]

Sigel (1979) also studied beliefs about active citizenship among 17-year-old Americans. Nearly all students were found willing to take at least some action in response to government actions of which they disapproved, but many were initially unaware of standard avenues of protest like writing letters to congressional representatives or organised pressure groups.

Zellman and Sears (1978) found that young Americans from 9-14 years, like American adults, tended to assert free speech as a generalised virtue of democracy, but to deny it to Communists and Nazis. There appeared little developmental change in these beliefs over the period studied. Zellman and Sears say that 'Early political socialization in this area does little or nothing to keep the child from exercising a natural proclivity to derogate and repress those with differing or rejected values and ideas' (p. 133). In this, as throughout their paper, they fail to point out that many Americans consider both Communists and Nazis as people who set out to destroy free speech. Thus intolerance of these groups may not imply intolerance for other minority opinions.

LEGAL STUDIES

Tapp and Kohlberg (1971) described two studies of the development of legal understanding.[21] They asked children and adolescents the following questions:

- What if there were no rules?
- What is a rule of law?
- Why should people/why do you follow rules?
- Can rules be changed?
- Are there times when it might be right to break a rule?

Three levels of answers were distinguished, held to correspond to Kohlberg's levels of moral reasoning.

At the preconventional level, predominant among elementary school children, laws are seen as preventing physical harm to people and securing physical necessities. Rules and laws are to be obeyed to avoid punishment rather than out of respect for law. The authority of rules derives chiefly from that of authority figures like the parents or President. Laws are considered as fixed and permanent and there is no differentiation between the legal and the moral.

At the conventional level children think laws restrain bad people, guide the weak and secure personal control over greed. Society cannot exist without rules, which exist to maintain social order. Obedience to the law is confused with stereotyped norms of what is socially desirable for a given role, say husband or child. It is recognised that laws may be unfair and may be made by uncharitable persons. Some moral rules are recognised as providing a justification for laws, such as the preservation of life. This level of reasoning is predominant throughout adolescence and among college students.

At the postconventional level human beings are viewed as self-regulatory, acting from general moral principles which provide a justification for laws. Law may be seen as an instrument for the maximising of social welfare. Alternatively, general principles such as the maintenance of life or liberty are used to justify laws. When laws violate moral principles it is right to break them.

Tapp and Kohlberg also report a cross-national study of the development of these ideas involving children from Denmark, Greece, India, Italy and Japan. Results were substantially similar to the United States study, although the US sample showed a greater emphasis on the ideal of personal liberty than that from other countries.

In their recommendations regarding legal education, Tapp and Kohlberg emphasise that participation in legal decision-making is valuable both through discussion of possible legislation to deal with topical social issues and through involvement in discussion of school rules. However, Kohlberg has since admitted that too great an expectation of children in deciding and enforcing their own rules can lead to difficulties (Tomlinson, 1980). It is worthwhile pointing out here that the rules of an institution depend very much on its purposes and children may differ radically from adults in their preferred aims for school life, particularly when having fun conflicts with schoolwork.

Gallatin and Adelson (1971) report a study of legal guarantees for individual freedom. Following a popular seventeenth century model for political and legal debate, they presented adolescents with the hypothetical situation: a thousand people, dissatisfied with their government have moved to a Pacific island to form a new society. The interview schedule then posed a large number of questions about how laws should function on this island. Their sample included American, British and German adolescents.

Fifteen and 18 year olds were found to generally have a greater concern for the rights of the individual as against younger age groups (11 and 13 years). Thus when asked if the government should have the right to suspend laws in an emergency, about 50 per cent of 15 and 18 year olds said either that free speech should be maintained or that such suspension be of a qualified nature, as against less than one-quarter of 11 and 13 year olds.

National differences in this study were quite fascinating. When asked which laws should be made permanent, 71 per cent of American adolescents referred to one or more of the liberties guaranteed by the Bill of Rights (freedom of speech, of the press, etc.). When American adolescents agreed to the suspension of laws in a crisis many mentioned the phrase 'in the interest of national security'.

British adolescents, apparently following the lead of Thomas Hobbes, wanted the state chiefly to enact laws to protect its citizens from one another. Such laws are to be suspended or relaxed in emergencies. For the British, freedom was largely a negative 'freedom from'. The German adolescents steered a middle course between this and the American emphasis on positive rights.

In a separate discussion of the results of the American part of the Gallatin and Adelson study, Adelson *et al.* (1969) emphasise some other facets of the results. Between 13 and 15, law shifts from being regarded as restrictive, even by the American adolescents, to being seen as positive in intent. They suggest that in moving out of the world of childhood into that of adulthood the child goes from submission to benign authoritarianism to a personal autonomy that produces a more positive attitude to law as a means of enhancing the life of the individual.

Fifteen and 18 year olds were also found more likely to mention the possibility of amending laws and more likely to appreciate that the existence of law has a moderating effect on the disposition to individual selfishness as well as on the incidence of injury to others in the cause of self-gratification.

This completes the major generalised studies of growth in understanding laws.[22] It is of interest, however, to describe a separate tradition of studies that have examined the role of mitigating circumstances in influencing children's views of breaking rules or laws. Piaget (1965) claimed that children of less than about 7 or 8 years took no account of intention in judging the rightness of action. If a child broke some cups, the magnitude of the offence was considered as proportional to the number of cups broken, accidental breakage being ignored as a mitigating circumstance.

Later research has shown that children as young as 5 or 6 years will occasionally take intention into account in such cases, their tendency to do so increasing progressively with age.[23] Likewise, emphasis on consequences was found to decline with age. Children of less than 7 or 8 years are more likely to ignore intention and stress consequences when either the rule-breaker was not provoked or the consequences were severely damaging.[24] Elkind and Dabek (1977) found that younger children in a kindergarten grade judged personal injury to be more serious than property damage, while older children used intent as a criterion.

Darley et al. (1978) examined the effects of legally defensible mitigating circumstances on suggested sentences for offenders among first graders, fourth graders and adults. A large majority at all ages advocated reductions in sentences for such mitigating circumstances, particularly when it was argued that the accused had been forced to commit the crime by necessity.[25]

Radosevich and Krohn (1981) undertook a similar study involving hypothetical trials such as one involving arson in which the defence was based upon lack of intent. Mitigating circumstances were presented involving denial of responsibility (e.g. insanity at the time of crime), denial that harm had been done, argument that the crime involved no victim and appeal to higher loyalties than that to the law. Among all age groups all appeals had some influence, with denial of victim most effective in influencing moral judgements about the crime. Reductions in severity of recommended sentences were found less consistently and were found among a smaller percentage of those taking part.

Participants' predominant level of moral reasoning was determined by Rest's (1974) paper and pencil alternative to Kohlberg's moral issues test. Those operating at Kohlberg's stages 5 and 6 were found less likely than others to alter moral evaluations or suggested sentences, apparently because they tended to regard moral principles as applying regardless of mitigating circumstances.

Darley et al. (1978) examined the effects of age on reaction to mitigating circumstances for a crime among children and adults from 5-44 years. The circumstances cited were necessity, public duty and provocation. To their surprise, 5 and 6 year olds did not differ from adults in tendency to reduce suggested sentences. It is not clear why this study differs from some of those cited previously which have found a greater tendency to consider intention with age. The authors suggest the simplicity of their stories may have helped the younger children.

There have been a number of studies of the impact of law schools on beliefs and attitudes among law students that may provide a clue as to how legal education at school affects students. The focus of interest in these studies has been the suspicion that legal education might act to promote an attitude of enforcing legal technicalities rather than reflecting on moral or ethical concerns. Overall, this contention has received only moderate support.[26] Tapp and Levine (1974) found law students had a greater tendency to give conventional (Kohlberg's stages 3 and 4) as opposed to post-conventional replies on moral issues than college students or teachers. It may be, however, that law students begin their careers with this tendency.

In conclusion, one weakness of existing research for the purposes of curriculum construction in the legal area should be mentioned. Because of Kohlberg's overwhelming influence, emphasis has been on the understanding of basic concepts and situations rather than on the influence of legal complexity on level of understanding. In devising a curriculum, the level of legal complexity in such activities as sifting evidence or considering laws with great internal complexity will be of considerable significance and studies of these topics would be welcome.

CONCLUSIONS

A number of general principles for approaching teaching in this area can be suggested with some confidence. Students tend to interpret larger social phenomena in terms of their own immediate experience; they tend initially to think some adult arrangements are immoral because they judge morality in terms of a 'fair bargain' for the immediate face-to-face participants in a transaction (reciprocity); in late adolescence the newly acquired ability to imagine ideal forms of alternative social arrangements often encourages enthusiasm for utopian social theories.

A number of weaknesses in research in this area must also be pointed out. Firstly, research has tended to concentrate on the pre-adolescent age group. Secondly, in dealing with adolescence it still leans too heavily on the idea, originating in the writings of Piaget, that we can effectively describe adolescent thinking in terms of generalised stages (Furth's work is an example of this). Thirdly, there has been too much emphasis upon general styles of moral evaluation and not enough on the conceptual complexity of subject matter.

I end with some speculative comments about how a more effective view of adolescent social reasoning could be derived. If we return to the general principles governing adolescent reasoning outlined in the Introduction, the following appear relevant. In adolescence the ability to discover and conceptualise functional relations between variables emerges. It is likely that functions involving three or more variables are considerably more difficult to comprehend than those involving only two. This is probably the origin of a difficulty well known to economics teachers but ignored by researchers: many children in the 14 and 15 year age groups still have great difficulty in grasping curves relating demand, supply and price because there are three variables involved. A plausible way to remedy this is to first of all introduce functions with three variables in an immediately visible situation, like the covariation of size, composition of an alloy and weight of a body. This could then be drawn up as a three-dimensional surface. The economic variables could first be explored in concrete situations and then drawn up (either as a drawing or a model) as a three-dimensional surface. This is only one example of the possible effects of a particular type of conceptual complexity and a way to remedy its effects. Teachers need to be aware that complexity is an issue that often needs to be taken into account.

Few studies in this area have compared the effectiveness of different methods of teaching. Much current practice rests on very similar principles to those outlined in the Introduction for teaching concepts generally, particularly in the use of periods of exploration, concept instruction and application. In teaching about social arrangements we have the added circumstance that students can participate in the rules and situations in addition to simply observing or manipulating them. As in learning about physical laws, observation alone may have attractions, particularly when the phenomena observed are intrinsically interesting or cannot be effectively reproduced in the classroom. Thus a film or video about economic arrangements in a tribal society may be valuable in these respects. At the same time, actual participation in a simulation of economic activity in a tribal society or in one of the many games simulating the economics of capitalist societies will often produce greater attention to the details of the process.

FURTHER READING

On Kohlberg's theory of moral judgement see particularly Kohlberg (1984), other useful surveys being Rest (1979), Tomlinson (1980), with Snarey (1985) providing an excellent survey of cross-cultural applications; on Turiel's work see Turiel (1983); on Elkind see Elkind and Bowen (1979) and Gray and Hudson (1984); on Selman's work see Selman (1984); on Furth see Furth (1980). On economic concepts Strauss (1952) is still required reading, while of more recent studies Jahoda (1981), Cummings and Taebel (1978), Leahy (1983a,b) and Schug (1983) are of most interest; on political concepts Hess and Torney (1967), Connell (1971), Jennings and Niemi (1974), Torney et al. (1975) and Sigel (1979) should all be looked at; for legal studies Tapp and Kohlberg (1971), Gallatin and Adelson (1971), Darley *et al.* (1978), Radoswich and Krohn (1981), Willging and Dunn (1981) and Ackerman *et al.* (1984) are all worth a look.

NOTES

1. Kohlberg (1963, 1967, 1969, 1976, 1981, 1984), Levine *et al.* (1985).
2. See also Enright *et al.* (1983), Rest and Thoma (1985), Haan (1985), Schlaefli *et al.* (1985).
3. Peck and Havighurst (1960), Hoffman and Saltzstein (1967), Holstein (1968).
4. Simpson (1974), Peters (1975), Crittenden (1978, Ch. 4).
5. Davies (1980), Lasswell (1960), Murray (1945).
6. Kohlberg and Kramer (1969), Kohlberg (1974), Kohlberg (1976), Kohlberg *et al* . (1977), Graham (1972), Weinreich (1977), Edwards (1975), Parikh (1975), White (1975), Rest (1974), Kohlberg (1984), Snarey (1985), Gibbs *et al.* (1984), Weinreich-Haste (1983), Snarey *et al.* (1985), Walker (1984), Rest (1979).
7. Arsenio and Ford (1985) also found that young children regard breaking moral rules as more upsetting than breaking conventional rules. See also Smetana (1983, 1985a,b), Davison *et al.* (1980).
8. Turiel (1977, 1978, 1983).
9. Elkind (1967, 1968), Elkind and Bowen (1979), Gray and Hudson (1984).
10. Elkind and Bowen (1979), Muuss (1979), Enright *et al.* (1979, 1980). For a critical view of the theory see Lapsey and Murphy (1985).
11. Selman (1971, 1976a,b, 1977, 1984), Selman and Byrne (1974).
12. Selman *et al.* (1983) have also shown a relation between social understanding and communicative competence.
13. Lee (1971), Keasey (1975), Langford and George (1975), Black (1976), Kuhn *et al.* (1977), Zeidler (1985), Pellegrini (1985).
14. The results of Sutton (1962), Burris (1976), Ward *et al.* (1977), Fox (1978), Jahoda (1979) and Berti and Bombi (1981) further confirmed earlier findings. See Berti *et al.* (1986) for a training study on young children.
15. Langton (1969), Greenstein and Tarrow (1970), Schwartz and Schwartz (1975), Stacey (1978), Jennings and Niemi (1981), Gallatin

(1980).

16. Remmers and Radler (1962), Almond and Verba (1963), Jennings, Langton and Niemi (1974), Jennings, Ehman and Niemi (1974).

17. Litt (1963), Cox and Cousins (1965).

18. Jennings, Langton and Niemi (1974).

19. See also Durio (1976), Rogers (1976).

20. See Kramer and Kramer (1975), Sigel (1979).

21. Thomas *et al.* (1984) have replicated these studies and also shown a connection between the stages described and Kohlbergian levels of moral judgement.

22. Osterweil (1982) replicated several of the earlier results.

23. Armsby (1971), Costanzo *et al.* (1973), Rule *et al.* (1974), Surber (1974), Suls and Kalle (1979).

24. See, respectively, Hewitt (1975), Armsby (1971), Rule and Duker (1973).

25. Ackerman *et al.* (1984) found severity of sentence tends to decline somewhat during adolescence even without mitigating circumstances.

26. Erlanger and Klegon (1978) and Kubey (1976) found a slight movement in this direction, though Steele (1970) and Willging and Dunn (1981) failed to find such an effect.

Chapter 4

HUMANITIES SUBJECTS

HISTORY

Studies of children's ideas about history have passed through the same kind of historical evolution as studies in other areas. Interest in the application of Piaget's ideas has given way to a realisation that in some ways these ideas were limiting. In the study of children's ideas about history this has taken the particular form of a shift from the interest in historical causation stimulated by E. A. Peel and Piaget to an interest in how children understand the ideas and motives of historical actors. As Shemilt (1984) has pointed out there is no necessary conflict between these two ways of looking at history. We may well believe that given the particular cast of mind, motives and historical situation of a particular actor we can predict with a fair degree of accuracy their likely course of action. The average reaction of large groups of people is likely to be even more predictable and thus to give rise to general causal explanations. It is, however, true that some historians tend to prefer a primarily causal, 'covering law' approach (see Hempel, 1959, 1963, 1966), while others tend to prefer to think of history primarily in terms of empathising with individual actors.[1] According to the second view the business of the historian is to immerse him or herself in enough of the writings of the period, to survey enough of the archeological sites and look at enough of the battle plans and lists of munitions to be able to intuitively feel why someone did something and to know what kinds of things they were doing when their actions are not recorded.

While this second way of looking at history is not necessarily philosophically incompatible with the first, it does lead to considerable differences in the practice of the historian and in the kinds of practice that historians induct others into, including school children. Such differences are in the first instance matters for the professional historian. Developmental psychology can, however, comment upon the likely results of trying to teach these two approaches to children at various points in their development. Before turning to this issue directly, I will cover some of the earlier studies of the growth of historical ideas about time and a number of scalogram studies looking at developmental ordering. My reason for including these first is that they don't fall neatly into the dichotomy of causal explanation versus empathy with the individual, but they are still of practical interest to the history teacher.

The Concept of Historical Time

The period of time that children regard as either memorable or foreseeable ('experienced time') changes from including yesterday, today and tomorrow in 5-6 year olds, to a span of three seasons for 10-11 year olds and of three years in the adolescent (Jahoda, 1963).

Cohen *et al.* (1954) found that within experienced time 'as the actual intervals increase logarithmically, (the child's) estimates increase in linear fashion'. Beyond the bounds of experienced time children, however, seem able to relate periods of historical time to a spatial 'time line', with equal periods of time being allotted equal intervals on the line. Peel (1967a) concluded that even quite young children can be introduced to ideas about historical time as related to a time line, which is in accordance with the practice of history teaching at the primary level.[2]

Lello (1980) has recently reviewed studies in this area, arguing that the modern Western idea of measured time as evidenced by clocks and calendars investigated by these studies represents only one, culturally specific, view of time. The question of whether we ought or ought not to teach our own culture raises questions beyond the scope of this book. The interested reader may consult Lello's article for further details.

Some Studies of Relative Difficulty

Some of the early studies of history concepts gave children words like 'trade' or 'king' and asked what they thought they meant.[3] It was generally found that children gradually shift from a concrete understanding of the terms based on their own experience to a more abstract view. Typically, we find three, four or more steps in the development of understanding such words can be found between the primary years and adolescence. Thus Coltham (1960) found three steps in the understanding of the concept of 'king' among primary school children. In the first children thought of a king as a person with great pomp, ceremony and a majestic presence; at the second as a person with great power to compel others to do things; only at the third stage did children mention that the functions of kingship have changed during modern European history. Even at this last stage ideas about changes in the functions of kingship were often crude, with one child, for instance, saying 'Kings used to have power but not now.'

We need only reflect on this for a moment to realise that there must be further steps in understanding the full complexity of the functions of kingship and the specific kinds of changes that have occurred over time in particular countries. Such steps would presumably roughly parallel those found in children's understanding of the functions of government in contemporary society (see Chapter 3), though of course greater familiarity may mean that contemporary government is understood better than historically existing forms of government.

Similarly, Coltham (1960) found that understanding of the term 'trade' went through four steps among his subjects, similar to those found for the growth of economic concepts generally (see Chapter 3).

While this style of study has gone out of fashion among research workers in recent years, some familiarity with it is, I think, desirable. Learning about history is, among other things, learning about how social institutions have changed historically. This may seem too obvious to be worth saying but in our enthusiasm for looking at other aspects of historical thinking it can be forgotten. In their day such studies served the useful function of reminding history teachers that even though quite young children may be able to parrot a phrase like 'Trade was an important issue in the Long Parliament', they may be far from understanding the full implications of this. Another useful lesson from such studies is that they discourage the facile notion, which has occasionally gained ground in more recent years, that one cannot teach anything worthwhile about history until senior secondary school as only then can children test historical hypotheses. Much history learning is not about testing historical hypotheses, but rather about learning the detailed operation of customs and institutions. A child is never too young to start learning about institutions, though with young children we need to gradually develop such an understanding from what children already know and are interested in.

Understanding Historical Causation

The general approach of those interested in children's and adolescents' ideas about historical causation can be appreciated from the following passage in Peel (1967a):

> When we understand the dynamics of chemical reactions, involving forward and reverse reactions and the intervening states of chemical equilibrium, when we can predict what will happen when a level is balanced about a point of suspension, when we understand plant ecology or can explain the post-Napoleonic situation in Europe or the current economic problems of South-East Asia, we not only know the contents of each problem and are able to select ideas to explain them but we have also insight into the inter-relatedness of the factors making up the situation and we have the mental equipment to conceive action and reaction. (p. 187)

Here we are to understand that the balance of forces between the great powers achieved by Metternich after the Napoleonic wars resembles a balance of forces in physics. Equally, the current economic problems in South-East Asia might, in one aspect, involve the various factors influencing investment in the region, such as a cheap and relatively compliant labour force, being offset by negative factors like political instability and poor infrastructure. Notice that in both cases the claim that such factors are in equilibrium would often not be backed up by any quantitative demonstration that this was so, nor even by any demonstration that the factors mentioned were indeed operative, such as was involved in the physics problems given to adolescents by Inhelder and Piaget (1955). In these studies adolescents were, for instance, shown a beam balance on which varying weights could be hung at various distances from the central fulcrum, and asked under what conditions balance was achieved. In such a case the adolescents could alter the two factors of weight and distance from the fulcrum, which is of course usually impossible when we are dealing with balances of historical forces. However, with this qualification we can accept Peel's comparison between the interaction of forces in physics and that encountered in historical causation.

A number of studies showed that the attainment of the 'formal operations' ability to deal with historical factors systematically was not usually found as a predominant mode of reasoning among adolescents until at least 16 years of age.[4] Hallam (1975, 1978) went on to show that even adolescents exposed to a course designed to foster this kind of thinking did not seem to improve significantly, though children in the upper primary school were more affected by a programme designed to advance their level of thinking.

Some of the detailed application of scoring criteria in this research can be faulted, but in general the conclusions mentioned above seem fairly well established. However, their implications for history teaching remain rather contentious. One conclusion that can, for instance, be drawn from this is that children of less than 16 years benefit most from a purely narrative approach to history (see Watts, 1972). Yet this does not at all follow. Not only can a good deal be taught about institutional structures, but some discussion of factors is likely to be understood by adolescents in the mid-secondary school. Hallam's chief index of 'formal operations' thinking was 'Holds certain factors constant and varies others systematically in order to discover which explanations are true.' Yet this kind of thinking is really rather peripheral to history proper. Peel (1967b) gives an example of thinking involving factors occurring when adolescents are asked why the outline of the walls of a Roman building appear when corn growing on top of the building is photographed from the air. Here various factors that may make the corn above the walls lighter, such as lack of soil, poor drainage and chemical changes in the soil, can be suggested and in principle experiments devised to test this. However, when it comes to the causes of the American Civil War or the Russian Revolution, things are different. We can never repeat the American Civil War without the slavery issue or the Russian Revolution without the Social Revolutionaries. In one sense we can admit that to really understand the statement 'Slavery was the main cause of the American Civil War', we would have to know it means that had the slavery issue been absent and all other aspects of the situation remained the same, then the war would have been much less likely. However, we know that quite young children understand 'A causes B' to mean that B regularly follows A. In the case of the slavery issue we can also surmise from work on empathy that young adolescents could empathise with the feelings of indignation which some Northerners felt towards the South as they probably feel the same way about the slavery issue themselves. For both these reasons, 'Slavery was the main cause of the American Civil War' can be understood with a reasonable degree of accuracy considerably before adolescents can actually construct systematic experiments, though we need to remain aware of the limitations of their thinking.

Empathy and Understanding the Individual

Lee (1978) and Dickinson and Lee (1978) have described results from a research programme designed to investigate how children learn to empathise with the motives and reasoning of historical actors. They distinguish five levels as follows:

- Initially (at Level 1) the action is treated as inherently unintelligible.
- At Level 2 (Category 2) action is seen as chiefly motivated by convention. Thus a king might be expected to act in a certain way to fulfil the role of king. Sometimes conventions applying to the student are also projected onto historical figures. At Level 2 (Category 3) the possibility of various alternative courses of action begins to be appreciated, which undermines the simplistic conventional reasoning of Category 2 and causes an inability to understand actions. Often the student fails to distinguish between the viewpoint of the historical actor and various possibilities suggested by hindsight, thus further contributing to an inability to decide why a particular action was decided upon.
- At Level 3 (Category 4) the student has learned to separate the historian's hindsight from the viewpoint of the historical actor and thus to produce an explanation for a particular course of action. Conflicting intentions on the part of the historical actor are seen as resolved in favour of the actual course of action. Action tends, however, to be seen in terms of local and immediate goals rather than as part of large-scale and long-term planning. At Level 3 (Category 5) this wider context is introduced but as it cannot be properly integrated with the local and immediate goals of action the student is perplexed by contradictions that cannot yet be resolved.

- At Level 4 (Category 6) action is explained by the resolution of potential conflicts between local and immediate goals and wider planning. The historical actor is seen as having resolved such conflicts in favour of a particular course of action.

Dickinson and Lee (1978) gave students from 12-18 years of age a passage describing Jellicoe's action during the battle of Jutland in turning away the British fleet to avoid a German torpedo attack, together with a series of questions about this action. The immediate goal of the action was to avoid the torpedo attack, which, according to the passage, Jellicoe might have thought was larger than it was. Jellicoe's uncertainty over this produces a potential conflict between the hindsight of the historian and the knowledge of the actor. The wider result of the action was that Jellicoe allowed the German fleet, which was numerically smaller, to slip past him and reach port. To achieve a Category 6 score, students had to relate this overall strategic consideration to the immediate goal of avoiding the torpedos.

It was found that the most common level for students of 12 and 13 years was Level 2, for those of 15 and 16 years, Level 3. For those of 17 and 18 years the most common response was still Level 3, but nearly one-third scored at Level 4, with few at Level 2. For those of 15 and 16 years, over one-third scored at Level 2, with few at Level 4.

Dickinson and Lee (1978) noted that some of the adolescents in their study seemed to advance in their level of thinking about the Jutland problem during a discussion after the test. They are consequently optimistic that greater factual knowledge of the background to historical action, together with discussions, perhaps sparked by historical games, can allow students to advance with relative swiftness from one level to another.

Dickinson and Lee (1984) have taken this observation somewhat further by tape recording some discussions of unfamiliar historical material by students in the upper primary school. They describe these as passing through three phases. The first is dominated by puzzlement and contempt, the second by initial attempts at understanding and explaining, the third by further progress in understanding. Most of their analysis here is quite impressionistic and requires further development to marry it up with the four levels of explanation described in their earlier article. Their later work does, however, show that quite young children can pass from initial shock and puzzlement at the unfamiliar worlds of the past quite rapidly to sympathetic understanding.

Some Other Recent Studies

Two other groups of recent studies are notable for their attempts to develop our understanding of the causal style of historical reasoning studied by Peel.

The first, reported in Booth (1978, 1980), points to an interesting problem but fails, I think, to solve it. This involves the drawing out of inductive conclusions from historical material. This often involves problems that are conceptually close to the type of causal situation looked at by Peel. If we are to look for 'covering laws' in history, then we have to accept the relevant examples of such laws found in history. Thus we might propose as a historical 'law', 'Every revolution is followed by a reaction'. Specific material on various different revolutions, particularly those in modern times, might well suggest this. Unfortunately, however, Booth's tests for historical-inductive thinking involve presenting the student with rather disparate pieces of information. The student then uses ingenuity or imagination to relate them. While this might conceivably have some value as a test of ability, it does not relate at all closely to the kind of induction from evidence used by professional historians. For this reason Booth's findings should, I think, be viewed with some scepticism.

Studies by Shemilt (1976, 1980) seem to provide a more valid extension of Peel's ideas. In one of these he looked at the idea of historical change, which Peel (1967b) mentions but does not examine in detail. He assessed the extent to which it was understood that (a) development entails both change and continuity; (b) it is seldom steady or linear; (c) it is often negative as well as positive in result; (d) it is not always continuous; (e) it may take place within more than one tradition. Among fourth formers (mainly 15 year olds) it was found that for those not given the Schools Council Project 'History 13-16', (a) was easiest, with 84 per cent success, the other categories ranging in difficulty down to (d) (discontinuity), which was understood by 1 per cent and (e) (different traditions) 0 per cent. Among those taught the 'History 13-16' materials, percentages were greater for all categories of understanding except (e) (also 0 per cent) and ranged from 97 per cent for (a) down to 7 per cent for (d).

An assessment was also made of the same students' ability to spot four kinds of fallacy: change as an explanation (things changed because they changed); intentionalism (change occurred because people wanted to find out the truth); technologism (change occurred solely because of inventions); and reification (things changed because there was 'progress'). Thus, for instance, students were shown the statement, 'The development of man's astronomical ideas took place because of progress' (the reification fallacy) and asked to assess it. Among students not taking 'History 13-16', 84 per cent detected the 'change as an explanation' fallacy, with percentages successively declining for the other fallacies, down to 52 per cent for 'reification'. Percentages for students taking the project declined in the same order but were all higher than those for the controls, ranging from 90 per cent to 85 per cent.

Shemilt (1980) found that the following types of causal reasoning appeared in the order stated:

a. realisation that statements about cause and effect are not identical with those about intention and action;

b. realisation that several causes may be involved in producing a change (younger children tend to think there is always one major cause);

c. cause must come before effect, but not necessarily directly before it;

d. because something followed something else this does not necessarily mean one caused the other; and

e. causal statements relate two different events and we can never say 'A caused itself' (this is similar to the 'things changed because they changed' fallacy).

Shemilt (1980, p. 47) thinks this ordering results largely from the purely logical relations between these various kinds of thinking, a kind of developmental ordering discussed more generally by Brainerd (1978).

CONCLUSIONS

The bare outline of the development of historical thinking given here will be difficult for many teachers to relate concretely to classroom history lessons. To be able to actually work effectively with these ideas would need more attention to the original sources and a lot of work with particular examples and particular types of lesson. Given such experience it is possible to gain a better understanding of pupils' difficulties from general theory and also to provide some pointers as to how to remediate them.

On the research side many of the studies described are, by their authors' own admission, pilot studies and in some cases the detailed application of scoring schemes can be queried. A further extension of the methods used to ensure that they are assessments of what historians do rather than importations from the study of physical science would also be welcome.

GEOGRAPHY

Map Reading

While much theorising about the map-reading curriculum has been, and continues to be, based on a rather dated faith in Piaget's view of the growth of spatial understanding, the empirical and theoretical basis of Piaget's ideas here have been the subject of much critical comment in recent years by psychologists.[5] One problem has been that Piaget used only tests involving small-scale environments, that is, those that the child could take in at a glance.[6] The problem of understanding a map of such an environment is considerably easier than that of comprehending something like a road map where direct experience of the area is had a bit at a time. On the other hand, some other aspects of the tasks used by Piaget and his associates may have made things rather harder than they would otherwise have been. Their requests for children to draw shapes involved motor skills that may have hampered performance. A further problem with Piaget, Inhelder and Szeminska's (1960) studies was that they used a very exacting test of understanding angles, arguing from this that children learn the concepts of Euclidean geometry relatively late. However, more commonsensical indexes of the ideas of length and angle would suggest that these appear in middle childhood at around 6 or 7 years of age (Langford, 1979). Siegel (1981, 1982) found that when a map-making task presented only minimal performance difficulties even 5 year olds could code Euclidean properties like distances and angles into a model. Their success in this, however, depended upon having an external framework to relate to the positions of objects (in this case the walls of a room). The problem of relating positions to imaginary co-ordinates like north-south and east-west is still a considerable one for 5 and 6 year olds. From this point of view we may still take Piaget and Inhelder's (1967) three mountains problem as indicating one sort of difficulty faced by children.

In this study children were shown a model consisting of three mountains and then asked to judge which of several pictures represented the view of the mountains seen by an observer with a vantage point different to that of the child. It appeared from interviews with children that success depended upon being able to code their own view along the dimensions left-right and front-back and then to transform these dimensions depending on the viewpoint of the other person.[7] Thus if the child sat on the south side of the model, an observer from the west would see the child's left as front, the child's right as back, the child's front as right and the child's back as left. Piaget and Inhelder claimed that most children were 8 or 9 years of age before they could do this.

Also relevant to the growth of map-making skills are the ideas about cognitive maps developed by Siegel and Gladwin.[8] According to the Siegel and White (1975) model, the internal representation of a large-scale environment not visible at a single glance is built up from an initial awareness of landmarks, followed by awareness of routes linking the landmarks and finally 'configurations', that is, patterns of landmarks connected by routes. Anyone who has observed their own mental processes in exploring a new city will recognise this process. Evidence reviewed in Siegel (1981, 1982) shows that even quite young children can build up cognitive maps of a local area in this way. The Gladwin (1970) model centres more on the process of finding one's way by an internal map. This is held to consist of the consecutive processes of orientation (finding out which way you are facing in relation to your mental map), route choice (choosing which route to start on), route monitoring (checking on which way to go at choice-points) and recognition of destination (a trivial but necessary step). The Gladwin (1970) model effectively assumes that a configurational map of the area travelled has already been formed. While intended for use with internal 'mental' maps, the Gladwin model also provides a sequence of skills that are needed for reading a paper map.

It is interesting to compare the resulting idea of map use with the 'four basic map-reading skills' of Salt (1971) and Ghuman and Davis (1981). These are finding compass directions, distance measurement, height interpretation and reading map co-ordinates. Ghuman and Davis (1981) found that performance on these skills was poor from ages 12-15. Furthermore, there was little improvement over this period. However, before being too pessimistic as a result, it is worth pointing out that Ordnance Survey maps were used and height would probably be easier to assess on a colour-coded map. On the other hand, comparison with Gladwin's (1970) list of skills must induce a degree of pessimism. Neither route choice nor route monitoring were included in the studies of Salt and Ghuman and Davis. Common experience would suggest these are at least as difficult to master as the skills assessed. A further skill implied by Gladwin's (1970) model that was assessed by Ghuman and Davis (1981) was the ability to relate an actual three-dimensional environment to a two-dimensional map. They commented that 'It cannot be taken for granted that young secondary school children can accurately relate the immediate environment to even the simplest plans.'

In conclusion the findings of research support those of common experience: reading a map of a large unfamiliar area is found to be difficult even by adults. Such difficulty does not, however, seem to arise so much from inability to understand abstract co-ordinates as from inability to use this and other ideas in the particular conditions that obtain with map reading. For this reason, Ghuman and Davis (1981) recommend more attention be paid to the provision of real life experience in map-reading skills. In a study with college students, Slack and Larkins (1982) found such skills were improved far more by practical exercises than by classroom instruction.

Geographical Thinking

The best-known early study attempting to apply the ideas of Inhelder and Piaget (1955) to geographical thinking was that of Rhys (1966, 1972). This can perhaps best be appreciated from the following example.

Secondary school children were shown an aerial photograph of a small town built on the intersection of a road and railway in the Canadian wheat belt. The students were asked, 'Why has this small town grown up just here, where the main road and railway cross each other?' Younger students had little idea of how to solve this problem, saying, for instance, 'Because the land is flat and they build houses on flat land usually.' This mentions only one of the factors facilitating the growth of a town, namely flat land, while ignoring the influence of the road and the railway. Between the mental ages of approximately 13 and 13½ years this was the most common type of explanation. From 14-14½ years of mental age, several factors were typically included, as in, 'Because you can get to the wheat here by railway and road, and seeing how the railway goes straight through, it can pick up all the wheat from the farms.'

Rhys claimed that following this it was possible to detect a further level of reasoning involving 'Comprehensive judgement based on hypothetico-deductive reasoning'. It seems from the examples he gives that this is effectively a further elaboration of the multi-factor explanations of the previous level.

Rhys examined other examples of factors influencing a geographical result, including the settlement pattern of Japanese farmers, of crofters on the Island of Lewis in the Outer Hebrides, the seasonal migration of the Masai tribe in Nasok, East Africa, and soil erosion in Magdalina Valley, Columbia. He found that in general the ability to think of several factors as having influenced the result in question appeared at around mental age 14 years. This is close to the age of about 13 years of chronological age mentioned by Inhelder and Piaget (1955) as marking the onset of testing multi-factorial hypotheses in physics and chemistry, although more recent studies show that Inhelder and Piaget's subjects were probably of well above average intelligence (see Chapter 5).[9]

A very different approach to conceptual development in geography was taken by Mackenzie and White (1982), who based their study on the model of Gagné and White (1978). The Gagné and White model assumes that people store in long-term memory verbal knowledge, intellectual skills, images and episodes. The recall of each of these categories of knowledge is assisted by linkage with items from other categories. Mackenzie and White (1982) argue that geographical field-work trips will assist in the retention of more abstract verbal knowledge and intellectual skills by linking them to episodic memories of the field trips. This effect was substantiated in their study. It should, however, be added that memory for both images and episodes is known to be considerably better than that for abstract verbal knowledge and probably for intellectual skills (see Paivio, 1969). It was perhaps this, in addition to interlinkage as such, which contributed most to Mackenzie and White's results.

CONCLUSIONS

Map-reading skills improve gradually from the early primary years on. It is likely that much of what is known is a product of teaching and everyday experience in map use rather than of spontaneous development. Understanding maps is probably easiest when the 'map' is a model of environmental objects (e.g. the furniture of a room) and the whole area mapped can be seen from a single vantage point (again a room is an example, or a city seen from a skyscraper). From this children move to understanding paper maps of an immediate environment to paper maps of a large area. Specific skills like understanding scales and aligning compass bearings with the map are a product of gradual learning. Most junior secondary school students are still very weak in these and other skills involving large-scale maps.

Thinking about geographical problems often involves investigating a number of causal factors that may have contributed to an effect, such as the causes of a settlement pattern or of soil erosion. Ability to frame such problems adequately and to pose convincing means of testing hypotheses about causation has been assessed as normally appearing spontaneously about 14 years of age, though studies in other areas suggest this may be optimistic.

FURTHER READING

For early work on historical thinking see Peel (1967a,b) and Hallam (1967); on more recent work see Lee (1978), Dickinson and Lee (1978) and Shemilt (1980); on spatial skills and understanding maps see Siegel (1981, 1982) and Ghuman and Davis (1981); for other aspects of geographical thinking see Rhys (1966, 1972) and Mackenzie and White (1982).

NOTES

1. See Dray (1957, 1964), Wright (1971).
2. Ault (1982) reached the same conclusion about geological time.
3. Alilunas (1967), Coltham (1960), Wood (1964).
4. Case and Collinson (1962), Lodwick (1959), Hallam (1967), Peel (1967b, 1971), Jurd (1978).
5. For the former approach see Rushdoony (1968), Bartz (1970), Hall (1975), Naish (1982); for the latter see Liben et al. (1981), Cohen et al. (1982).
6. See Piaget and Inhelder (1967), Piaget, Inhelder and Szeminska (1960).

7. The coding of features in this task probably takes place through sub-vocal speech (Ives and Rakow, 1983).
8. See Siegel and White (1975), Siegel *et al.* (1979), Gladwin (1970), Downs and Stea (1977). See also Cousins *et al.* (1983).
9. Rhys's (1966, 1972) findings were largely confirmed by Ghuman and Davis (1981).

Chapter 5

SCIENCE

SCIENTIFIC METHOD

Designing Experiments

Inhelder and Piaget (1955) reported a number of studies relevant to secondary science teaching. Of these, two experiments on the separation and exclusion of variables are of great importance in understanding how adolescents think about the design of experiments.

The topics of separation and exclusion of variables are quite similar. In both cases the problem involves a situation in which a number of variables operate. In the case of the separation of variables all variables influence an effect, the problem being to find the amount of influence exerted by each. In the exclusion of variables some variables influence the effect, others do not; the problem is to find which variables have an influence and which do not.

In both these situations the most common strategy used by successful investigators is called 'the schema of all other things being equal', which is the strategy of holding all variables but one constant in order to find out whether it has an effect and if so how much.

In their main study of the separation of variables Inhelder and Piaget showed adolescents rods of differing lengths, materials, thicknesses and cross-sectional shapes. The problem was to find how much each of these influenced flexibility. The apparatus provided to assess flexibility was a clamp that held the rod parallel to the surface of a bowl of water. Three different weights could be screwed to the end of the rod and if the rod touched the surface of the water under any of the weights it was said to show 'maximum flexibility'. It is worth pointing out that this is a rather clumsy and indirect way of measuring flexibility and this could have influenced results.

From about 8 years we find methods based on classification and ordering of the rods and weights which do not, however, usually lead to a correct solution. Various combinations of length, material, cross-section and thickness are tested and the results correctly reported and listed. However, because the data are not gathered according to a systematic plan the child is unable to go on to correctly deduce the relative influence of the factors. From 12 or 13 years there is a significant improvement. Now children try to select rods for test on a systematic basis and usually make tests with the intention of trying out a particular hypothesis. They have an inkling of the schema 'all other things being equal' but do not implement it consistently. Thus the child may compare a round rod of thickness 10mm with a square rod of thickness 16mm, thus confounding thickness and shape. On the other hand, in dealing with the influence of material the same child was found to compare a copper with a steel rod while holding all other factors constant.

From 14 or 15 years the adolescent learns to apply the strategy of holding all factors other than that under investigation constant in a consistent manner.

Rather similar findings emerged from the experiment on the exclusion of variables. Here the problem was to find out which from a number of possible factors influence the rate of oscillation of a pendulum. The possible factors are: length of string, weight of bob, amplitude of swing and the force of push used to release the pendulum. In reality only the length of string has an influence, with a longer string producing a slower oscillation.

From about 8 years children can register and list findings in this situation but they tend to vary several factors together and if an effect is observed will conclude that all are responsible. Thus one child compared a weight of 100 grams with a string of two units to a weight of 50 grams with a string of one unit. On finding that the former pendulum went more slowly the child concluded that heavier weights cause a slower swing when in fact this was produced by the greater length of string.

From 12 or 13 years the child is able to arrive at a correct solution when an adult uses the method of holding all factors but one constant to collect information. When observations are devised by the child, however, we continue to find that while some factors may be held constant, more than one is varied at a time and when effects are observed they are attributed to all the factors varied. Finally, from 14 or 15 years adolescents successfully implement the strategy of holding all factors constant but one and draw correct conclusions from observations made in this way.

The method of holding all factors but one constant will yield correct results only if factors do not interact in producing an effect. In cases where factors may interact we must use a more complex experimental design in which several levels of each factor are systematically combined with several levels of all the other factors. This design is usually called a cross-classification factorial design and results from such designs are commonly analysed by analysis of variance techniques.

One problem used by Inhelder and Piaget to study the adolescent's approach to interactive effects involved chemical reactions. Adolescents were shown five chemical solutions: (1) dilute sulphuric acid, (2) water, (3) oxygenated water, (4) thiosulphate, and (5) potassium iodide. Oxygenated water oxidises potassium iodide in an acid medium producing a cloudy yellow precipitate. Thus (1) + (3) + (5) produces a yellow colour. Further addition of (2) (the water) has no effect, but the addition of (4) (thiosulphate) causes the yellow precipitate to disappear. Thus in factorial terms the presence of factors (1), (3) and (5) is necessary for any effect to appear at all. This is different from the effects in the flexibility and pendulum experiments which were produced by factors that influence the effect when taken singly and do not interact.

At the start of the chemicals experiment the adolescent is shown that a yellow colour is possible and asked to investigate the conditions responsible for its production. From about 8 years children began quasi-systematic approaches to the problem, usually based on the physical appearance of the containers. The thiosulphate, unlike other items, was kept in a smaller flask and had to be added using a dropper. Many children at this stage test all combinations of thiosulphate with the other chemicals (i.e. (5) + (1), (5) + (2), (5) + (3), (5) + (4)). Chemicals are mixed together three and four at a time, but in a haphazard manner that prohibits solution of the problem. From about 9 years combinations begin to be more systematic but are still incomplete and insufficient to lead to the answer. From 12 or 13 years systematic testing of all possible combinations of chemicals begins. Many children begin with all combinations by twos ((1) + (2), (1) + (3), (1) + (4), (1) + (5), (2) + (3), (2) + (4), (2) + (5), (3) + (4), (3) + (5), (4) + (5)), then go on to all combinations by threes ((1) + (2) + (3), (1) + (2) + (4), (1) + (2) + (5), (1) + (3) + (4), (1) + (3) + (5), (1) + (4) + (5)) and so on to combinations by fours and fives. From this it is usually concluded that only the following combinations produce colour: (1) + (3) + (5), (1) + (2) + (3) + (5). The only improvement that occurs in older adolescents is that they are more systematic in their tests and more likely not to make a mistake. However, even from 12 and 13, children are reported as writing down the various combinations and results in an effort to be exhaustive.

Subsequent studies have, virtually without exception, confirmed the broad outline of Inhelder and Piaget's (1955) sequences. They have also added more detailed information on a number of descriptive issues. First of all, level of achievement on one of the three tasks described has often been found to be quite strongly correlated with level on the others (for reviews and some particularly relevant data see Lawson, 1977, 1979, 1982).[1] Secondly the conditions of testing can influence results. Shayer (1979) for instance found that, while a paper-and-pencil version of the tests was of about the same level of difficulty as the original clinical interview method the latter method resulted in appreciably greater variability in scores. Pulos and Linn (1981) and Linn, Pulos and Gans (1981) found familiarity with the situation presented was of assistance.[2] Thirdly, it has been found in studies of large samples of students using both paper-and-pencil and clinical interview techniques that Inhelder and Piaget had seriously overestimated the level of achievement of the average child.[3] It appears from Shayer's (1980) review that only 25 per cent of 15 year olds in either Britain or the United States could be expected to show even inconsistent application of the schema 'all other things being equal' on separation and elimination of variables problems. Only about 10 per cent could be expected to show consistent application of the schema.[4]

Studies of teaching the control of variables strategy have used four main methods of instruction: practice alone, practice with feedback about success, explanation, and attention to variables. Sometimes more than one method is given simultaneously, practice plus an explicit explanation of the control of variables strategy being especially popular.

Practice alone involves simply giving students more problems to solve involving the control of variables strategy without feedback as to correctness of findings. The basis of the attention to variables method is to ask a student to devise a test of the origins of an effect and then if two or more variables are varied simultaneously to draw attention to this fact.

Studies have shown that, as we might expect, all four methods can be applied successfully.[5] Comparisons of practice with practice plus feedback, and of practice with practice plus explanation, have had mixed results, two studies finding no difference, one finding practice plus feedback superior to practice alone.[6]

Notwithstanding these last findings, the teacher and curriculum designer would be best advised to incorporate all four kinds of learning experience in a programme on this topic. As in the case of other fundamentally new conceptual strategies, learning the control of variables strategy is a long and arduous task, with most of the studies reported above only recording modest gains. It is thus best to use all possible opportunities for learning.

A recent study by Wollman (1983) shows that a particularly effective way to achieve transfer of the control of variables strategy from one problem to another may be to give explicit instruction in the idea of similarity between problems. However, as Wollman's procedure went so far as to point out the similarities between two tasks in great detail it would need to be modified for classroom application.

It would also be advisable for future teaching projects to take note of recent work by Lawson on the early origins of the control of variables strategy. Lawson (1983a,b) suggests that these lie in situations where only one variable is considered in relation to production of a single effect. Thus Lawson (1983a) gave students the following problem. It is suspected that feeding them lipids makes rats fat. If this is true, would you expect to find (a) thin rats fed lipids become fat, (b) thin rats fed lipids stay thin, (c) thin rats fed food without lipids become fat, (d) thin rats fed food without lipids stay thin? Lawson (1983a,b) found that success on this series of questions was over 40 per cent at 12 years and was a precondition for the acquisition of other 'formal operations' concepts including the control of variables strategy.

While more attention could be paid by schools to experimental design in general and the control of variables strategy in particular, we should not be over-optimistic about the results. There is already considerable attention paid to this in science curricula, though students' spontaneous use of the strategy remains abysmal. One question, asked by Coulter *et al.* (1978), is particularly perplexing: 'If large numbers of students . . . are unable to think scientifically, why would teachers continue to teach material that students don't understand?' In their study these authors asked teachers to devise tests of scientific reasoning for adolescents and compared performance on such tests with that on the Piagetian control of variables tasks. Success on the teacher-devised tests was considerably greater. This appeared to be because teachers had previously drilled students in how to approach problems in a relatively standardised verbal format and they then set problems conforming to such formats.

Problem Finding and Hypothesis Generation

There are a number of other intellectual skills involved in secondary science besides the design of experiments. Some of these, particularly those dealing with relationships between variables expressed as quantitative functions, are dealt with in Chapter 6. The skills of problem finding and hypothesis generation will be dealt with in this section.

Arlin (1974, 1975, 1977) suggested that the ability to find scientific problems represented a possible fifth stage of intellectual development beyond that of Piagetian formal operations. Inspection of her method of indexing problem-finding ability shows, however, that it did not involve adolescents in posing the kind of questions most relevant to science educators at secondary level, which would be those where the student became interested in a general topic, thought of an experiment to test some conjecture about the situation and was then able to test it. There have been a number of criticisms of Arlin's study on this and other grounds and in addition a further study failed to replicate her findings.[7]

On a more speculative level Moshman and Thompson (1981) have suggested that a further stage of cognitive development beyond that of formal operations might involve the following features: realisation that for a theory to be meaningful it must be 'applicable' (one example of this kind of thinking being the idea that theories must be testable); realisation that the theoretical preconceptions of the scientist influence the search for and perception of facts or 'data'; a realisation that there are limitations to both the logical positivist philosophy (seeking to test theories by verification) and the falsifiability view of science associated with the writings of Karl Popper (1959). Moshman and Thompson are rather vague about just how the problems of verifiability and falsifiability can be resolved, but the ideas of Feyerabend (1975) and Kuhn (1970) are used to illustrate how philosophers of science have tackled these problems.

My own view is that to be of interest to the secondary science teacher we need to look at something more complicated than Arlin but less rarefied than Moshman and Thompson. Designing experiments to investigate a self-generated hypothesis would seem the most likely candidate here, but as yet there have not been formal studies of this.

The same problem of identifying levels of problem finding has bedevilled the few reported studies attempting to train such abilities. Pouler and Wright (1980) and Volk and Hungerford (1984) were successful in training students to generate more hypotheses and problems, but they did not encourage them to evaluate or investigate their suggestions. Hartford and Good (1982) accepted such a wide variety of reactions as evidence of problem finding that it is hard to interpret their results.

PHYSICS CONCEPTS

Statics

Inhelder and Piaget (1955) reported two studies of how children conceive the equilibrium of forces. One investigated the equilibrium of two weights on a balance at unequal distances from the fulcrum, the other those factors that cause some bodies to float and others to sink. Both studies involve the discovery of quantitative functional relationships, in the first case the law that $w_1 \times l_1 = w_2 \times l_2$ (where w_1, w_2 are the weights at distances l_1 and l_2 from the fulcrum), in the second the law that bodies whose weight per unit volume is less than that of water float, which involves some conception of density as equal to w/v. The difficulty of understanding functional relations of this sort seems to lie chiefly in conceiving the function in question, which will vary with general complexity and other factors described in Chapter 6.

In their study of the beam balance Inhelder and Piaget (1955) gave adolescents a beam balance and weights that could be suspended on either side at various distances from the fulcrum. It was not until around 11 or 12 years that subjects discovered it is always true that $w_1/w_2 = l_2/l_1$ where w_1 and w_2 are the weights suspended on either side of the fulcrum and l_1 and l_2 their respective distances from the fulcrum.[8]

In the experiment on floating and sinking children were given various objects and asked to predict which would float and which would sink.

They were then asked to find out in practice if their predictions worked. Between 7 and 9 years, approximately, children based their predictions on some kind of consistent distinction between the objects, usually that 'light' objects will float and 'heavy' ones will sink. These categories generally refer to the material from which the object is made. Thus iron is 'heavy' and wood is 'light'. While Inhelder and Piaget, as so often, stress the failures of children at this age, it is evident from their interviews that many of the children from 7-9 years were able to suggest an approximate solution to the problem based on material, while the younger children failed to do so because they based their predictions on absolute weight and would thus suggest that a needle would float because it is light. When the child of over 7 years goes wrong in using a similar method of prediction such errors are often put right. Thus Bar (aged 9 years) included a large block of wood among the heavy objects along with keys and needles. On seeing that the large block of wood floats he says this is because it is too wide. Subsequent answers show that he thinks that water pushes on the bottom of objects to make them float and on the top to make them sink. Thus the area of the object on the bottom and the top has to be taken into account. This hypothesis, though incorrect, shows that the child is prepared to engage in a strategy of adding in extra qualifications to a hypothesis, shifting from a rather poorly defined 'weight' to the relation between this weight and area. This seems to be the beginning of Bruner, Goodnow and Austin's (1956) focusing strategy for dealing with conjunctive concepts defined by the simultaneous presence of several characteristics. It would be interesting to know more about the details of the emergence of this strategy.

Rowell and Dawson (1977a,b) have reported studies aimed at pinpointing the level of developmental readiness necessary for successful teaching of the density concept and its relation to floating and sinking. In both studies it was found that instruction in density and floating and sinking by lectures and demonstration for ninth graders resulted in highly successful learning for students who already conserved both weight and volume. Fourteen year olds who did not conserve weight or volume or both were unlikely to profit from such instruction. (Conservation of weight and volume means an understanding that the weight and volume of a malleable lump of clay or plasticene remain constant despite deformations of shape.)

Rodrigues (1980) looked at children's understanding of Archimedes's principle (upthrust equals weight of fluid or gas displaced by a body) in connection with balloons in air as well as in objects floating on water. While broadly agreeing with Inhelder and Piaget's (1955) descriptive conclusions she points out that it appears to be the complexity of Archimedes's principle (upthrust equals weight of fluid displaced) that defeats the younger child rather than the fact that this principle is a physical law. Younger children can cope with simple physical laws but not with one of this complexity.

This leads us finally to enquire why it was that Rowell and Dawson (1977a,b) achieved such spectacular success in teaching about the relation between floating and density; for among children who had weight and volume conservation they achieved almost 100 per cent success in a relatively short time. This tells against the Piagetian view that the step from the concepts of weight and volume to density requires a wide-ranging qualitative transformation of the child's thinking from 'late concrete operations' to 'formal operations'. It rather supports Rodrigues's (1980) argument that the law of floating bodies is one slightly more complex law among others that may be fairly rapidly learned by children who already understand its component concepts of weight, volume and arithmetical division.

We now turn to studies of the resolution of forces. Piaget (1974) reports a number of enquiries which confirmed, in line with earlier explorations, that when two forces pull in exactly opposite directions it is understood from about 7 or 8 years that they will be in equilibrium if the two forces are equal. The equilibrium of two equal weights hung on a balance at equal distances from the fulcrum is also understood.

Three experiments on the composition of forces acting at an angle to one another are also reported, of which the most interesting was as follows. Three strings pull on a ring from three different directions. Each string is attached to a pulley from which is suspended a weight. Thus the forces produced by the weights are transmitted by the three strings and act on the ring by pulling it in three different directions.

Those trained in classical mechanics will recognise that to find when the forces are in equilibrium we normally resolve them into two directions at right angles to one another and see if there is equality of forces acting in

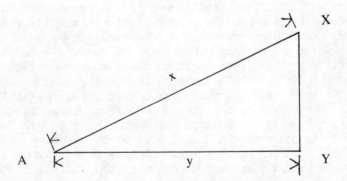

Fig. 1. *The Resolution of a Force*

the two directions. This in effect simplifies the problem to a form where it could be understood by an 8 year old. The formulæ for resolving the forces make the process more complicated, being based on the rule that to resolve a force in a direction at an angle θ to the force we use the formula x Cos θ where x is the magnitude of the force.

The usual way to visualise this process is by means of length vectors. In Figure 1, if x represents the magnitude of the force along AX then y will be its magnitude along AY.

Common observation suggests that few adolescents spontaneously think of using the analogy of length vectors or of the formula x Cos θ. Nor do they spontaneously discover the parallelogram of forces used to resolve two forces into a single resultant.

Piaget's (1974) studies seem to confirm these surmises as he makes no mention of his subjects using any of these methods. Instead they employ intuitive and non-quantitative fragments of them. Thus one part of the study using the ring apparatus is shown in Figure 2.

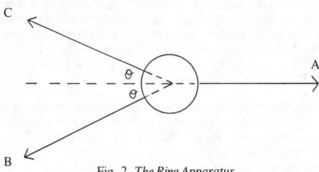

Fig. 2. *The Ring Apparatus*

Here B and C oppose A, acting at angle θ to the line of A. Even from about 5 or 6 years it is understood that as θ gets smaller the resultant of B and C acting against A gets larger, that it is at a maximum when θ = 0° and it reaches zero when θ is 90°. Piaget claims that there is a further advance from 11 or 12 when 'the angle is considered'. However, as the angle is considered in a non-quantitative manner from 5 or 6 years and there seems no progress towards real quantification (resultant = Cos θ) at 11 or 12 we are entitled to wonder if Piaget is not simply fitting his observations to a predetermined scheme.

Another part of this experiment involved finding the angle at which a force must pull to balance out the resultant of two unequal forces at an angle of 150° to one another. From about 7 or 8 years children chose either to bisect the angle of 150° or to place the counteracting weight opposite the direction of the larger of the two forces. From 11 or 12 years it is reported that children chose 'the correct' direction. Although the description of the study is unclear it appears that a number of alternative pictures were offered and the children now chose the correct one. It seems most likely that they did this by realising that the resultant of two unequal forces acts in a direction that gets closer to the direction of the larger force the greater the disparity between the forces, rather than by understanding the formula Resultant = x Cosθ.

Piaget's (1974) studies of the composition of forces do not appear to have attracted replication attempts.[9] Most of the results described are relatively unsurprising and although it seems likely that the age at which the average child attains these ideas is rather later than claimed by Piaget, the general sequence of events is probably as described. The chief message of these studies seems to be that while fragmentary intuitions about the resolution of forces appear in early adolescence, these require considerable development by the mechanics teacher. The traditional strategy of encouraging the representation of forces by length vectors has much to commend it, though this is unlikely to be discovered spontaneously. It enables forces to be visualised in a way that is intuitively satisfying and leads on to the quantitative formulæ used in resolution.

Dynamics

Inhelder and Piaget (1955) also reported two experiments on dynamics. The first concerns intuitive conceptions of forces acting on a body in motion and their relation to inertia. Children were shown balls of varying sizes and densities being propelled along a groove by an impulse from a spring mechanism. They are asked to say which balls will go furthest, to see which do and to explain their results.

A result already noted by Piaget (1929, 1930) was repeated here; children up to the age of 9 or 10 tend to think that for an object to remain in motion it must be continuously acted on by a force. When objects slow down this is because the force acting on them weakens. These ideas presumably originate from everyday experience. To make a body resting on a surface move, whether it has wheels or not, requires us either to push it, or for a motor or string to propel it. To a physicist these forces push against the counteracting effect of friction, but friction is not appreciated by the child. When the driving force starts to act the body starts to move; when it stops or weakens the body slows. Aristotle also thought of the motion of bodies in this way and such a naive belief is often called 'Aristotelian physics'. The chief difficulty that emerges from everyday experience to oppose such a theory is when a body is given an initial push and then moves for a while before stopping, as when marbles are rolled across a table or a stone is thrown through the air. In these cases there is a tendency for young children to argue, as did Aristotle, that while the body remains in motion a force must be acting on it. So they say that air displaced at the front moves around to the back and pushes the body along by a process of 'reflux'. Inhelder and Piaget (1955) describe this theory as being common until 11 or 12 years of age.

From about 7-9 years children centered attention on the force that initially impels the balls in this experiment. They reason that the impulse from the spring is always the same and will make a light ball go faster than a heavy one. Thus light balls are predicted to go further than heavy ones. This shows a conception of inertia, but its application is limited to the starting-off process. From about 10-11 years greater interest is shown in the slowing down process. It is now sometimes predicted, again on the basis of inertia, that the heavy balls will go further. From 11 or 12 years interest in the slowing down process becomes predominant and it is often predicted that heavy balls will travel a greater distance.

To understand how further progress is made it will be necessary to explain the physics of the problem. To approach the problem of the balls by using momentum we can try to argue that when the spring strikes a ball it provides a constant amount of momentum mv, where m is the mass of the ball and v its initial velocity. This tells us that heavier balls will start at a slower speed. We can, however, only deal with the slowing down process by using energy conservation principles. The initial kinetic energy of the body is $\frac{1}{2}mv^2$ and this will be cancelled by the work performed by friction, fd, where f is the force of friction and d the distance travelled. If we assume friction is a constant then the kinetic energy of the smaller faster balls will be greater than that of the larger slower ones and thus the smaller balls will go further (if $m_1v_1 = m_2v_2$ then if $v_1 > v_2$, $\frac{1}{2}m_1v_1^2 > \frac{1}{2}m_2v_2^2$). This won't solve the problem exactly as friction varies both with speed and with mass, but it is as far as we can get without more information. However, we know that adolescents do not have a natural intuition that kinetic energy is given by $\frac{1}{2}mv^2$ and thus the problem is insoluble on the basis of natural intuition (see next section).[11]

Inhelder and Piaget's description of what happens at the final stage of comprehension among adolescents is both confused and confusing. On the one hand they say that a few subjects discovered the conservation of momentum for themselves. Yet none of the protocols cited show such comprehension, nor on its own would it lead to solution. It seems from remarks in Piaget (1974, p. 81) that what is really intended in regard to 'conservation of momentum' is an intuitive version of Newton's first law of motion: that bodies remain in a state of rest or uniform motion in a straight line unless acted upon by a force. This is indicated in the child by the shift from interest in the starting process to interest in the forces that act to stop the body. This is of course some way from a quantitative belief in the conservation of the quantity mv (the formula for momentum).

From the protocols cited it seems the best that most adolescents of 13 years and over managed was to see that there was a problem of weighing the greater initial speed of the light bodies against the greater momentum of the heavier bodies. As in the statics experiments intuitions derived from everyday experience leave the student far short of that understanding of quantitative functional relationships that is the goal of the science teacher.

A second experiment reinforces this conclusion. Here balls of different weights were placed on the surface of a metal disc at varying distances from the circumference. The disc is then gradually accelerated until the balls begin to move outwards under the influence of the centrifugal tendency. Inhelder and Piaget do in this case point out that discovery of the law that governs the magnitude of centrifugal tendency was beyond even the oldest subjects. This is given by mw^2r, where m is the mass of the ball, w its angular velocity and r its distance from the centre. Their study shows that from 12 or 13 years the adolescents were able to use the method of holding all other factors equal to show that balls fly out sooner the heavier they are and the further they are placed from the centre. The formula mw^2r was not discovered.

Piaget (1974) reports a further experiment on the direction of motion that results from a force acting on a body. Even from quite a young age it is realised that when a single force acts on a body the body moves in the direction of the force. When two forces are acting (in Piaget's experiment these were transmitted by strings attached to the object) the younger child is confused, thinking the body will move towards one or the other. From 8 or 9 years if two equal forces are involved most children know that the direction of motion will be midway between the forces, but it is not until 11 or 12 years that the average child knows that the greater the inequality of the forces the closer to the direction of the larger force the body will move.

Piaget (1974) studied children's ideas of action and reaction first of all by having child and adult sit on opposite sides of a piece of clay while each pushes a coin into the clay. Up to about 5 years children evaluate only the forces exerted by the child and adult, ignoring the force of resistance exerted on each by the clay. Then up to around 6 or 7 years the 'holding back' force of resistance is mentioned if prompted but its relation to the inwardly thrusting forces is ignored. After about 7 years until about 11 the forces of resistance are mentioned but their numerical relationship is not appreciated. After 11 years children apparently try to explain a case in which the two coins penetrate to equal depths by saying 'When you were pushing I was holding back and when I was pushing you were holding back.' Piaget thinks this is correct physics, which it is not. The 'equal and opposite reactions' mentioned in Newton's first law are in this case actually the forces of friction exerted by the child's and adult's feet (or the feet of their chairs) on the floor. The situation in the lump of clay (whether suspended off the table or sitting on it) is an unbalanced system of forces that may well result in the two coins penetrating to different depths.

Other experiments on air being expelled from balloons and on pressures and forces in a hydraulic system are also used to show, this time with rather better physics, that it is not until around 11 years of age that Newton's first law is understood. Thus it is at around this age that children realise that when air is expelled from the nozzle of a balloon this acts to push the balloon forward.

We have already seen that adolescents often fail to grasp Newtonian dynamics. Viennot (1978, 1979) has attempted to formalise the implicit dynamic theories of adolescents and adults and has shown that rather than being a rather garbled view of Newtonian dynamics they are organised into a system of beliefs remarkably similar to those prevalent in European science in the three centuries before Galileo and distinctly different from the dynamics of Galileo and Newton.[10]

The main reason Viennot is able to describe this dynamics in more detail than Inhelder and Piaget is that she looks at a variety of more complex examples of motion than those used in the earlier studies. Thus Figure 3 shows the paths of three identical balls thrown into the air by a juggler.

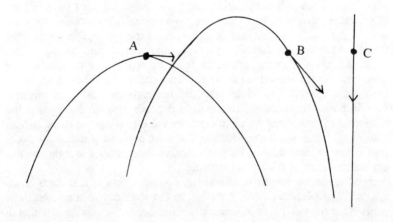

Fig. 3. *Three Balls Thrown by a Juggler*

According to Newtonian dynamics the forces acting on the three balls are all equal (ignoring air resistance) and are just the weights of the balls. Each ball is acted on only by the force of gravity which pulls it earthward. According to about 50 per cent of French and British school leavers, however, the forces are unequal and act in the direction of motion of the balls. This is an example of a generalised belief that any object in motion is being acted upon by a force in the direction of its motion and proportional to its speed.

This naive belief is common in attempts to understand everyday situations like those involving the juggler's balls. When faced with abstract questions, posed about 'masses', 'velocities' and 'accelerations' on the other hand, a greater number of students recall their Newtonian training (if any) and answer correctly. One question was, 'If the same force acts on two identical masses, are the motions necessarily identical?' Eighty per cent of first year university students were able to say (correctly) that the accelerations would be equal but the velocities would depend upon the initial velocities.

The tendency to associate certain kinds of explanation with particular situations is seen in a third conception of force applied to cases where for instance cars stop or corner suddenly and the passengers are thrown forward or sideways. Viennot calls this 'inertial force'. In the case of the car passengers it is said that a force throws them forwards or sideways, though in reality it is the car that alters its motion, not the passengers. The notion of 'centrifugal force' is invented for the case of swinging an object in a circle attached to a string. It is argued that the centrifugal force is acting outwards and the pull of the string acts inwards, giving a net force of zero in the radial direction, thus explaining why there is no motion along the radial direction. This reasoning is based on the theory that force is proportional to velocity and thus where there is no apparent velocity there is no force. It must also draw sustenance from the tug on our hand when we swing an object around on a string. This theory is virtually universal among adolescents and adults who are not especially adept at physics. This is probably because its refutation depends upon realising that the relevant direction along which to consider velocity is not the string (which is moving) but a stationary direction. Once we consider a stationary direction it is soon clear that the body does move away from a straight line under the influence of the tug of the string.

Another reason why it is difficult to convince people that there is acceleration involved in circular motion is the tendency to think that 'impetus is curvilinear'. This misconception has been investigated in adults in a number of studies by McCloskey and his associates, who found it very widespread even among those with a university education.[12] According to this theory a kind of perverted version of Newton's second law operates such that 'Every body remains in a state of uniform motion in a straight or in a curvilinear line unless acted on by a force.' Thus a body moving in a circle will naturally continue to do so even if not acted upon by a force. This theory is no doubt based largely on the fact that when bodies are thrown through the air their motion is curvilinear although there is apparently no force acting upon them.

Viennot's (1979) advice for teachers is well worth heeding:

> If the spontaneous scheme is to be replaced or overcome, a major teaching effort is needed which goes beyond the conventional teaching of the Newtonian scheme alone. As we have seen, the latter results merely in juxtaposing academic knowledge and the intuitive system, laying one on the other without conflict between the two. Teaching of the Newtonian scheme will only be fully effective when students are led to look at the discrepancies between it and their spontaneous ideas.

> It follows that students should be helped to make explicit their own intuitive reasoning with all its consequences, and to compare this with what they are taught. This is essential if students are to play an active role in the process of abstraction, and if they are to understand the nature of a formal model. Indeed, during the investigations reported here, a very real measure of satisfaction was found amongst students who, through tackling the questions, arrived at a clearer view of their own thoughts.

Work, Heat, Energy

Energy as understood by physicists exists in a number of different forms of which the most important from the point of view of secondary school physics are work, kinetic energy, potential energy and heat. It is most plausible to think that initially these four kinds of energy are understood from an intuitive point of view and some examples of cases where one form of energy is transformed into another are known. The law of conservation of energy depends upon being able to obtain accurate measurements of the amounts of various kinds of energy existing in a system before and after transformation and it could only be discovered in general in a laboratory of considerable technical sophistication. This has usually led to explanations by the textbook and teacher that experiments have been able to demonstrate conservation of energy in certain situations rather than to actually carrying out such experiments.

We may begin by considering whether some of the four forms of energy mentioned are more easily understood than others. Inhelder and Piaget (1955) showed children the situation diagrammed in Figure 4.

Here, W_1 is a toy wagon that is hauled up rails at an incline θ to the horizontal by a weight W_2 suspended from a string attached to W_1 and passing over a pulley. W_1 and W_2 can be varied by using a set of weights and θ can be adjusted. The physics of this situation can be understood by:

a. the resolution of forces,
b. by noting that (assuming zero friction) the work done in hauling W_1 up the incline must equal the potential energy released by the fall of W_2, or
c. purely empirically by finding either that $W_1 \sin \theta = W_2$ (which can be derived by either of methods a) and b)) or the qualitative equivalent of this which says that as θ gets smaller the ratio W_1/W_2 gets larger.

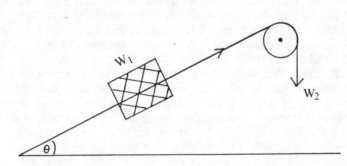

Fig. 4. *Hauling Weights Up an Incline*

From about 7 or 8 years children began to attempt to find relations between W_1 and W_2 but they tended to assume that to produce situations where W_1 would be drawn upwards, it was necessary to add or subtract equal weights from W_1 and W_2. From 9 or 10 years children realised that W_1, W_2 and θ were all involved. This leads to the idea that more work is needed to pull W_1 up a steeper slope than up a gentler one. This general approach persists until about 13 or 14 years, when the idea emerges of relating W_1, W_2 and the height through which W_1 rises per unit fall in W_2. Denoting this by h, the law $W_1 h = W_2$ is now discovered, often in the ratio form $W_2/W_1 = H_1/H_2$, where H_1 is the rise of W_1 and H_2 either the fall of W_2 or the distance W_1 moves along the track.[13]

This study gives an interesting insight into the origins of the idea of work. It suffers from two limitations. The first is that ideas about work are indexed by understanding of quantitative relationships. Surely non-quantitative ideas about work as an effort involved in raising an object or walking up a hill will emerge much earlier. The second is that, as Inhelder and Piaget point out, their apparatus tended to direct attention to the angle of the incline to the vertical rather than to the height through which W_1 is raised. Thus the idea that the work involved in raising an object is directly proportional to the vertical distance it is raised may really appear some-what earlier than they estimate, though we certainly would not expect a quantitative understanding before 7 or 8 years.

A study by Piaget (1974) bears this out. Children were asked to say how many equal weights would need to be lifted one step up a staircase to e-qual the work expended on carrying one weight up four steps. Even children between 5 and 7 years would judge the work either by the height alone or by the weight alone. It was not until around 12 or 13 years that they used the formula work = weight x height.

Archenhold (1979) looked at the relation between concepts of work and potential energy. An example of a test of the work concept was to lift a ½ kg weight from the floor onto a table and then ask 'What do you under-stand when I say "You have to do work?"' A question involving potential energy was to push a weight off a table and ask 'Explain carefully in terms of potential energy what happened when you pushed the iron ball over the table.'

Results showed that the idea of work (defined as force x distance) among students who had passed GCE O level physics and mathematics (an examination taken at 16 years) was considerably more developed than the concept of potential energy (differences in potential energy being defi-ned as height travelled x weight). Archenhold suggests this was because the concept of potential energy includes the concept of work, requiring in addition the concept of mass.

This claim was based on a number of questions in which students were required to discuss situations in which space probes moved through large distances in the earth's gravitational field. In this case of course the student must not only understand the concept of mass (as distinct from weight) but must also use the formula that the gravitational attraction between two bodies m_1 and m_2 at distance d is given by Gm_1m_2/d^2, where G is the uni-versal gravitational constant. It is hardly surprising that such questions are much harder to answer than those involving simple work, both because they involve the notion of mass and because of the complexity of the func-tion involved. Unfortunately Archenhold does not discriminate between such situations and the more elementary ones where the simplified idea that increase in potential energy equals height x weight was involved. It may be that even in the latter situations potential energy is rather harder to grasp because it is 'potential' and only becomes visible and touchable when it is realised, whereas work is both visible and can be experienced when we push, pull or lift something.

Piaget (1974) also reported a study of the transfer of kinetic energy. This used the apparatus shown in Figure 5.

Here two pendulums are linked by a piece of elastic. Ball A is moved to the left and the subject asked what will happen if it is released. It is then released and as A swings the elastic transfers motion to B. Subjects are again asked to predict what will follow. Eventually A stops and B has acquired all its kinetic energy. At this point prediction is again invited and then observation continues as A begins to swing with increasing amplitude and B slows down. Eventually B stops and then the process begins again.

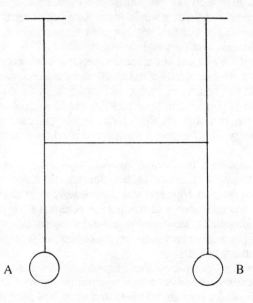

Fig. 5. *Linked Pendulums Experiment*

From 7 or 8 years the transmission of motion from A to B is predicted but not the reverse. When observed it is explained as a transfer of motion. From 9 or 10 the reversal is predicted but not further cycles. From 13-15 the whole process including the continued cycles of transfer is predicted.

The main problem with this experiment is that it presents a situation in which kinetic energy is transferred by a rather complex mechanism. Are the subjects confused about the concept of kinetic energy or about the actual forces acting along the elastic in different parts of each oscillation and in different phases of the cycle? Surely the concept of kinetic energy would be approached more directly in the case of a single force acting to produce motion? Here we might expect that the experience of trying to slow down moving objects would give rise to a non-quantitative idea of kinetic energy as 'needing a braking force to slow down'. As for potential energy, we might expect this to be rather more difficult than the idea of work, as kinetic energy is in this sense 'the capacity to do work when slowed down' just as potential energy is 'the capacity to do work when released from a height'. On the other hand, while kinetic energy is not directly 'touchable', it is visible and this may make it a little easier to grasp than potential energy.

Piaget's (1974) study shows that given the rather complex situation presented, children do not predict that kinetic energy will be transferred from A to B until 7 or 8 years, but common observation shows that they know that moving objects often require braking forces to slow them down from an early age. The essential problem for the younger child is to relate braking forces and inertia to their idea that rest is in some sense natural and velocity is proportional to force exerted. According to Viennot (1978, 1979) these two notions are kept rather distinct until well into adolescence and are not felt (except perhaps on exceptional occasions) as involving any contradiction.

The next step in understanding kinetic energy would be the formula kinetic energy = $\frac{1}{2}mv^2$. Piaget (1974, p. 100) found, as we might expect, that his subjects never attempted to apply this formula to the linked pendulums. Even in simpler situations it would be surprising to find more than a tiny minority discovering this formula for themselves even if a suitable apparatus were provided, e.g. rolling balls down an inclined groove onto a flat groove and timing the speed of the ball along the flat using two observers or an electronic timer linked to photo-electric beams. In theory this would generate the relation $d = Kv^2$ where d is the distance fallen and v the velocity on the flat. Such carefully graded experiences cannot, however, be described as 'spontaneous discovery' and in their absence we should not expect (and certainly do not find) even intuitive beginnings of the formula kinetic energy = $\frac{1}{2}mv^2$.

Recognising the excessive complexity of Piaget's (1974) apparatus Shultz and Coddington (1981) looked at understanding of the conservation of kinetic energy using the colliding pendulums apparatus of Figure 6.

Here one ball is drawn back to a point measured by the scale and when released collides with the other, which then swings to a degree also measured by the scale.

Shultz and Coddington also tested children on the Piaget (1974) connected pendulums apparatus. On both set-ups children were tested in a perceptual condition where the whole apparatus was visible and in a conceptual condition where the motion of one ball was hidden behind a screen. This second condition was introduced to try to break up judgements based on perceptual symmetry.

Success for both problems was judged by the ability to say that when the ball set swinging initially had come to a standstill (either after a single initial collision or after gradually transferring its motion to the other pendulum via the elastic) the other ball would then swing as high as the first ball had initially. About 50 per cent success was achieved at age 9 years

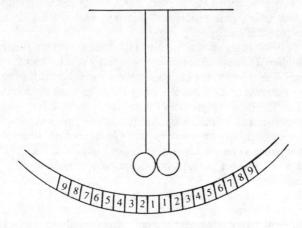

Fig. 6. *Colliding Pendulums Experiment*

for both conditions on both problems. These results show that in a fairer testing situation than that used by Piaget (1974) quantitative conservation of kinetic energy appears on average around 9. This does not of course alter the conclusion that understanding of the formula for kinetic energy $\frac{1}{2}mv^2$ is not a spontaneous acquisition and requires teaching. It also seems quite possible that in both experiments children focused more on equal weights rising through equal heights (potential energy) than on the transfer of kinetic energy.

Piaget (1974) looked at children's understanding of the transfer of heat by dipping a hot steel ball into a bath of cold water and asking what would happen. Many of the youngest children (6 years) appreciated that the water would heat up and the ball cool down, though they were sometimes reluctant to say that heat transferred from one to the other. One-third of 6 year olds thought the water would heat up without the ball cooling. From 7-11 years it is gradually realised that heat passes from one body to the other, but only from 11 and 12 years is it understood that the ball will end up at the same temperature as the water. Another similar experiment confirmed these conclusions.

While we may expect the equalisation of temperatures following the transfer of heat to be understood in early adolescence, the idea that the total amount of heat in a closed system remains constant would be very hard for an adolescent to discover without extensive guidance. Temperature is something we assess directly when we touch a body or look at a thermometer. The amount of heat in a body is, on the other hand, hard to assess by touching it and we do not use instruments for assessing it in everyday life. The closest we normally come to an intuition of heat is the experience of immersing objects in a bowl of water or ice. Small objects have less effect on the bowl than large ones. Despite this, the relative influence of the material, size and temperature of the body on the rise or fall in the temperature of the water in the bowl are not normally the subject of spontaneous investigations by adolescents, which would in any event require insulating containers to discover accurate relationships.

Erickson (1979, 1980) interviewed and questioned children about a variety of situations involving heat transfer. He assessed their ideas about the composition of heat (e.g. is it a substance?), its movement, effects and source. These were clearly separated from questions about temperature, which asked children to describe it, to explain changes in temperature and its relation to heat. He concluded that three kinds of explanation are used by students in the range 10-14 years. The children's viewpoint is represented by the ideas that heat is related to the size, shape or material in a body, as in the common belief that large bodies are colder and contain less heat. Here heat is hardly distinguished from temperature and both are related to chance aspects of warm or cool bodies. The caloric theory holds that heat is a substance, likened to a fluid or gas, which passes from one body to another. The expansion of hot bodies is explained by the addition of this substance. Finally, the kinetic theory, held by contemporary science, holds that heat is the degree of molecular agitation in a body and that during heat transfer by contact this agitation passes from one body to the other.

Few students consistently adopted only one of these three theories. There was a tendency for students in the range 10-14 to shift with increasing age to more explanations based on the kinetic theory and less on the children's viewpoint. There was no detectable alteration in use of the caloric theory with age.[14]

Thus 10 year olds tended to say that a hot body put in cold water cools because there is a lot of water or because water cools things. By 14 years more were likely to say that the vibration of molecules in the hot body is transferred to the water or the water slows down the vibration of the molecules in the hot body.

A training study by Stavy and Berkovitz (1980) was successful in helping children of 9 years overcome their confusion between temperature and amount of liquid in a vessel and over what happens when mixtures occur. Thus if asked what will be the temperature of the water in a bath when two equal amounts of water at 20°C are poured in, many younger children say 40°C. Feedback by measuring the result after performing this and similar experiments helped them overcome this problem.

We may summarise the foregoing by saying that when shown certain demonstration situations young adolescents, and sometimes younger children, show evidence of understanding that work, potential energy and kinetic energy are quantitatively conserved under certain kinds of simple transformation. Evidence regarding the conservation of heat is more equivocal, but the widespread early adolescent belief that heat is a substance would suggest something similar.

Against this optimistic view of capacities we must place the fact that young adolescents rarely have any exact idea about how kinetic energy or heat are defined in physics. Work (force x distance) and potential energy change (simplified as weight x height) have intuitively accessible definitions involving the multiplication of observable quantities. Kinetic energy (½ x mass x velocity squared) and heat transferred (specific heat x mass x temperature change) are both complex and, in the case of specific heat, not easily observed.

The only way to reconcile these two aspects of adolescent thinking is to admit that the ideas young adolescents have about kinetic energy and heat are intuitions that are more closely related to everyday experience than to the definitions of physics. In addition all the situations used to index conservation of these forms of energy (even Shultz and Coddington's half-screened apparatuses) to some extent suggest conservation to the subject.

The studies described so far centre on transformations within the same form of energy, as when kinetic energy in one pendulum becomes kinetic energy in another. The belief, held by physicists, that energy can be transformed from one form to another, probably also emerges quite early. Thus quite young children know that rapid friction causes heating in such things as bicycle brakes and high-speed drills; that when objects fall from a height they gain speed; that the application of a push to a body (work) produces movement. There seems to have been no study of whether children spontaneously develop intuitions about the quantitative conservation of energy when converted from one form to another.[15] The only case where this is at all likely is in the transformation of the work involved in raising a body into potential energy. Any case of transfer involving kinetic energy or heat is likely to be made difficult by the problem of knowing how much of these forms of energy the body has.

The adolescent's conception of heat as a distinct substance is likely to hinder understanding of the transformation of heat into other forms of energy, just as it did among eighteenth century scientists. For this reason instruction in the kinetic theory of heat should precede treatment of transformations involving heat.

Electricity and Magnetism

Primary age children often have difficulty in understanding that electric current must flow around a closed circuit. While many children understand this by age 11, difficulties remain even for a simple circuit with elements connected in series. Shipstone (1984) found that four models of current flow were present in this situation among secondary students.

1. Current leaves both terminals and is used up by the time it reaches the middle ('clashing currents').
2. Current flows around the circuit in one direction, but is weakened as it goes so that the elements it reaches first (e.g. lamps) work best (e.g. the lamps are brighter).
3. Current is shared between elements in the circuit, e.g. if there are five identical lamps each will have one-fifth of the current.
4. The scientific model (the entire current is present in each element).

It seems that in model 2 current is likened to an energy that diminishes through exhaustion as it goes around the circuit. In model 3 the fact that this does not occur is appreciated but the idea of dividing up this energy between the various elements persists. Much of the difficulty experienced in these models seems to be due to a tendency to confuse current with intuitive notions of work or energy. Shipstone found that model 1 was held by nearly 40 per cent of students at age 11 but declined sharply after age 12; model 2 did not decline to under 40 per cent until age 16; model 3 reached its greatest popularity (25 per cent) at age 14; model 4 increased steadily from 10 per cent at age 11 to over 60 per cent at age 16.

When students begin to understand current flow, it is often as a result of being told that there is a fluid or little particles that flow around the circuit. Further progress in understanding circuits will often be accompanied by continued use of such analogies.[16]

Gentner and Gentner (1983) point out that two of the most common analogies used by physics texts and by teachers are the hydraulic model and the crowd-flow model. According to the hydraulic model electric current in a wire is like water flowing in a pipe. Voltage is likened to the pressure, current to the amount flowing, resistors to constrictions in the pipe and batteries to pumps. According to the crowd-flow model voltage is likened to the pushing of the crowd down a confined road or laneway, current to the number of people passing a given point, resistors to constrictions in the road. Batteries are hard to explain in the crowd-flow model. Gentner and Gentner (1983) found that among adults and high school students 'naive about physics' those who used the water model found it relatively easy to understand the effect of equal resistors connected in parallel (less resistance than when used individually) and of equal voltage batteries connected in parallel (same voltage as when used individually). Those using the crowd-flow model found it harder to understand these effects, with understanding of batteries in parallel particularly badly affected. This conforms with the lack of a proper battery analogy in the crowd-flow model. It appears from these results that the water-flow analogy is likely to prove more beneficial, although among younger adolescents there

may well be difficulty in understanding that the result of combining two e-
qual pressures will be the same pressure.[17]

The topic of magnetism has attracted little formal study. Haupt (1952)
described a preliminary study of primary age children. He found that understanding of magnets varied widely, perhaps due to differences in experience of them. Some children in all grades knew that magnets are made
of iron, and north attracts south. Lower grade children tended to explain
magnetic phenomena as something 'just naturally belonging' to magnets
(the view of Aquinas). Higher grade children tended to explain them as
due to a vapour or gas given off by the magnet (the view of de Cusa, Des-
cartes and others).

For explaining the simpler properties of magnetism there is much to be
said for the Aquinas view—magnetism is just an invisible force, like
gravity, that acts under certain conditions. This can lead on quite naturally
to the development of quantitative formulæ describing the size of this
force. The main further intuitive development that takes place is based on
the picture adolescents form of lines of force in a magnetic field, a picture
often aided by seeing the lines that appear when a magnet is held under a
piece of paper covered with iron filings. Many students in mid adolescence
will be capable of realising that such lines of force are fictions, though for
others this will need considerable re-emphasis.

A study by Selman et al. (1982) looked at the concept of invisible force
in more detail. This study focused on concepts of electromagnetism and
gravity and detected four stages in their development. At Level 1 (from
about 3-5 years) phenomena such as the falling of bodies towards the earth
or magnetic attraction are explained either by superficial similarities or
coincidences or by God. At Level 2 (5-7 years) the idea of an unseen force
develops, but only one such force is considered at any one time. At Level
3 (7-12 years) a number of interacting forces can be conceived. At Level 4
(12 years on) the idea of interacting forces being in equilibrium takes root.

While there is no doubt that Selman et al.'s (1982) study is a valuable
contribution to understanding the development of the concept of an unseen
force, their claim that their findings support Piagetian theory is an odd one.
Piaget describes young children's thinking as dominated by animism and
other unscientific tendencies until around 8 years of age, while Selman et
al. (1982) clearly show that the scientific conception of an unseen force
appears earlier than this. Secondly Selman et al. (1982) concede that individual children may show a variety of levels of reasoning depending on
the topic and other conditions. Piaget (1929, 1930) argued in favour of
very coherent stages, though in his later work he admits more fully that
different topics may produce different levels of thinking. Thirdly Selman
et al. (1982) relate their levels to a number of Piagetian indices of general
logical thinking, while admitting that the correspondence between scores
on these tests and scores on the concept of unseen forces scale is quite

loose. In summary, Selman *et al.*'s (1982) findings show only that the concept of unseen force passes through what appear to be a sequence of loosely defined levels. To give this the description 'Piagetian' is rather misleading. As Brainerd (1978) has pointed out we often find sequences in conceptual development that are largely a reflection of the kind of logical necessity that no theory could avoid. The concept of unseen forces scale is a perfect example of this. It is logically necessary that a child who knows about two or more unseen forces, knows about one and that a child who understands the equilibrium of forces understands situations involving at least two forces. Thus to claim this scale is a success for Piagetian theory is misleading; any theory that recognises that some kinds of logical understanding necessarily entail others would predict exactly the same thing.

CONCEPTS IN CHEMISTRY

States of Matter

Piaget and Inhelder (1941) showed children sugar dissolving in warm water and asked them to explain what happened. From about 7 years children believe the sugar has disintegrated into tiny particles that float around in the water. From about 9 years they think the amount of sugar is conserved following solution and that the same quantity of sugar could be recovered if the water were evaporated. Piaget (1974) claims that this corpuscular model of matter is formed at a particularly early age for substances that dissolve. For other bodies and substances, including explanations for changes in the states of matter (e.g. water into ice), the corpuscular theory only emerges around 11 or 12 years. Now children argue, probably following instruction by adults, that the molecules (or 'atoms') of ice are less mobile than those of water. As usual we may suspect that Piaget's average ages for adolescent achievements are rather optimistic here. We have already seen that even up to 14 years only a minority of students explain heat as due to molecular motion.

In a controlled study of conceptions of the gaseous state Novick and Nussbaum (1978) found that among 13 and 14 year olds who had already received formal instruction in the particulate theory of matter and its application to gases, only about 60 per cent of students thought gas was composed of invisible particles. Only just over 50 per cent knew that there is empty space between the particles and that they are in an intrinsic state of motion. In a study involving a wider age range Novick and Nussbaum (1981) found that about 30 per cent of junior high school and 10 per cent of senior high school students thought that the particles in a gas are static. On the other hand, 70 per cent of junior high school students explained the liquefaction of air as being due to the slowing down and coalescence of the particles.

One of the chief problems in teaching the particulate theory of matter is that it involves entities (particles) that cannot be seen or touched. The most usual method of instruction is therefore by definition and use of diagrams or models said to represent in visible or touchable form the invisible entities. Thus an ideal gas may be defined as a collection of particles of zero size and finite mass moving at random inside a container. Their motion is completely random with respect to direction, only partially random with respect to velocity, there being a median velocity and a distribution around this. A picture will often be offered in support of this kind of definition, as in Figure 7.

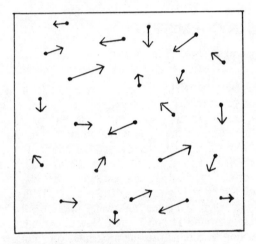

Fig. 7. *Diagram of an Ideal Gas*

Here it is understood that the directions of motion are shown by the arrows, velocity being indicated by length of arrow. Each invisible particle is represented by a visible dot. Cantu and Herron (1978) call such diagrams 'pseudo-examples'. Contrary to the way scientists usually view diagrams, as somehow directly representing an ideal model, Cantu and Herron (1978) suggest they are seen by students simply as examples of the intended concept. Aspects of the illustration that may appear transparently circumstantial to the expert, like the shape of the container in the above example, may initially be taken by the student as essential to the concept. Thus diagrams with few irrelevant elements and sequences of diagrams that vary the irrelevant elements may be helpful. In their study they successfully taught the concept of an ideal gas using a sequence of such diagrams, with students asked to distinguish between diagrams showing ideal gases and those not showing them. This appeared superior to teaching that relied more exclusively on definition.

Molecular Structure and Chemical Reaction

Most junior secondary school students have some rudimentary idea that matter is composed of invisible particles. The problem for the chemistry teacher is how to refine this idea into a detailed understanding of molecular structure.

The use of concrete materials to allow students to build molecular models of families of chemical compounds has been popular with science teachers for several decades. Presentation of such models, photographs of them and two-dimensional diagrams of molecular models have an even longer history. A third method suggested by Cantu and Herron (1978) is to apply their method of pseudo-examples mentioned in the previous section.

Studies on the application of the molecular manipulation and pseudo-example methods of instruction show they are both superior to methods involving no concrete illustration.[18] More significantly Gabel and Sherwood (1980) found that the addition of molecular manipulation to traditional chemistry instruction using only diagrams was beneficial.[19]

It seems likely that the pseudo-example method would also prove superior to the inspection of diagrams. Both it and the manipulation method have the advantage of focusing students' attention on relationships between molecules and the reasons why only certain kinds of molecules are possible, why only certain kinds of chemical reaction occur and how reactions occur. An example of this last kind of insight is given by Goodstein and How (1978a):

> For example, students initially made models of one hydrogen molecule and one oxygen molecule and were asked to use them up to make water molecules. The students only gradually came to realize that another hydrogen molecule was needed to use up the oxygen, thereby producing another water molecule. From this simple exercise came an improved understanding of the balancing of a chemical equation.[20]

CONCEPTS IN BIOLOGY

Relative Difficulty

Much learning in biology is either descriptive (often involving classification and nomenclature) or involves the application of methods of experimental testing already dealt with. A study of the relative difficulty of topic areas has shown that certain topics cause particular difficulty:

a. water transport in organisms (osmosis, water potential and water balance),
b. energy conversions during metabolism,
c. genetics, and
d. the mechanism of evolution (Johnstone and Mahmoud, 1980).

These are all topics involving idealised models of processes in which the entities and processes used in the models (molecular diffusion, chemical reactions, genes) cannot be seen or touched. The difficulties involved in a. and b. are similar to those encountered in the last section in dealing with chemical concepts. Energy conversions at the molecular level may well add the further difficulty that they are based on two topics that are themselves inherently difficult—energy and chemical reaction. The remainder of this section will deal with studies of topics c. and d. (genetics and evolution).

Genetics and Evolution

Deadman and Kelly (1978) found that in students between 11 and 13 years of age who had not formally studied heredity, concepts of inheritance were largely confined to the notions either that organisms resemble one of their parents or that they resemble a mixture of the two. Most of their ideas seemed to be based, as we would expect, on inheritance of characteristics within human families. They also found a widespread belief in the inheritance of acquired characteristics, such as amputated limbs. Kargbo *et al.* (1980) further discovered that while such beliefs are also characteristic of the 7-10 age range, after 10 years a small number of students become aware that heredity is probabilistic and when asked about the characteristics of offspring will say 'It depends who they take after.' Explanations about the mechanisms of heredity in the under 10s were based on:

a. the actions of the parents (e.g. a dog licking its pups),
b. the influence of parts of the body (e.g. the colour of the brain, blood or teats of the parent will influence that of the offspring), and
c. natural law explanations ('That's the way it happens').

A few of the over 10s gave explanations appealing to genes and their presumed effects.

Stewart (1982) looked at the solving of Mendelian genetics problems in 14 year olds who had studied genetics and achieved a high level of proficiency in problem solution. One problem was, for instance, to explain the possible genotypes found in offspring from parents with genotypes H (hard bones) h (soft bones) and h (soft bones)H (hard bones). Most could draw up a matrix as in Figure 8 and from this they successfully solved the problem.

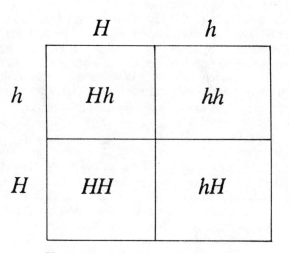

Fig. 8. *Matrix for Monohybrid Problem*

Here the letters denoting columns are the possible first position genes and those denoting the rows are the second position genes. Yet over half these students could not explain why they had labelled the rows and columns as they had or why they were able to get the correct answer or the relation between their method and the re-assortment of genes through the processes of meiosis (chromosomal division) and fertilisation (recombination of the divided chromosomes). This was despite their familiarity with the topics of meiosis and fertilisation as such. For large numbers of students the only explanation they could give for Figure 8 was the all-too-familiar 'That's the way we do them.'

Stewart (1983) substantially replicated these findings on a 14-18 year old sample. One plausible method of remediating such difficulties would be to have students discover the matrix procedure from the manipulation of concrete materials so as to model the re-assortment of genes.[21]

Turning to concepts of evolution, Jungwirth (1975) questioned 15 and 17 year old Israeli high school children of above-average ability who had studied evolution. When shown statements about evolutionary processes he claimed that teleological (e.g. plants adapt to their environment in order to survive) and factual (e.g. plants adapted to their environment) statements were most often chosen and about equally popular, while a lesser number actually opted for anthropomorphic statements (e.g. plants adapt to their environment because they want to). Jungwirth points out (with several examples) that high school textbooks are themselves prone to teleological and anthropomorphic statements.

So Burnett and Eisner (1964) say 'Thus terrestrial creatures . . . have devised mechanisms that minimise water loss . . .' Even the university biology students studied by Jungwirth had come to regard such statements as acceptable. It seemed from interviews that both high school and university students did not merely view these descriptions as acceptable shorthand but, particularly for teleological statements, they were actually unable to point to their shortcomings when pressed on the matter.[22]

Deadman and Kelly (1978) in their study of 11-14 year olds found that evolution was usually explained either through the 'wants' or 'needs' of animals (anthropomorphic and teleological explanation), through a generalised push towards 'improvement' or as due to environmental changes. Students were aware that some species (e.g. kinds of dinosaurs) had existed in the past but were now extinct, but they did not relate this to the process of natural selection. There was very little understanding of the role of chance either in the guise of the chance appearance of variations in characteristics or in that of chance of survival.

Brumby (1979) questioned university biology students who had passed A-level biology (a year 12 external exam) about the development of resistance to insecticides and disease in various animals. Only 18 per cent explained that such changes began from spontaneous mutations that enabled individuals to survive the insecticides or disease. Most of the remainder thought that the mutations were in some way triggered off by the insecticides or disease in such a way as then to be beneficial to the animal. While it is of course arguable that this second theory is actually correct, its adoption appeared not from any deliberate attempt to oppose the orthodox view, but rather from a mistaken belief that this was the orthodox view.[23]

One reason for students' difficulty in grasping the neo-Darwinian view of evolution is probably that we can't see the process of evolution occurring and that attention tends to focus on the evolution of species over huge periods of geological time and on examples like the appearance of lungfish and the evolution of apes into human beings. In such cases emphasis is often given to environmental changes (drying up of pools, appearance of savannahs) and thus the idea takes root that these are the origin of evolutionary changes. A plausible antidote to this would be more emphasis on animal breeding, which generally begins from chance mutations. More concerted explanation of the role of environmental change in offering opportunities for natural selection would also be advisable.[24]

CONCLUSIONS

Inhelder and Piaget's most important contribution for the science educator was their investigation of the rule of 'all other things being equal' and of cross-classified factorial designs. The chief amendment to their work here has been the finding that a majority of 16 year olds in Britain and the United States do not acquire an ability to apply these techniques for themselves despite the instruction in science they receive.

In dealing with adolescents' understanding of functional relationships between variables Piaget's work is often quite misleading due to two tendencies. One is to argue that as understanding reaches a final period of equilibrium in mid adolescence all understanding of functions has reached completion at this point. Thus more difficult functional relationships that appear after the typical achievements of mid adolescence are ignored. At the same time there is a tendency to argue in relation to topics like kinetic energy and heat that functional relations of moderate complexity are acquired spontaneously by mid adolescence, when in reality they require teaching to emerge at all.

Recent work has also improved our understanding of areas not investigated in detail by Piaget, particularly magnetism, electricity, chemical reaction, genetics and evolution.

FURTHER READING

Inhelder and Piaget (1955) is still essential reading on experimental design, with Shayer (1980) and Lawson (1985) providing reviews of more recent material, while among recent studies Wollman (1983) and Lawson (1983a,b) are of particular interest; on problem finding and hypothesis generation Moshman and Thompson (1981) is of interest (given the reservations expressed in the text). On statics see Inhelder and Piaget (1955), Piaget (1974), Viennot (1979, 1985), Anderson (1983), McCloskey (1983); on work, heat and energy see Inhelder and Piaget (1955), Piaget (1974), Archenhold (1979), Shultz and Coddington (1981), Erickson (1979, 1980); on electricity and magnetism see Gentner and Gentner (1983), Shipstone (1984), Haupt (1952), Selman *et al.* (1982); on the states of matter see Piaget and Inhelder (1941) (the English translation is titled *The Child's Construction of Quantities*, Routledge & Kegan Paul, London, 1974), Piaget (1974), Novick and Nussbaum (1978, 1981); on molecular structure and chemical reaction see Goodstein and Howe (1978a), Hackling and Garnett (1985) and Yarroch (1985). On the relative difficulty of concepts in biology see Johnstone and Mahmoud (1980); on genetics concepts see Deadman and Kelly (1978), Kargbo *et al.* (1980), Stewart (1982); on concepts of evolution see Deadman and Kelly (1978), Jungwirth (1975), Brumby (1979, 1984), Hackling and Treagust (1984).

NOTES

1. Pulos and Linn (1981) found quite low task intercorrelations, but this was probably because topics varied widely in familiarity.
2. Wollman (1977a,b) reported tasks that appeared dramatically easier, but the high guessing level and suspect scoring criteria must have largely contributed to this. Tschirgi (1980) reports that some problems presented as stories were much easier but it was again quite possible that these were answered correctly for the wrong, or at least insufficient, reasons.
3. Dulit (1972), Lawson and Renner (1974), Sayre and Ball (1975), Shayer and Wylam (1978), Shayer (1980).
4. Violino and Di Giagomo (1981) found similar results in Italy; even among Italian college students consistent control (3B) was only found in 50 per cent. Chiappetta (1976) was similarly pessimistic about older students. While the unfamiliarity of topics may have contributed here, even with familiar topics understanding is not much improved (Pulos and Linn, 1981, Linn et al., 1981). Lawson and Bealer (1984) found that certain social environments facilitate success, but again effects were relatively small.
5. See Kuhn et al. (1979), Wollman and Chen (1982), Bredderman (1973), Siegler and Liebert (1975), Linn (1978), Rowell and Dawson (1984), Stone and Day (1978), Day and Stone (1982), Wright (1979), Lawson et al. (1974), Blake and Nordland (1978), Howe and Mierzwa (1977), Gabel and Sherwood (1981), Ross and Maynes (1983), Wollman and Lawson (1977).
6. Bredderman (1973), Kuhn and Angelev (1976), Strawitz (1984a,b).
7. See Fakouri (1976), Cropper et al. (1977).
8. For replications and the influence of task variables see Kishter (1979), Pumfrey (1968), Tomlinson-Keasey (1972), Lawson et al. (1974), Sayre and Ball (1975), Juraschek and Grady (1981), Maloney (1983).
9. Aguirre and Erickson (1984) have reported some slightly different studies of vector resolution leading to similar conclusions.
10. Anderson (1983) has also shown that college students fail to arrive at the correct formula for specifying the time taken for a ball to roll down an inclined plane or other mildly complex dynamics laws.
11. For a methodological discussion see Viennot (1985). See also Disessa (1982).
12. McCloskey et al. (1980), McCloskey (1983), McCloskey and Kohl (1983), Caramazza, McCloskey and Green (1981), Kaiser et al. (1986).
13. For a replication see Ferretti and Butterfield (1985).

14. For a cross-cultural extension see Hewson (1984). Shayer and Wylam (1981) claimed to find distinct stages in the understanding of heat, but this seems to have arisen chiefly because they concentrated on amount of heat and temperature and neglected qualitative explanations of heat.

15. Maloney (1985) has reported some preliminary work on college students, but his tasks suffer from the same problems as those used by Piaget for within-form energy transformations.

16. On scientific analogies more generally see Zeitoun (1984).

17. See also Joshua (1984).

18. See Goodstein and Howe (1978b), Cantu and Herron (1978) respectively.

19. On the influence of model manipulation during testing see Staver and Halsted (1985). For some difficulties with molecular models see Seddon and Moore (1986).

20. It has also been shown that ability to draw diagrams is closely related to ability to balance chemical equations (Yarroch, 1985). On chemical equilibrium see Hackling and Garnett (1985).

21. See also Smith and Good (1984), Thomson and Stewart (1985).

22. Tamir (1985) shows such confusions are common in other areas of high school biology. See also Clough and Wood-Robinson (1985a).

23. Brumby (1984) repeated these findings with senior high school students.

24. See also Hackling and Treagust (1984), Clough and Wood-Robinson (1985b).

Chapter 6

MATHEMATICS

CONTENT AREAS

Functions, Equations, Algebra

In algebra y is said to be a function of x if there is some defined relationship between values of y and values of x such that for every value of x in a stated range there is a value of y and if $x_1 = x_2$ then $y_1 = y_2$; that is to say, for every value of x there is only one value of y. Typical functions we meet in secondary school algebra are those expressed in the equations $y = 5x^2 + 1$ or $y = x/2 + 1$. In more complex cases y may be a function of several variables, as in the equations $y = r^2 + 2rt + t^2$ or $y = r/t$.

An important series of studies on the function concept was reported in Piaget *et al.* (1968). These studies evidently posed some problems for Piaget, who takes up the last chapter of his book trying to relate his own ideas to the results of the studies, which in some respects contradict his general theoretical conceptions. For present purposes it will, however, be sufficient to note that the studies reported in this monograph have not met with the kind of critical assault that has greeted many of Piaget's studies in recent years and they stand to some extent outside the structure of Piagetian ideas that many now regard as dubious.

In one of their studies Piaget *et al.* (1968) showed children two rows of differently shaped objects inserted into two rows of holes (Chapter 3). In one part of the study the position of an item in the second row was arrived at by the rule $y = x + 1$, where y is the number of the hole being used on the second board and x the number of the hole on the first board. This rule was appreciated by induction from a number of examples from roughly 7 years on, but the rule $y + 2 \times x$ was not generally mastered until after 11 years of age.

In another study, which is similar to one reported earlier in Inhelder and Piaget (1955), Piaget *et al.* (1968) investigated children's understanding of equilibrium on a beam balance. Here the distances at which two weights w_1 and w_2 are hung on a beam from the fulcrum (point of support) may be denoted by 1_1 and 1_2. It is a physically ascertainable law that these four values are related such that $w_1 \times l_1 = w_2 \times l_2$. From around 10-12 years of age we find that when asked to explore this situation there is 'search for a law of progression'. This may involve the exploration of equations involving first additions or subtractions of equal lengths or weights, moving on to the exploration of equations involving multiplication and finally at 11-12 years, the discovery of the equation involving division of magnitudes $(w_1/w_2 = l_2/l_1)$. While this experiment might equally be considered a study of the equation concept, it remains true that every variable can be expressed as a function of the others.

While these and the other studies reported in Piaget *et al.* (1968) can with considerable ingenuity be accommodated within the framework of Piaget's overall theory, to an uncommitted observer they suggest the following generalisations. Firstly that functions involving only addition and subtraction are easiest, with multiplication next and division hardest. Secondly, that the number of variables in the function has an interactive effect on difficulty. This observation arises from comparison of the two experiments just discussed. In the first y is a function only of x; in the second each variable is a function of three others. Addition and subtraction hypotheses are considerably easier in the first experiment than the second, while multiplication seems to be around the same difficulty for both. However, the two studies, like the others reported, are so dissimilar in so many respects that we must take this as only a very preliminary suggestion.

A more recent study of the initial development of the concept of a linear function $(y = kx + c)$ by Ricco (1982) has indicated that elements of this begin quite early in the period 7-11 years, and that the presence of the constant c causes, as might be expected, difficulties over and above those presented by $y = kx$.

Siegler (1976) has reported two studies in which children were given training in the skills necessary to solve the balance beam problem. He concluded that the main reason that young children fail to profit from instruction here is that they do not notice the relevant aspects of the problem.[1] This study implies that we could teach functions involving multiplication and division somewhat earlier than 12 years by using concrete situations, provided that we carefully point out the variables involved, which in the case of the balance beam experiment would mean emphasising that the size of the weights and the distances from the fulcrum were the relevant aspects of the situation.

A second influential study of the function concept has been that of Thomas (1975). This was carried out on American children taking SSMCIS mathematics, which introduces functions through arrow notation and in addition to the generalised arithmetic interpretation of functions also introduces a mapping interpretation from the outset. The significance of this will become clearer as the stages in the development of the function concept discerned by Thomas (1975) are outlined.

At stage I (concrete-intuitive), children could understand the generalised arithmetical interpretation of functions, but not the mapping interpretation. Thus in arrow notation $n \rightarrow 3n + 4$ means, in 'old-fashioned' notation, $f(n) = 3n + 4$ or y is a function of n such that $y = 3n + 4$. The interpretation of $n \rightarrow 3n + 4$ is unique only in that it emphasises the instruction to perform an arithmetical computation.

'Multiply by 3 and add 4' is a typical student explanation of the meaning of this statement at stage I. This is the generalised arithmetic interpretation of the function, which is treated as an instruction to perform certain arithmetical operations once given a value of n. The mapping interpretation (not found at this level) would be involved in understanding that relations like 'is the father of' and 'is one inch to the left of' can be considered as functions. In such cases there are no arithmetical operations involved yet statements like 'Bill is the father of John' still relate pairs of values (in this case Bill and John) in a way that satisfies the definition of a function.

Thomas gives no typical age range for this first stage, but as her sample included students from 11.6-14.5 years we may take it that this is typical of the lower end of this age range and that the succeeding stages follow through the range.

Stage II involves an understanding that $n \rightarrow 3n + 5$ means 'take any number, multiply by 3 and add 5'. Thus the statement is still understood as primarily a 'do something' instruction, but the variable is explicitly stated to involve 'any number'. At the same time mapping interpretations of the function concept begin to be understood. In such interpretations if $y = f(x)$ then y_1 is said to be the image of x_1 under the mapping $x \rightarrow f(x)$, where y_1 is a particular value of y corresponding to x_1. If the function were $x \rightarrow 2x + 1$ then if x_1 is 1, y_1 is 3. The concepts of domain and range also begin to be understood at this stage. The range in the case just mentioned would be some restriction on values of x, such as the stipulation that x lies between 0 and 10. The corresponding domain of y (set of values corresponding to available mappings of x) is then values between 1 and 21. In addition to arithmetical mappings, non-arithmetical mappings such as 'assign as the image of x, x's father' also begin to be understood.

At stage III students are able to distinguish mappings that are functions from those that are not. We recall here that y is only a function of x if for every value of x there is a unique value of y. Thus if the mapping is 'y is the father of x' then for every child there is one unique father. On the other hand, if the mapping were 'y is the offspring of x', y would not be a function of x as in many cases there would be several values of y for a single x.

Further sophistication appears in IIIB and IIIC, notably in IIIC with understanding of composition of functions. Here it is understood that if y is a function of x and z is a function of y, then z is a function of x. At the final stage IV, students were in addition able to translate different ways of representing functions into one another. Thus rules given in arrow notation can, where appropriate, be related to both line-to-line graphs and standard Cartesian graphs (x and y axes at right angles). Line-to-line graphs illustrate functions with two parallel lines; values on the lower line are mapped onto their images on the upper line. In addition the following problem is mastered. 'If h maps 10-23 and j o h (composition of mappings j and h) maps 10-47, then j maps ?-47?' The difficulties experienced by students at stage III here seem to have been chiefly caused by attempts to interpret these arbitrary functional assignments in terms of arithmetical operations. Thus h was thought to be 'add 13', j o h to be 'add 37', j to be 'add 24'. Thus the missing value was 24. The correct interpretation is 23 as what is asked for here is the missing element, not a missing, and in this case fictitious, operation.

One question that emerges here is as to the influence of the particular mathematics programme followed. Thomas herself notes ·that some obscurities in the programme may have caused difficulties. In addition, the introduction of functions through mappings may have caused some problems as many students seemed to want to interpret them as examples of generalised arithmetic.

Both Thomas (1975) and similar early studies of functions used Piagetian theory as an adjunct to their empirical work.[2] Suarez (1977) in reporting his own studies objected to this on the grounds that a variety of factors seemed to contribute to the developmental difficulty of function concepts, including the general complexity of the functions involved. He argued that function concepts begin with notions of direct proportionality in late elementary school ($y = kx$), continue into inverse proportion ($y = k/x$), then quadratic functions ($y = ax^2 + b$), through the polynomials and conics of secondary school mathematics, then on into topics like functions of a complex variable that are explored fully only in the university.[3]

Dreyfus and Eisenberg (1982) systematised this kind of approach further by arguing that tests of function concepts differ along four dimensions. The first dimension is the various notational and diagrammatic representations, such as the arrow, line-to-line and Cartesian graph representations used by Thomas. The second dimension is the constituent concepts involved in the mathematical statements used, such as those of image, e-quality, particular arithmetical operations and so forth. A third dimension is the number of variables involved, while a fourth is the nature of the variables (whether discrete or continuous and presumably the level of measurement involved in numerical elements).

Dreyfus and Eisenberg (1982) suggest that progress along the first dimension (notation and diagrams) represents 'horizontal transfer of learning'. They imply that this might be fairly easy to achieve. Vertical transfer of learning is said to apply to the third and fourth dimensions (number and nature of variables). It is only along the second dimension (constituent concepts) that we may speak of the development of fundamentally new concepts.

In a questionnaire study involving a large number of children from sixth to ninth grade (11-14 years), Dreyfus and Eisenberg (1982) found that on the first dimension (notation and diagrams) a diagrammatic presentation similar to Thomas's (1975) line-to-line diagrams was harder than either Cartesian graphs or a table showing pairs of corresponding values one under the other. These last two were of similar difficulty. The second dimension (constituent concepts) was also found to have a considerable influence, with questions on the concept of image being answered best, those on the concept of slope worst. Unfortunately the authors did not include a range of values along the third and fourth dimensions, but common experience would certainly suggest that these are also influential.

An interesting additional finding was that the first two dimensions interacted quite strongly. For image and extrema (limits of the range) the table presentation was preferred, while for pre-image, growth and slope the Cartesian graph presentation was preferred. When set alongside the earlier suggestion of an interaction between number of variables and type of arithmetical operation (part of Dreyfus and Eisenberg's constituent concept dimension) in Piaget *et al.*'s (1968) study this emphasises the need for further exploration of the interactions between the various dimensions of difficulty in function concepts.

An influential study of the concept of equation has been Collis (1975). Here Collis distinguished two kinds of dimension along which equations containing only one unknown could vary. The 'operational structure' dimension separated equations requiring only one operation or one operation and its inverse from those requiring two operations, one not being the inverse of the other. Thus $4 + 6 - 6 = x$ is in the easier 'concrete' department because though it has two operations ($+ 6$ and $- 6$) one is the inverse of the other. $6 - 2 = x - 6$ would on the other hand be 'formal' on this dimension because we (for instance) first of all simplify the left hand side ($4 = x - 6$) and then add 6 to both sides (or, according to an often decried rule, move the 6 to the left hand side and change its sign). Alternatively we can perform these steps in reverse order.

The other dimension is called the element dimension. Here concrete elements are small numbers, while abstract elements are large numbers or algebraic letters standing for variables. Some examples of items categorised according to the two dimensions are given in Table 1.

Three groups of students were given a selection of items based on the criteria just described. The youngest were of average age 10.6 years, the middle group of average age 13.4 years and the oldest group of average age 16.7 years. In general the prediction was verified that items with concrete operations and concrete elements were mastered by the youngest

Operations Dimension

	Concrete Level	Formal Level
Concrete Level	$8 \times 3 = 3 \times \triangle$ $8 + 4 - 4 = \triangle$	$7 - 4 = \triangle - 7$ $4 + 3 = (4 + 2) + (3 - \triangle)$
Formal Level	$a \times b = b \times \triangle$ $4283 + 517 - 517 = \triangle$	$576 + 495 = (576 + 382) +$ $(495 - \triangle)$ $a \div b = 2a \div \triangle$

Elements Dimension (row axis label)

Table 1. *Classification of Problems by Operations and Elements*

group; items in the formal operations with concrete elements and concrete operations with formal elements categories were mastered by the middle group; while only the oldest group could master items in the formal operations, formal elements category. Two points are worth noting initially. Subjects were all girls, whose mathematical attainment may well have been lower than that of boys; in addition the criterion for achieving mastery of a category was rather lax, with success by .6 of the children being considered as evidence of mastery. To some extent these two biases may have cancelled one another out. In addition it was noted that abstract elements with concrete operations was a rather easier category than concrete elements with abstract operations.

Studies reported in Collis (1975) of the concept of the equals sign in equations, of working within given assumptions within mathematical systems and of combinations of operations, reinforced the conclusions of the first study. In general younger children find it hard to accept a letter in an arithmetical equation unless they can think of it as denoting 'the answer'; this must also be an answer that can be arrived at rather directly. They tend to interpret the equality sign in this light too. As far as they are concerned, a statement like $\triangle = 8 + 5$ means 'do the sum $8 + 5$' and the $\triangle$ and the $=$ are just instructions to perform this computation.[4]

Other studies of understanding the = sign in primary age children have confirmed Collis's (1975) conclusions that it is viewed primarily as an operator, a 'do something' instruction.[5] Denmark *et al.* (1976) tried to remedy this poor grasp of the concept by illustrating equality of weights on a balance and by using the = sign from the start in a variety of contexts, but achieved only slight success.

While similar difficulties have been found to persist into the secondary years, studies by Herscovics and Kieran and associates have been more successful in remediating the problem in the age range 12-14 years.[6] Their methods first emphasised that operations can be found on both sides of the equality (e.g. $2 \times 6 = 10 + 2$) in order to get over the idea that the right hand side represents 'the answer'. Following this, algebraic equalities with multiple operations on both sides were introduced.

Other studies have focused on the concept of variable in equations and functions. Wagner (1981) showed that when asked, before solving the equations, if W was bigger than N in $7 \times W + 22 = 109$ and $7 \times N + 22 = 109$, many students even in the age range 15-18 years were unable to say without solving the equations. Similar difficulties were found when the letters denoting variables in a function were altered. Interestingly Wagner found that comparing the age ranges 10-15 and 15-18 years, age had no statistically significant effect on such understanding, though students exposed to a semester of algebra were superior regardless of age. Kuchemann (1978, 1980) found that among 14 year olds a number of concrete interpretations of variables in equations were still present. Letters were replaced with particular irrelevant numbers, were ignored as nonsensical, were thought to name objects (2a means two apples), or were thought to stand for a specific but unknown number.

A much more detailed approach to the development of algebraic as well as other mathematical concepts and skills has been taken by the Concepts in Secondary Mathematics and Science project at Chelsea College, London. While this uses tests that incorporate demands on skills and knowledge as well as fundamental concepts, in a sense this makes their work even more relevant to the classroom teacher. One result seems to stand out as significant. Within the secondary mathematics curriculum they were able to discern four levels of difficulty in the three areas of ratio, algebra and fractions, and three in the study of graphs. However, the points at which a given student was ready to switch between levels in the different areas were widely discrepant and not predicted by a battery of Piagetian tests.[7] This kind of result confirms the general theoretical and empirical arguments against Piagetian theory and suggests that to make theory really relevant to the classroom teacher we need specific diagnostic tests for specific topics and textbooks or sequences of activities that are ordered in a developmental sequence.

Geometry

According to Piaget and Inhelder (1956) and Piaget *et al.* (1960) there is an evolution from topological conceptions of geometry, found in the pre-school years, to on the one hand, projective geometrical concepts, typical of 'early concrete operations' and on the other hand, the somewhat later acquisition of Euclidean conceptions, found in 'late concrete operations'. The chief motive force underlying these transitions is the child's attempt to co-ordinate its own spatial perspective with that of others.

Piaget and his collaborators make the kind of assumptions about the growth of geometrical concepts found in other areas. They assume that the three kinds of geometry appear as *structures d'ensemble* (structures of the whole) in which all the various axioms and theorems as well as constituent concepts like those of line, angle or neighbourhood appear together. Hardly any evidence is used to back this underlying theory, with the empirical studies concentrating on constituent concepts like those of the length of a line, of parallels and of angle. In dealing with the notion of angle in particular, Piaget *et al.* (1960) require the child to pass a very demanding test of measuring an angle that effectively forces the child to think in terms of co-ordinate systems, which is not of course necessary. Thus the same kind of problem about the level of difficulty of tests that we have found in other areas appears here.

Another problem with their work relates to their claims about the necessary priority of topological concepts in geometrical understanding. Here some of the tests they used seem to have been vitiated by reliance on children's drawings, where problems of motor skill in execution become entangled with those of conceptual understanding (Freeman, 1980). In other tests more subtle problems appeared (see Darke, 1982, for a recent review).

While criticism of Piaget's work on geometrical understanding along the lines just mentioned has been widespread, a number of other difficulties with the Piagetian view have not received sufficient attention. Three may be mentioned as most important. Firstly, there has been very little work on the development of intuitions about such basic Euclidean axioms as that 'corresponding angles' are equal when straight lines intersect. There has been a similar neglect of theorems. These difficulties apply to topology and projective geometry as much as to Euclidean.

Secondly, much recent work has followed Piaget in his interest in a transformational as opposed to a traditional axiomatic and proof-centred view of geometry. A typical task in such studies may involve asking a child to visualise what a shape will look like when 'flipped' about a vertical or horizontal axis (reflection transformation) or when rotated or displaced. We find, as might be expected, that success in such tasks improves throughout the primary years, with the complexity of the task, the direction of the transformation and the mode of presentation all influencing results.

The problem with this kind of study from the point of view of the mathematics educator is that it is not clear where to go from here. Partly inspired by Piaget and partly by Klein's (1872) 'Erlangen Programme', some people have suggested that geometry be presented from a 'transformational perspective'. The result of this is to train children in what is essentially naming their own intuitions. Before undertaking such a course, for instance, a student may know intuitively that a square and a circle are 'topologically equivalent' because they are both closed figures and can thus be transformed into one another. On the course they learn to name this intuition.

Opponents of this kind of thing would argue that it isn't really mathematics at all. It was mathematics for Klein and his followers as they used the algebraic theory of invariants to approach geometrical transformations in a rigorous manner by converting them into problems in analytic geometry. The difference between this and intuitive judgements about equivalence based on looking at pictures is enormous from a mathematical point of view.

We can underscore this difference by just thinking of a few theorems in geometry. It is a theorem in topology that any 'map' (division of the plane) can be coloured using four colours. To prove this counter-intuitive result we need mathematical methods, not intuitions about transformations. To pick examples closer to the standard secondary curriculum we could think of the following Euclidean theorems: the squares on the sides of a right-angled triangle have the relation specified in Pythagoras's theorem; angles in a circle subtending chords of equal length are equal. Neither theorem is intuitively obvious from intuitions about transformations or anything else. More importantly, the only simple ways I know to encourage acceptance of these theorems would be (a) by induction from a lot of examples, and (b) by deductive methods from axioms. Neither method is remotely transformational. The plain fact is that the transformational methods of algebraic invariance theory are very hard to intuit and are undoubtedly a lot harder for adolescents to understand than 'old fashioned' deductive methods in geometry.

The third area of difficulty in the Piagetian view of geometry teaching leads on from this last point. According to some Piagetians (e.g. Copeland, 1979) we should teach topology first, projective geometry second and Euclidean geometry third, as this is their developmental order of difficulty. Two things can, however, be said against this. Firstly, there have been a large number of studies critical of this ordering (see Darke, 1982). Secondly, if we mean topology as developed from its axioms this will involve us in highly abstract ideas about continuity, neighbourhoods and limits that are certainly harder to grasp than elementary Euclidean geometry (see next section). To be fair to Piaget he does try to separate the initial 'spatial' intuitions about topology that develop in the early primary years from 'geometry', which he associates with developed ideas about measurement (see Piaget *et al.*, 1960). However, more recent work on continuity and limits shows that he tended to underestimate the difficulty of these latter concepts, which really seem to be more appropriate to the later secondary school years.

These considerations lead us back to the traditional commonsense view of the development of geometry. This maintained that Euclidean geometry was easiest to grasp, then projective geometry and finally topology. The key difference between this view and the Piagetian view is that this is based on the difficulty of grasping the basic concepts, axioms and theorems of the system. In one version of the traditional view, geometry was to be developed deductively, in a more recent variant, inductively from examples. In educational terms this remains a potent issue. A recent review of geometry teaching in British secondary schools, for instance, found that both are still widely used methods (Lang and Ruane, 1981). Yet whichever method we use there seems to be a considerable difference in the difficulty of, on the one hand, Euclidean and projective geometry and on the other, topology, produced by the constituent concepts themselves. The constituent concepts of 'real' topology are abstract and counter-intuitive. The points and lines of Euclidean and projective geometry are abstract and not generally understood in their mathematical sense until the secondary years, but they are not as difficult to grasp as those of topology.

I conclude with a qualification of some of the above comments. So far I have been talking as though we should restrict ourselves to material the student already finds intuitively acceptable. Yet every mathematics teacher knows that the things that most interest students are often those that arouse surprise, even disbelief. The trick here seems to be to arouse a certain amount of disbelief, but not too much. There seems so far to be no work on this important topic. One speculation might be that a student needs to understand enough about a mathematical system to make the general language of the system intelligible and enough of its results must be intuitively plausible so as not to undermine belief in the system as a whole. Within this context surprising results may then have the result of encouraging the student to think more deeply about reasons for believing in surprising results.

A related issue is involved when we move into the senior secondary school. Here we begin to have to accept things about limits, differentials and functions that are counter-intuitive to the average adult. Adult mathematicians actually vary rather widely in their attitudes to such things. To some they are just things about which we suspend disbelief for the sake of a coherent system. For others there seems to be a point at which intuition alters so as to accept the surprising result. Some work on this kind of difficulty has been reported (see next section) but at present there is little information about this in the area of geometry.

Infinity, Limit and Calculus

The earliest studies of the development of concepts of infinity in children failed to distinguish potential infinity from completed infinity, although this has traditionally been an important distinction in mathematical philosophy (Boyer, 1939). Potential infinity is involved in such notions as that mathematical operations can be indefinitely iterated or that there can be no largest or smallest number. Completed infinity is involved in the concept of an infinite set or an infinite decimal. The concept of a limit can be considered from either point of view. If it is said that a function can be brought indefinitely near a limit point, this is a statement about potential infinity. If, on the other hand, we speak of the limit of an infinite sequence being reached, that is a statement about completed infinity. It seems likely that concepts of potential infinity develop before those of completed infinity as many adults have difficulty with completed infinity, but not with potential infinity.

The earliest study was that of Piaget and Inhelder (1956). Their task involved showing children a figure—either a square, triangle or line—and requesting them to draw repeated bisections of the figure. When the figure became too small for further bisection the child was asked about the possibility of continuing the process in his mind. Questions were asked about three aspects of this process. First, to see if the child appreciated the operation of bisection could be continued indefinitely. Then to see whether he thought the end product of the process would have a shape, or whether it would be a point. Finally, to see whether the child thought the original figure could be reconstituted from its 'constituent' points. It was found at 11 or 12 years of age children believed in the possibility of indefinite bisection of the figure, that the end result would be a point and that the original figure could be reconstituted from its 'constituent' points. If valid, these figures would indicate that children develop concepts of potential infinity, in this case indefinite bisection, at the same time as they develop concepts of completed infinity, in this case the notion that the end product of the bisection would be a point. However, the children's notion that the original figure could be reconstituted from points provides immediate occasion to doubt this conclusion. This erroneous idea would indicate that the child had failed to appreciate that the nature of a point is to have no extension. This doubt about Piaget and Inhelder's conclusions will be returned to later.

Taback (1969) again used tasks involving indefinite iteration of operations other than bisection, including operations that increased the size of the figure as well as those that diminished it. He concluded it was only at age 12 that a majority of children were able to conceive of indefinite iteration or the limit point of a sequence. He points out that there was, however, a very marked discrepancy between results on his various tasks testing for the concept of limit point. He suggests that in tasks involving representation of the limit point in the figure shown to the child, such as in a task involving bisection of a line, children do much worse than in tasks where the limit point is not represented, as where a series of figures are drawn one inside another.

Langford (1974) reported two studies in which questions asked about the end result of indefinitely iterated processes were clearly separated from those asking about the process of iteration itself, particularly whether it could 'go on forever'.

Under the most favourable conditions a majority of 9 year olds could conceive of the arithmetical operations of addition, subtraction and multiplication being indefinitely iterated when applied to numbers. In the case of division this is put off until age 13. The way in which children answer questions about indefinitely iterated division indicates that it is not until age 13 that a majority of children have a concept of limit. Even at age 15 the overwhelming majority of adolescents continue to think of limits from the standpoint of potential rather than that of completed infinity. This points to the conclusion that while concepts relating to potential infinity develop between the ages of 9 and 15, concepts of completed infinity do not develop until after this period. It also indicates that the claim of Piaget and Inhelder (1956), based only on results from tasks involving division, that the concept of indefinite iteration does not develop until the period of formal operations, needs to be reassessed.

Fischbein et al. (1979) reached substantially the same conclusions about potential infinity, though their questions concentrated on division and other operations that were not understood as being capable of indefinite iteration until about 12 or 13 years. These investigators also found that teaching appeared to have a positive effect upon the indefinite iteration of division, but a negative one on some other geometrical processes. They suggest that the demands of symbol manipulation may in some cases actively discourage thinking about basic concepts, which in the topics of infinity and limits can lead to conceptual contradictions that are actively dysfunctional in relation to symbol manipulation.[9]

Two studies of concepts of integration and differentiation by Orton (1983a,b) found, as might be expected, that even students taking senior secondary high school calculus tended to interpret the limit process involved in obtaining the integral and differential of a function as a process of indefinite approximation. A minority appeared to accept that an exact value for the integral and differential could be derived and this may indicate attainment of a concept of completed infinity. An earlier study by Sellwood (1973) on non-mathematically trained adults and adults with a mathematics degree found that most of the mathematicians but few of the non-mathematicians interpreted limits in terms of completed infinity.

Ratio, Proportion, Probability, Combinations

The concept of ratio is found in a wide variety of situations of great practical importance. If we compare the numbers of two types of objects in a collection, such as the number of black balls compared to the number of white (where all balls are black or white), we talk of the ratio of one to the other (in this case, the ratio of black to white). Apart from this most elementary situation there are a large number of standard units of measurement obtained as ratios, including speed (ratio of distance travelled to time taken), density (ratio of weight to volume of a body) and steepness of an incline (ratio of distance travelled vertically to distance travelled horizontally). A fraction is the number of equal parts present out of a whole (e.g. 5/8 is 5 from 8 parts). It is worth noting that probability is not a ratio but a fraction, being the expected number of times event A happens out of a total number of events A + B, where B are all relevant events that are not A. When two ratios are compared (for instance two speeds, densities or gradients) the result is called a proportion.

Having defined these terms we might imagine that ratios and fractions would develop before proportions. It is also plausible to think that ratios and fractions dealing with comparisons of whole numbers of objects, like black and white balls, would differ from ratios and fractions involving continuous quantities and that continuous quantities where the different parts are visible (e.g. slices of a cake) would be easier than those where the different parts are not visible (e.g. speed and density). We might further speculate that ratios would be easier than fractions, as we know from Piaget's (1952) studies of class inclusion that children find it easier to compare two parts of a collection than to compare a part with the whole.

It is unfortunately not possible to provide a complete confirmation of this sketch of levels of difficulty in this area as most of the early work was conducted piecemeal and Piaget and his colleagues tended to assign the findings of their own studies to the various stages predicted by Piagetian theory. My first aim in the present section will be to show that the results both of the early Piagetian studies and of recent, better-controlled studies can be accommodated within the outline just given. Some approximate ages at which the various abilities appear will also be given.

A further initial difficulty is that the term ratio is rather ambiguous. If a child sees six apples and two pears, then a concrete understanding about the relative number of apples and pears might be simply directly counting that there are six apples compared to two pears. However, particularly during a mathematics lesson, we might be inclined to ask for this to be expressed in its simplest form, namely that there are three apples for every pear. This second kind of 'simplest form' ratio requires an understanding of the idea that there are two ratios here that are equal to one another, thus introducing the idea of proportion (6 to 2 equals 3 to 1).

The simple perception that there are A xs in relation to B ys (concrete ratio) is presumably a fairly early one and probably appears soon after children learn to count. This compares with the successful conception of fractions in relation to continuous quantities (e.g. dividing a cake) at around 10 years of age, according to Piaget *et al.* (1960) The procedure adopted there was to ask children to divide a paper 'cake' into a number of equal slices using pencil lines. This is not usually achieved for six pieces until about 10 years, though division into three parts is achieved at 6-7, and into two as young as 4½ years. Considering the very wide span of ages, we are entitled to ask whether the difficulties with the large numbers of slices are not primarily of a technical variety.

The rule that most adults would probably use to divide a cake would be to imagine the circumference divided into a number of equal sections and then to cut slices of that width at the circumference. This involves both a rather complex strategy and highly developed estimation skills. For these reasons we should, I think, be rather suspicious of cake-cutting as an index of fraction concepts.

Another way to test understanding of a fraction would be to present the child with several already-divided cakes and ask the child to select, say, two 'one-fifth' parts of a cake when confronted with cakes cut into various numbers of equal parts. Provided the meaning of 'one-fifth', 'one-sixth' and so on are carefully explained beforehand, many children seem to be able to do this in an informal way from 7 or 8 years.

The relatively scant attention paid to concrete fractions and ratios probably reflects the absence of great difficulty for the child in grasping these notions before they are introduced in the school curriculum. In contrast, the idea of a comparison of ratios in a proportion is much more difficult and has received considerable attention.

The idea of an abstract ratio or proportion is often involved in understanding standardised measures involving ratios such as those of speed, density and inclination. In such cases the actually measured values are usually converted to a standard unit defined by the divisor; thus kilometres per hour, grams per cubic centimetre. To understand this the student must know that the original ratio (say, 3 miles in a quarter of an hour) can be converted to an equal ratio with the desired divisor (12 miles in one hour).

Piaget (1971) reported a number of experiments dealing with movement and speed. In one experiment, for instance, a child was shown objects moving along a line and asked to time the interval between starting and finishing. The paths of the moving objects are sketched and the times taken to move along these lines entered beside them.

Generally speaking children of less than 12 years tend to avoid the problem of dealing with the ratio of time to distance by answering questions as if 'faster' or 'more quickly' meant 'longer' or 'more time'. It is not until after about 12 years of age that actual numerical division is used to compare ratios, though somewhat earlier there seem to be non-numerical intuitions of this. Thus a 12 year old compared 8 cm in 6 sec. with 5 cm in 5 sec.: 'It's the first one that goes faster because if the second one had gone the same distance it would have gone longer.' This appears to be based on using arithmetical approximations to effect a rough comparison.[10]

A number of studies have confirmed Piaget's view that proportion concepts are acquired during early adolescence, though content can have a considerable influence on difficulty.[11]

Recent studies of proportional reasoning have tended to move away from the idea of proportion as a static concept towards working within a problem-solving framework. Most such studies of proportion involve asking subjects to solve some kind of problem, sometimes asking which of two ratios is larger, sometimes for reduction to a standard unit or to a ratio that cannot be further simplified. Some studies have used qualitative intuitions (e.g. if ratio A is greater than B, how do A and B compare with some third ratio derived from them, as when liquid mixtures of different strengths are mixed?). Two recent studies will provide examples of this shift in focus.

Quintero (1980, 1981, 1983) has reported a number of studies of one-step and two-step ratio problems. In the 1983 study the one-step problems were of the kind, 'In the store they sell 12 candies in each box. Mary bought 4 boxes of candies. How many candies did Mary buy?' This needs only one step for solution (4×12). A two-step problem was, 'In a store they give 6 lollipops for every 2 chocolate bars you buy. John bought 10 chocolate bars. How many lollipops did they give to John?' Here the children could either go, (1) 3 lollipops for 1 chocolate bar. (2) So for 10 chocolate bars 10×3 lollipops. Or, alternatively, (1) 5 lots of 2 chocolate bars in 10. (2) So 5×6 lollipops. In this example both solution routes involve whole numbers, but the numbers given can make either or neither route involve whole numbers, which influences difficulty.

Quintero (1983) concluded that understanding the concept of ratio was one source of difficulty for 10-12 year olds. One index of this concept was ability to choose a picture representing the appropriate ratio. However, as might be expected, understanding of ratio was not the only source of difficulty and number of steps, preferred solution route as well as ability to understand and represent problem information apart from the ratio information all appeared to influence success in finding a solution.

It is interesting that Karplus *et al.* (1983) were also led to a problem-solving view of ratio and proportion problems emphasising a variety of sources of difficulty from their study of rather different problems involving pouring liquids of two different concentrations into the same vessel. Questions were then asked about the strength of the resulting mixture. Their view of the problem-solving strategies involved in such problems was even more complex than that of Quintero (1983). They suggest that the first strategic decision is whether to apply direct proportion, inverse proportion or arithmetical operations other than multiplication or division. The next level of decision is whether the ratios involve whole numbers or not (a problem that, it will be recalled, Quintero's subjects also faced). The third level of decision involves implementing actual computations. They suggest that for an expert problem solver the first decision can be taken firmly but the middle-level decision is partly left open while details of the bottom-level decisions are worked out, which may then later cause some middle-level decisions to be revised. As we can see from the solution methods used in Quintero's (1983) two-step problems, some of the details of both solution methods can be worked out and the solver can then discover whether integral ratios are involved. Having discovered that a particular route involves an integral ratio, the solver could then decide to choose that route rather than one involving a non-integral value. However, both children and adults tend also to try to short-cut this process by comparing the numbers involved to see if there are any integral ratios before working out the computational details. This will be beneficial if it leads to the rejection of hard solution routes and the acceptance of easy ones, but it can lead to error if the computational method is then determined solely by the desire for integral ratios. For instance, consider the problem, 'In a store they give 5 lollipops for every 2 chocolate bars you buy. How many lollipops for 15 chocolate bars?' Here some children will try to use the fact that 5:15 is an integral ratio, though neither of the correct solution routes uses integral ratios.[12]

Before describing some studies of the development of probability concepts something should be said about probability in general. Mathematical philosophers have looked at probability in a variety of ways and without some appreciation of this we may unintentionally fall into a rather narrow view of the topic. Three particularly important distinctions are as follows. Firstly, some judgements about probability seem to be made on the general principle that if there is no apparent reason why any one from a number of events should be more probable than another, then all are equally probable. Examples of this are the fall of a dice or the drawing of a particular card from a pack of fifty-two. On the other hand, there are probability judgements based on more intangible grounds, often dealing with unequal probabilities. Examples here might be estimating the probability of a given person performing an action on a particular day or estimating the chances of a horse winning a race. The key distinction between these two kinds of probability judgements is that in the first case the judgement is based on an explicit principle, while in the second we are dealing with a kind of guess, probably based on past experience, but seldom involving any systematic review of that experience or process of logical inference.

A second important distinction is between dependent and independent probabilities. The chance of rolling a six on a dice or drawing the ace of hearts from fifty-two cards is (we like to imagine) independent of previous throws or draws. The chance of a horse winning a race is usually not thought to be independent of the weather or its state of training.

A third distinction is that between what Cohen (1970, 1979) calls Pascalian and Baconian views of probability. As most school work on probability is based on the Pascal model most of what follows will deal with that. Cohen's writings have, however, served to point out the existence of another way of looking at probability that is quite at variance with the usual, Pascalian, model. He may also be right in thinking that in some situations adults use the Baconian rather than the Pascalian theory, though this remains controversial (see Tversky and Kahnemann, 1974, 1979).

The Pascalian model assumes that all conditions relevant to an event are specified in the evidence to hand; the Baconian model assumes that some are not. Consider, for instance, the familiar problem of drawing black and white balls from an urn containing equal numbers of each. Pascalian probability assumes that we know that the only relevant factor (the fumbling of the hand in the urn) is random; in addition, we know that the numbers of balls of different colours are equal. The Baconian view would, however, be relevant either if we suspected the hand to be capable of colour perception by synæsthesia or were ignorant of the number of balls of each colour in the urn, or both. In many situations, Cohen argues, we are faced with problems much more like the second situation than the first. Thus in testing a drug, we may try it on a particular human sample and then generalise the probabilities of the various outcomes to 'people in general'. We are at first tempted to say that this is just incautious. Thus if a group of male New Yorkers from the advertising industry were used we might restrict our probabilities to this group. The disconcerting thing is that this does not eliminate the problem. We still don't know how representative our sample was even of that group. We may always be deceived by any sample defined intensively, that is, by definition of the types of individuals in it. Thus our drug sample could have over-represented homosexuals, smokers or any other characteristic even within male New York workers in the advertising industry. One way we can stop this is to define the sample extensively, that is, name each person, but that prevents us from generalising at all. Worse, we may find that freak weather conditions or atmospheric pollution influenced the reactions of the particular people involved, which would have been different on any other day. We end up just stating facts about what happened to particular people on particular days and not talking about probability at all; that always involves generalisation to the unknown.

Bearing these distinctions in mind, I now turn to Piaget and Inhelder's (1951) study of the development of concepts of probability. Briefly, their conclusion was that before about 7 years, children tend to think that every event has a particular, in-principle, knowable cause. Particular events in the future may be predicted, such as 'This throw will be a six', but the idea of a long-run distribution of sixes, fives, etc. is foreign to the young child. This view of in-principle predictability is disrupted after about 7 years by the discovery of chance; that some events, like dice throwing, are in principle hazardous but subject to long-term prediction. In one study, for instance, children were shown two collections of white counters, each counter either with or without a cross on the back. Subjects were shown how many counters had crosses and how many did not in each collection and were then asked about the relative chances of turning up a cross in the two collections. In one condition (8) there was inequality of favourable cases (crosses) and equality of possible cases (number of counters) such that there were, for example, 1 from 4 versus 2 from 4 with crosses; in another condition (9) there was equality of favourable cases (crosses) and inequality of possible cases (counters), for example, 1 from 2 versus 1 from 3 with crosses. In both these conditions children from about 7 years were found able to make a correct comparison, arguing for (8) that there were more chances of success in the second collection and for (9) that there were more chances of failure (non-crosses) in the second collection. Thus a basic intuition that one event may be more probable than another exists at this age and an ability to compare arithmetical probabilities under the above conditions is present. However, when faced with the problem of comparing 2 crosses from 4 with 1 from 2, it is not until about 11 or 12 years that success is achieved owing to the difficulty of dealing with proportion. Even at this age comparison of 1 cross from 3 with 2 from 5 is found impossible in many cases because of the difficulty of comparing the fractions. To fit their results into a stage-like sequence Piaget and Inhelder try to gloss over this latter point by making out that the inadequate methods of comparison adopted involved some limited kind of success; the actual replies cited show, however, that 11 and 12 year olds really failed when asked to compare 1 cross from 3 with 2 from 5, showing that technical computational facility in the form of ability to reduce the two fractions to a common denominator plays a greater role than these authors are willing to allow.

Piaget and Inhelder argued, in a very vague way, that comparison of 1 from 3 and 2 from 5 is possible by means of looking at combinations between the two sets. Actually all this results in for the children is failure. Piaget and Inhelder then devote a long section of the book to some experiments on combinations and permutations and end by arguing that adolescent reasoning about probability involves a synthesis of ideas about combinations, probability and their own version of propositional logic.

Most of this we can immediately reject; their version of the advent of propositional reasoning is incorrect (see Chapter 1), while the linkages between combinations and probability are overplayed. It is true that in some situations involving a judgement that a number of combinations of events are equiprobable, we must first establish the number of combinations involved; for instance, in thinking about the possible outcomes of tossing two pennies we must think of two heads, two ways of having heads and tails and two tails. Piaget and Inhelder report a study of this kind of reasoning showing that assessment of possible combinations does not appear until early adolescence. However, this only establishes a linkage in situations where combinations are explicitly involved, not the very general linkage they wish to argue for.[13]

We may summarise Piaget and Inhelder's (1951) view as being that the difficulties that younger children have with probability are of relating a part (the target events) to the whole (all events). This is resolved during the primary years, but comparison of two probabilities remains difficult until 11 or 12 years owing to the difficulty of comparing ratios. Both the claimed stage-like nature of these developments and in particular the claim that children at 11 or 12 years are spontaneously able to compare ratios requiring reduction to a common denominator have been the subject of convincing criticism. The role of comparisons of part and whole in making difficulties for younger children remains unclear.

Two prominent alternatives to the Piagetian view will now be described. Fischbein (1975) differs from Piaget and Inhelder (1951) on two fundamental points. The first is partly derived from studies of probability learning. In these studies children are asked to guess which of a number of alternatives will occur and then discover whether they have chosen correctly. Probability matching occurs when children match their own relative frequency of choosing an alternative to that of the event. Studies by Siegel and Andrews (1962) and others show that probability matching can occur as young as 3 years of age. This led Fischbein to conclude that when assessed by non-verbal methods and not required to count relative frequencies or perform arithmetical operations preschoolers do have a primary intuition of relative frequency.[14] Hoemann and Ross (1971), however, argued that the non-verbal intuitive estimation of odds was not evidence of a 'real' or 'operational' concept of probability, thus upholding Piaget and Inhelder's original contention. This argument ultimately seems to devolve on what one means by a real concept of probability. On this point Fischbein (1975) prefers to distinguish the intuitive estimation of odds of the preschooler from the conceptual grasp of probability of the 8 year old.

Fischbein (1975) also provides evidence from his own experiments that adolescents are often inept at using combinations to solve probability problems. He argues that while they have a potential ability to do this, specific teaching is often required to perfect it.

A second important attempt to revise Piaget and Inhelder's (1951) view has been made by Brainerd (1981). He reports twelve experiments designed to systematically eliminate various hypotheses about probability judgements in children. In these studies the primary index of understanding was children's guesses about which colour a counter drawn from a container would turn out to be. Like Fischbein, Brainerd concludes that even preschoolers can match their choices to a knowledge of the relative numbers of counters of different colours in the containers. However, especially in younger children, the attempt to match frequency of choice with the relative number of counters of a given colour was imperfect. Brainerd attributes this imperfection primarily to failure to retrieve relevant information at the time a choice is made. This failure of retrieval is ascribed to the limitations of working memory space in the young child.[15]

A number of studies have looked at the question of whether children's understanding of probability can be influenced by teaching. Falk *et al.* (1980) found that teaching was able to improve understanding of elementary probability in the age range 6-11 years. Fischbein and Gazit (1984) found that many sixth graders (11 year olds) and most seventh graders were able to benefit from instruction in probability concepts. Myers *et al.* (1983) found in a study of college students that those taught the conceptual rationale for formulæ were superior in their application of the formulæ to story problems to those taught routine application only; however, both groups showed about equal facility with problems already expressed in formula form.[16]

Finally there have been a number of studies looking at the ability of secondary school students to grasp the more advanced applications of probability theory needed in secondary school mathematics. Ross and DeGroot (1982) gave adolescents two types of written problems involving combination of probabilities. An example of a conjunctive probability problem was 'You want to speak on a TV show. The chances you will be admitted are 50 per cent, the chances that if admitted you will be allowed to speak are 25 per cent. Your chances of both attending and speaking are approximately (a) 6 per cent, (b) 13 per cent, (c) 25 per cent, (d) 37 per cent, (e) 50 per cent?' Disjunctive questions asked about the chance of either one or the other of two events occurring (given by the formula $P(A) + P(B) - P(A) \times P(B)$ for independent events A, B). The correct answer for the conjunctive problems was given by $P(A) \times P(B)$.

Less than 20 per cent of students from 12-15 gave the correct answer to either kind of problem, which is below the chance level of responding (20 per cent). For 21 year old college students (psychology majors) nearly 50 per cent answered the conjunctive questions correctly, but still only 20 per cent answered disjunctive problems correctly. At the same time there was a significant increase on disjunctive items in the type of error produced by picking one of the values given in the initial part of the question.

Interviews with students suggested two kinds of reasons for the failure of the older students on disjunctive problems. One group tend to see the combination of disjunctive probabilities as impossible as they believe the first event must have occurred before a prediction can be made about the second. Other students see the question as a sophisticated attempt to get them to fall into the 'gambler's fallacy', which is in this case that occurrence of the first event makes the second event less likely. However, they are unable to go from here to a correct solution.

Another study dealing with combination of probabilities has been reported by Green (1983). He suggested that a box of drawing pins was emptied onto a table; 68 fell point up, 32 point down. Subjects were then asked which was the most likely result if the procedure were repeated: 36 up, 64 down; 63:37; 51:49; 84:16; or, 'All these results have the same chance'. Between 11 and 16 years the most common answer was the last, with the percentage giving this reply increasing from 58 at age 11-12, to 66 per cent at age 15-16. The correct reply (63:37) was given by 15 per cent at 11-12, rising to 20 per cent at 15-16. It appears from this that intuitive understanding of the likely distribution resulting from a large number of independent events emerges late, a result in accordance with both Fischbein's claim that the application of combinatorial analysis is often not undertaken spontaneously during adolescence and with Ross and DeGroot's (1982) finding that understanding of conjunction of probabilities does not emerge spontaneously even with late adolescence. It should be pointed out, however, that in some of Piaget and Inhelder's (1951) studies they found ability to comprehend distributions produced by independent events began in early adolescence. The factors producing this discrepancy were probably that Piaget and Inhelder's experimental situation encouraged a visual approach and the outlying arms of their distribution comprised individual events that were unlikely rather than combinations of individual events that were unlikely.[17]

For reasons of space, combinatorial reasoning will only be dealt with very briefly here. Roberge and Flexer (1979) found that contrary to Piagetian theory some kinds of combinations were successfully solved before some proportionality tasks. As usual, several specific kinds of testing difficulty may have contributed to this result, but the study illustrates the problems inherent in the Piagetian position. Likewise, Roberge (1976) found the inter-correlations between success on combinatorial reasoning tasks and conditional reasoning in early adolescence to be low. Scardemalia (1977) showed that the difficulty of combinatorial tasks depended upon the number of factors involved; she interpreted this as evidence of the influence of memory limitations, though variation in understanding of appropriate processing strategies was not ruled out in her study.

In general the most recent work on combinations emphasises the relative difficulty of tasks requiring different kinds of strategies and the large role of teaching in producing an understanding of the more difficult cases.[18]

PROCESS STUDIES

Problem Solving

This section will begin with a brief introduction to the view of problem solving taken by information processing theory, which has been the most popular approach to this topic in recent years.

It may help to begin with the example of arithmetical problems. Here the child or adult can be asked something like this: 'Jimmy has eight apples. He gives three apples to Bobby. How many does Jimmy have left?' Assuming a mental solution is required the first thing they must do is remember the information given. This is called the knowledge base. This is then acted upon by problem-solving strategies. The solution in this case depends upon taking three from eight; the answer to this may already be well known to the solver. Alternatively, the solver might try a different tack and count out eight fingers, remove three and then count the result. Both these solution methods are what are known as algorithmic solutions. This is to say that if implemented correctly they inevitably lead to a correct result. Another kind of algorithmic method used in solving more difficult addition problems is the familiar one of writing the numbers down with the tens under the tens and the ones under the ones, beginning with the right hand column, carrying any tens that accumulate, adding up the tens column, carrying any hundreds that accumulate, and so on.

A different kind of solution method can also be used in arithmetic, which involves heuristics. These are guides that recognise the problem as belonging to a certain type and that give a good chance of leading to a solution but do not necessarily do so. In arithmetic if we see the problem 25×40 we may think of trying to simplify it by extracting factors from each of the numbers that give a known answer when combined and then hoping that this known answer can be easily multiplied by the remaining factors. In this case the problem can be easily simplified by taking the factors 4 and 10 from 40: $25 \times 40 = 25 \times 4 \times 10 = 100 \times 10 = 1,000$. But if the problem had been 33×26 this kind of approach doesn't help us much. The sum can be expanded into the factors: $3 \times 11 \times 2 \times 13$. We can get a bit further by saying $3 \times 2 = 6$, $6 \times 11 = 66$. This reduces the problem to 66×13, but this is really no more manageable than 33×26. Thus the heuristic method of factoring numbers to be multiplied may help, but it may not.

Both heuristics and algorithms must have some way of recognising that the problem is an appropriate one to attack using the given method. In the case of the addition algorithm involving writing down columns of figures the recognition process is quite simple, being simply the rule that if the problem involves addition then use the addition algorithm. While this is obvious to us, young children may, of course, confuse problems with one another and start doing the wrong algorithm. Quite a common case here is to misread × as + and to do addition when multiplication was asked for. In this case the recognition procedure for the algorithm has broken down and the wrong one implemented.

Another kind of recognition mechanism is involved in retrieving information from the knowledge base to plug into the routines that have been chosen. Thus while a child might recognise the problem about Jimmy's apples as involving subtraction, they might well choose 3 as the number to begin the subtraction with. Then they might reason, 'Three take away 8. Can't do that. Try 8 take away 3. That makes 5. Answer 5.'

Mathematics teachers will recognise this kind of problem solving with a sinking feeling. The student knows what the information relevant to the problem is and knows the routine to solve the problem but can only match the two up by trial and error. An effective problem solver, on the other hand, would know that 'There is an initial number and something is taken away. We want to know what is left; take the something from the initial number.' When we explain this in words we see that the initial number and the something are tagged by these phrases in the first statement, so we know where to put them in the second statement. Somehow, perhaps using words or perhaps tagging the items of information in some other way, the problem solver knows which bits of information to plug into the problem-solving routines where.

One of the really novel things we have discovered from attempts to get machines to solve problems is that this process of finding the right information for our purposes is more of a difficulty than we might otherwise think. For one thing we probably tag all the information given initially about Jimmy and Bobby and the apples as 'relevant to this problem'. This would get around the task of having to search through all the millions of other things we know in order to find the information relevant to this problem. Solving problems using information not given recently but already stored somewhere in memory is generally more difficult, but we are still surprisingly adept at it.

One theory of how we are able to find relevant information so readily is that we have our memories organised into categories of information and the first thing we think of is how to get to the right category. Thus if I said to you, 'How many countries are there in South America?', you would either look under 'countries' or under 'South America'.

This actually points up rather well the dangers of following computer models too slavishly. Most computer-based information retrieval systems would have an index (or 'discrimination net') of information that listed items about geography under such things as 'countries', 'population statistics', 'continents', etc. However, when you ask most adults this question the first thing they think of is a picture of South America. Then they try to count the number of countries off the mental picture. If you try this with a continent you are fairly unfamiliar with (Africa or South-East Asia are good alternatives) something else interesting also emerges. Some parts of the picture are clear, but in the other parts you start falling back on names, which are dimly related to the picture.

So far I have talked about problem-solving strategies operating on an organised knowledge base to produce solutions. A number of clarifications to this general picture are now in order. The first is that as distinct from overall strategies, problem solvers also use more limited and stereotyped routines. Strategies are higher-order methods of organising the implementation of lower-order routines. Thus in arithmetic someone solving arithmetical problems might use the following strategy: 'Look to see if the problem contains one digit or many digit numbers. If one digit numbers, do you know the answer immediately (as addition facts)? If not, count on fingers. If many digit numbers, write them down and use the standard addition algorithm.' In this case the strategy is fairly simple, but in other cases it might be more complex. The routines in this case would be those of counting or of performing the addition algorithm.

Two more detailed concepts relating specifically to mathematical problem solving will now be introduced: subgoal and fixation. Most problems of any complexity usually seem to be tackled by setting up subgoals that, in one variant, reduce the distance between the initial situation and the solution. Sub-goals may either be set up by working forwards from the solution or backwards from the conclusion. A slight variant on this view of subgoals would be the idea that they are set up using highly intuitive, rapid and often inaccurate methods of guessing that a given route can be traversed that ignore all questions about advancing nearer to the problem solution. Full solution of the problem then requires retracing this route more carefully; in mathematics it usually involves writing down the detailed steps in the proof. It is likely that 'distance estimates' are used more in problems where some kind of estimate of distance can be obtained (planning a route on a road map would be a good example). However, in mathematics we must quite often begin by going in what appears to be 'the wrong direction' by setting up a subgoal that actually appears to increase the distance between sub-goal and final goal (or from starting point to subgoal, if we are working backwards).

Fixation of method is a phenomenon described by Luchins and Luchins (1959). In a typical case, the problem solver begins by solving a series of problems, all of which require the same method, that is, the same series of subgoals. When a problem comes along that needs a different method, the solver tends to try their old method first and may be unable to think of the new method while a person coming fresh to the problem would be able to solve it.

Both subgoals and fixation are relevant to a third term, which while not much used in the research literature has gone into popular usage: De Bono's (1967) 'lateral thinking'. This term is used when we have become fixated on a routine method or on one that seems to go in a straight line from start towards finish and then gets blocked. We then need to 'think off to the side' (lateral thinking) to avoid the obvious but wrong method and think of a non-obvious but successful one.

A number of recent studies have looked at the applicability of the general approach to problem solving outlined so far to school geometry problems. There is general agreement that it is applicable.[19] Of greater interest therefore are the ways in which teaching or other experiences can improve the operation of the various processes so far described.

Kantowski (1977) found that harder problems were more likely to elicit heuristics as assessed in an interview than easier ones.[20] Rather surprisingly she also found that the strategy of solving a problem, leaving the solution, then looking back and checking it, did not increase with experience of geometry problem-solving, though adult mathematicians recommend this and it has also been emphasised in school learning by Polya (1965). Kantowski also found that novice problem solvers began by using intuitive methods to go from one step in the proof to the next, but this was superceded by more rigorous logical deduction, a view earlier advanced by Van Hiele (1973).

A strong indication that this last finding may oversimplify the learning process can be found in Anderson et al. (1981), who found that even in successful solutions there was an initial phase of 'planning' during which the various subgoals to be obtained are mapped out, followed by a proof phase in which the individual steps are written out as rigorous deductions. While Anderson et al. do not mention this explicitly, it seems likely that during plan construction some evaluation of intended paths between subgoals takes place by intuitive means and this is then firmed up during the proof stage. Anderson et al. suggest that teachers often neglect the planning stage and try to get students going on the proof stage before they have a plan. They also suggest that explicit instruction about the proof phase could yield dividends.

Anderson et al. (1981) suggest that three kinds of learning are important in constructing geometrical proofs: from the textbook, by knowledge compilation and by knowledge optimisation. They begin by pointing out that textbooks are not explicit about the actual procedures used in problem solving. Rather, the learner must gather what they can from worked examples, general problem-solving techniques applied to the postulates and definitions of geometry, and the extension of general concepts to geometry. They argue that though students often work with plans derived by analogy from previously encountered examples, they generally fail to detect such analogies unless they are on a rather superficial level. Anderson *et al.* also suggest that many learners have considerable difficulty internalising the postulates and definitions of geometry because they look at a diagram illustrating, say, the side-angle-side definition of congruence for triangles, but only encode in memory part of the information presented, not noticing, for instance, that the relevant angle must be included between the two sides. Anderson *et al.* also believe that knowledge about definitions and postulates is encoded in the form of abstract propositions; it seems, however, plausible to suggest that some learners code the postulates as a schematic mental image that later becomes allied to visual recognition skills that detect examples where the postulate or definition is relevant.

As an example of the application of pre-existing concepts and schemas to a geometrical context, Anderson *et al.* give the problem below:

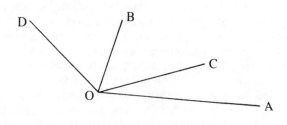

Fig. 1. *A Geometry Problem*

The problem is: given that <AOB and <COD are right angles, prove <AOC = <BOD. They found that some of their subjects compared this to the problem (overleaf) about line segments. Here the problem was given RO = NY, prove RN = OY. Notice that to make this particular transfer the learner must be able to adapt the solution to the slightly different structure of the geometry problem. In both cases, however, we use the fact that magnitudes remain equal when equal or identical elements are added to or subtracted from them.

Knowledge compilation is a term Anderson *et al.* use to describe the shift from 'knowing that' certain postulates and theorems are true in geometry to 'knowing how' to use these facts in the course of deductions. Their analysis here is, as mentioned previously, based on the notion that postulates and theorems are stored initially as propositions and then converted to 'how to' instructions that say how to use this knowledge; as al-

Fig. 2. Line-segment Problem

ready pointed out an alternative view might place more emphasis on moving from schematic images to visual recognition skills. Very little is explicitly taught about compilation of knowledge and we must assume that students learn about this largely by doing worked examples.

The third kind of learning involves 'knowledge optimisation', which consists largely of learning when to apply various heuristics both in the planning and the proof phases. An important cause of improvement in use of heuristics is, they suggest, the transition from seeing superficial resemblances between problems to being able to see that superficially dissimilar problems have the same underlying structure.

Hoz (1981) has reported a successful attempt to measure the tendency for individual ninth grade geometry students to suffer from rigidity of use of methods in geometry problem solving. He concludes that the tendency to rigidity contains two subcomponents, perceptual and conceptual. The perceptual component corresponds to Duncker's (1945)' functional fixedness and acts, for instance, to prevent a subject from treating the line giving the height of a triangle as simultaneously the side of a second triangle. Elements of the problem are seen to have a fixed rather than a variable function. The conceptual component of rigidity is similar to Anderson *et al.*'s (1981) observation that methods tend to be allied with particular problems and difficulty is experienced in uncoupling them and applying them to different situations.

Lewis (1981) has applied general notions about problem solving to the simplification of expressions in elementary algebra. He suggests that two processes are involved—strategies and procedures. Procedures are legal moves for simplifying expressions, like expanding a bracket or applying one of the four arithmetical operations to both sides of the expression. Strategies are chiefly arrived at by heuristics that tell the learner when given operations are likely to be of use. Thus $5/10 = (x-10)/(x-5)$ asks for a cross-multiplying operation, while $x + 2 = 5$ calls for subtraction of 2 from both sides. Surprisingly, Lewis found that while expert mathematicians differed quantitatively in ability to find the correct strategy and apply procedures from novice students, there was little qualitative difference.

Mayer (1982) found that when given algebra word problems college students tend to try to clear brackets before collecting unknowns to one side of the equation, whereas for problems given in symbolic form the students preferred to collect unknowns to the same side first. Thus for the problem $(8 + 3x)/2 = 3x - 11$, students would under the first strategy first multiply both sides by 2; under the second they might 'move' $3x/2$ across to the right hand side and $- 11$ to the left hand side. It is not presently very clear why this happens, but the phenomenon may ultimately provide the key to certain kinds of errors.[21]

Schoenfeld (1979) found that explicit instruction in five heuristics indicating strategies for solving elementary algebra problems produced quite marked improvement among university students, indicating that explicit teaching of heuristics can be beneficial. However, a later study by Schoenfeld (1982) produced more equivocal results in attempting to improve problem-solving skills in a wider range of mathematical problems. In general, reviews of controlled studies of the effects of problem-solving instruction have reported mixed results. While Suydam (1980) was optimistic about results, most are much more restrained.[22] Even in Suydam's review most of the studies reported only tentative results and throughout the literature one finds such methodological problems as those encountered when the control and experimental groups have different teachers, thus confounding programme and teacher. It is possible that the contrast between Schoenfeld's (1979) and (1982) results provides one explanation for so many equivocal results: many of the programmes investigated are of a general nature, as in Schoenfeld (1982), whereas more specific programmes of the kind reported by Schoenfeld (1979) would be expected to yield better results. A particularly successful attempt to teach problem-solving strategies for specific types of elementary algebra problems to junior secondary students by Malin (1979) reinforces this conclusion.

Finally, two reports of interactions between algebra teaching methods and ability have been made in recent years. Young and Becker (1979) found that high ability students benefited more from a 'figural' method of instruction that translated problems into number-lines, while poor ability students benefited more from being taught methods involving purely symbolic manipulation. This finding seems to suggest that while both high and low ability students need to know how to translate problems into symbolic form, symbol manipulation may be more easily acquired by low ability students if less emphasis is placed on its rationale. Eastman and Salhab (1978) have also reported a similar result in a study of two methods of solving equations.

Concepts of Proof

The previous section was concerned with the mechanics of manipulating mathematical expressions, which includes the process of giving a proof. The present section is concerned with what students think they are doing when they give a proof.

According to Piaget and Inhelder (1955) the ability to reflect upon processes of logical deduction belongs to the 'formal operations' of adolescence. This belief is based on general grounds, and specific studies of mathematical thinking were not undertaken. More recent studies have shown that 'metacognition' (ability to reflect on one's thought processes) is present in some degree from an early age. It requires specific study, however, to determine the actual ideas students of varying ages have about mathematical proof.

Van Hiele (1973), reporting on his own studies of geometrical proof, distinguished three 'levels of thinking'. At the 'ground level', typical of first contacts with geometry, thinking is restricted to particular figures. At the 'first level' of thinking this gives way to the idea that figures of a particular kind (such as trapezia) have certain properties, but thinking is still restricted to a particular class of figures. At the 'second level' the student is able to think more self-consciously about geometrical proof. While proof at the first level tends to be intuitive, at the second level the requirement that each step be carefully set out and based on explicit principles is realised.[23]

Bell (1976a) described three stages 'loosely related to age' applying to proofs more generally. At stage 1 patterns of relationships can be recognised, described and extended, but there is no attempt to explain, justify or deduce them. This predominated at ages 11-13 and appears to correspond to Van Hiele's first level. Stage 3 was found in only 10 per cent of children in the range 11-18 and this percentage did not increase much in older children. This consisted of an 'informal but acceptably complete' deductive argument or an empirical check on all possibilities inherent in the situation. The majority of students in the range 14-18 years produced stage 2 proofs, which were 'deductive arguments ranging from relevant but fragmentary remarks to almost complete arguments and empirical checks ranging from the consideration of one or two cases only to the testing of a variety covering most of the significantly different types of case' (Bell, 1976b).

Williams (1980) was similarly pessimistic about the ability of secondary students either to give or understand proofs, less than 30 per cent of 16 year olds being capable of these. He further found 70 per cent of this age group incapable of distinguishing inductive from deductive proof, 80 per cent failing to realise the significance of hypotheses and definitions, 60 per cent unwilling to adopt an apparently false hypothesis 'for the sake of argument', and 80 per cent unable to understand the significance of counterexamples. All this despite being enrolled in a mathematics programme designed 'to enable students to subjectively understand the nature and role of mathematics proof'.

Despite the rather widely differing demands that mathematics curricula place on students in regard to proof in different strands of national systems and in different countries (see Bell, 1976b) there is little doubt that students widely fail to gain all but the most elementary notions about proof in secondary schools. While the studies of Van Hiele (1973) and Bell (1976b) can be criticised for failing to discriminate sufficiently between the technical complexities of different kinds of proof, those of Bell (1976b) and Williams (1980) show that even taking this into account, proof is a difficult topic for the majority of students.

One way round the difficulty of deductive proof for the average student that has been widely adopted in recent years, especially in geometry teaching, has been to make some results that are hard to prove inductively plausible by providing a number of examples and having students discover the result by induction from the examples. This seems a reasonable first means of arriving at such results. At the same time it seems desirable to explain that these results can be arrived at by rigorous deduction and to illustrate deduction using simple examples.

CONCLUSIONS

Studies of the content of the secondary mathematics curriculum bear out two of the general weaknesses of Piagetian theory discussed earlier in the book. First, Piaget tended to exaggerate the extent to which disparate abilities emerge together as a 'stage'. Rather, the difficulty of constituent concepts as well as of the complexity of problems has been shown to have a considerable effect on the differential difficulty of problems. Second, Piaget tended to be over-optimistic about the spontaneous appearance of conceptual skills and awarenesses that have since been shown to require teaching for their emergence.

Studies of mathematical problem solving show that the general concepts of the problem-solving theories of Gestalt psychology and information-processing theory can be applied to problem solving in secondary school mathematics. Attempts to explicitly teach problem-solving skills suggest that the more specific the topic the more successful teaching is likely to be. Studies of awareness of the characteristics of proof show that this remains difficult for all but the most able students throughout secondary school.

FURTHER READING

On functions, equations and algebra see Piaget *et al.* (1968) (the English translation is titled *Epistemology and Psychology of Functions*, Hingham: Kluwer, 1977), Siegler (1976, 1984), Thomas (1975), Dreyfus and Eisenberg (1982), Collis (1975), Wollman *et al.* (1979), Kieran (1979), Herscovics and Kieran (1980), Kuchemann (1980) and Wagner (1981); on geometrical concepts see Darke (1982), Sommerville and Bryant (1985); on infinity, limit and calculus see Langford (1974) (also reprinted in Modgil and Modgil, 1976, Vol. 4), Fischbein *et al.* (1979), Orton (1983a,b); on proportion see Piaget (1971), Quintero (1983), Karplus *et al.* (1983); on probability see Piaget and Inhelder (1951), Fischbein (1975), Brainerd (1981), Ross and De Groot (1982), Green (1983). (French readers will also find Maury (1985) of interest.) On combinations see Roberge (1976), Scardamalia (1977), Hadar and Hadass (1981). (French readers will find Mendelsohn (1981) and Dubois (1984) of interest.) On problem solving generally see Newell and Simon (1972), Mayer (1977, 1983), Langley and Simon (1981); on problem solving in mathematics see Greeno (1983), Anderson *et al.* (1981), Lester (1980), Hayes (1980), Schoenfeld (1982); on concepts of proof see Bell (1976a,b), Hoffer (1983).

NOTES

1. See also Juraschek and Grady (1981), Ferretti *et al.* (1985).
2. See Orton (1970), Lovell (1971).
3. See also Häussler (1977) and Karplus (1979). Demonstrations that positive linear functions are easier to understand than negative ones had long been available for college students, but this was not generally related to the developmental literature (Björkman, 1965; Eade, 1967 ; Mayer, 1967; Naylor and Clark, 1968; Brehmer, 1973; Slovik, 1974).
4. Wollman *et al.* (1979) have shown that non-acceptance of lack of closure is partly due to memory load problems.
5. Ginsburg (1977), Behr *et al.* (1976).
6. On difficulties in the secondary years see Vergnaud *et al.* (1979); for Kieran's studies see Kieran (1979, 1980), Herscovics and Kieran (1980).
7. Hart (1981a,b), Kuchemann (1980).
8. Such as Moyer (1978), Schultz and Austin (1983), Kidder (1976).

9. The earlier findings were confirmed by Tall and Vinner (1981) and Fischbein *et al.* (1981).
10. Comparisons of variable speeds are more difficult. See Crépault (1978a,b, 1979, 1980). On metric conceptions of speed see Wilkening (1982). Levin (1979) showed that other irrelevant cues apart from distance can become the basis for erroneous speed comparisons in young children.
11. Lovell and Butterworth (1966), Lunzer and Pumphrey (1966), Fischbein *et al.* (1970), Strauss (1977), Karplus and Peterson (1970), Karplus and Karplus (1972), Hensley (1974), Kishta (1979), Case (1979), Noelting (1980a,b).
12. See also Tourniaire and Pulos (1985), Lawson *et al.* (1984), Le Halle and Savois (1985).
13. A number of studies have tried to gauge whether, as Piaget and Inhelder claim, the primary difficulty faced by young children is in coordinating part (frequency of target event) with whole (frequency of all events). To date no resolution has been achieved. See Goldberg (1966), Yost *et al.* (1962), Hoemann and Ross (1971), Chapman (1975), Perner (1979). Green (1978) showed that when non-verbal testing is used the stage-like character of development is reduced.
14. Fischbein was also influenced by the studies of Davies (1965) and Fischbein *et al.* (1971).
15. More on information-processing approaches to probability can be found in Wallace and Fonte (1984).
16. See also Hawkins and Kapadia (1984).
17. Maury (1985) has shown that even quite slight variations in the question can radically affect adolescents' ability to conceive independent probabilities.
18. See Mendelsohn (1981), Hadar and Hadass (1981), Dubois (1984), White (1985).
19. Kulm and Bussman (1980), Kantowski (1977), Anderson *et al.* (1981).
20. On the use of heuristics in geometry see also Greeno (1983).
21. See also Rosnick and Clement (1980), Sims-Knight and Kaput (1983).
22. See Lester (1980), Hayes (1980), Schoenfeld (1982).
23. For a review of research based on this model see Hoffer (1983).

BIBLIOGRAPHY

Chapter 1

Abraham, M. R. and Renner, J. W. (1986) 'The sequence of learning cycle activities in high school chemistry', *Journal of Research in Science Teaching*, 23, 121-43

Anderson, J. H. and Armbruster, B. B. (1984) 'Studying' in P. D. Pearson (ed.), *Handbook of Reading Research*, Longman, New York

Ault, R. (1977) *Children's Cognitive Development*, Oxford University Press, New York

Ausubel, D., Novak, J. D. and Hanesian, H. (1978) *Educational Psychology, A Cognitive View*, 2nd edn, Holt, Rinehart and Winston, New York

Bennett, N. (1977) *Teaching Style and Pupil Progress*, Open Books, London

Brainerd, C. J. (1983) 'Young children's mental arithmetic errors: a working memory analysis', *Child Development*, 54, 812-30

———— and Kingma, J. (1985) 'On the independence of short term memory and working memory in cognitive development', *Cognitive Psychology*, 17, 210-47

Bullock, M. *et al.* (1982) 'The development of causal reasoning', in W. J. Friedman (ed.), *The Developmental Psychology of Time*, Academic Press, New York

———— (1985) 'Causal reasoning and developmental change over the preschool years', *Human Development*, 28, 169-91

Case, R. (1979) 'The underlying mechanism of intellectual development', in J. Biggs and J. Kirby (eds), *Instructional Processes and Individual Differences in Learning*, Academic Press, New York

Dunn, C. S. (1983) 'The influence of instructional methods on concept learning', *Science Education*, 67, 647-56

Ennis, R. H. (1976) 'An alternative to Piaget's conceptualisation of logical competence', *Child Development*, 47, 903-19

———— (1982) 'Children's ability to handle Piaget's propositional logic: a conceptual critique', in S. Modgil and C. Modgil (eds), *Jean Piaget Consensus and Controversy*, Holt, Rinehart and Winston, London

Fischer, K. W. (1980) 'A theory of cognitive development: the control and construction of hierarchies of skills', *Psychological Review*, 87, 477-531

———— and Pipp, S. L. (1984) 'Processes of cognitive development: optimal level and skill acquisition', in R. J. Sternberg (ed.), *Mechanisms of Cognitive Development*, Freeman, New York

Gagné, R. M. (1984) *The Conditions of Learning*, Holt Saunders, New York, 4th edn

Halford, G. S. and Wilson, W. H. (1980) 'A category theory approach to cognitive development', *Cognitive Psychology*, 12, 356-411

Inhelder, B. and Piaget, J. (1955) *The Growth of Logical Thinking From Childhood to Adolescence*, Basic Books, New York

Karplus, R. (1980) 'Teaching for the development of reasoning', in A. E. Lawson (ed.), *1980 AETS Yearbook*, Eric, Columbus

Kennedy, J. H. (1983) 'Assessing the relationship between information processing capacity and historical understanding', *Theory and Research in Social Education*, 11, 1-22

Langford, P. E. (1974) 'The development of concepts of infinity and limit in mathematics', *Archives de Psychologie*, 42, 311-22

———— (1980) 'Review of J. A. Keats, K. Collis and G. Halford (eds), *Cognitive Development* (1978), Wiley, New York,' in *Australian Journal of Psychology*, 32, 69-71

———— (1981) 'A longitudinal study of children's understanding of logical laws in arithmetic and Boolean algebra', *Educational Psychology*, 1, 119-39

———— (1984) 'A critique of Halford and Wilson's approach to cognitive development', *Research in Mathematics Education in Australia*, 1 (2), 34-40

Lott, G. W. (1983) 'The effect of inquiry teaching and advance organisers upon student outcomes in science education', *Journal of Research in Science Teaching*, 20, 437-51

McKinney, C. W. *et al.* (1983) The effectiveness of three methods of teaching social studies concepts to fourth-grade students', *American Education Research Journal*, 20, 663-70

Norman, D. A. (1980) 'What goes on in the mind of the learner', in W. J. McKeachie (ed.), *Learning, Cognition and College Teaching*, Jossey-Bass, San Francisco

Novak, J. D. and Gowin, D. B. (1984) *Learning How to Learn*, Cambridge University Press, Cambridge

Osherson, D. N. (1974) *Logical Abilities in Children* (Vol. 1), Wiley, New York

Pascual-Leone, J. (1971) 'A mathematical model for the transition rule in Piaget's stages', *Acta Psychologica*, 32, 301-45

Piaget, J. and Inhelder, B. (1969) *The Psychology of the Child*, Routledge, London

Seltman, M. and Seltman, P. (1985) *Piaget's Logic*, Allen and Unwin, London

Siegler, R. S. (1981) 'Developmental sequences within and between concepts', *Monographs of the Society for Research in Child Development*, 46 (2)

Spiker, C. C. and Cantor, J. J. (1983) 'Components in the hypothesis-testing strategies of young children', in T. J. Tighe and B. E. Shepp (eds), *Perception, Cognition and Development*, Erlbaum, Hillsdale

Sternberg, R. J. (1979) 'Developmental patterns in the encoding and combination of logical connectives', *Journal of Experimental Child Psychology*, 28, 469-98

Tennyson, R. D. *et al.* (1981) 'Concept learning effectiveness using prototype and skill development presentation forms', *Journal of Educational Psychology*, 74, 329-44

Trabasso, T. (1978) 'On the estimation of parameters and the evaluation of mathematical models: a reply to Pascual-Leone', *Journal of Experimental Child Psychology*, 26, 41-5

———— and Foellinger, D. B. (1978) 'Information-processing capacity in children: a test of Pascual-Leone's model', *Journal of Experimental Child Psychology*, 26, 1-17

Whiteley, J. (1985) 'Control of children's observing responses during information feedback during discrimination learning', *Journal of Experimental Child Psychology*, 39, 245-69

Wilson, K. W. (1980) *From Associations to Structure*, North Holland, Amsterdam

Chapter 2

Anastasi, A. (1958) *Differential Psychology*, Macmillan, New York

Asch, S. E. (1936) 'A study of change of mental organisation', *Archives of Psychology*, 195

Bereiter, C. and Scardamalia, M. (1982) 'From conversation to composition: the role of instruction in a developmental process', in R. Glaser (ed.), *Advances in Instructional Psychology*, Erlbaum, Hillsdale

Billow, R, M. (1975) 'A cognitive-developmental study of metaphor comprehension', *Developmental Psychology*, 11, 415-23

Britton, J. *et al.* (1975) *The Development of Writing Abilities*, Macmillan, London

Brown, A. L. *et al.* (1984) 'Instructing comprehension—fostering activities in interactive learning situations', in H. Mandl (ed.), *Learning and the Comprehension of Text*, Erlbaum, Hillsdale

Burns, H. L. (1980) 'Stimulating rhetorical invention in English composition through computer assisted instruction', *Dissertation Abstracts International*, 40, 3734A

Collins, J. I. (1979) *Teaching Writing: An Interactionist Approach to Abbreviated and Idiosyncratic Language in the Writing of Secondary School Students*, Ph.D. Thesis, University of Massachusetts, Amherst

———— and Williamson, M. M. (1981) 'Spoken language and semantic abbreviation in writing', *Research in the Teaching of English*, 15, 23-35

Cometa, M. S. and Eson, M. E. (1978) 'Logical operations and metaphor interpretation: a Piagetian model', *Child Development*, 49, 649-59

Cook, L. K. and Mayer, R. E. (1983) 'Reading strategies training for meaningful learning from prose', in M. Pressley and J. R. Levin (eds), *Cognitive Strategy Research: Educational Applications*, Springer-Verlag, New York

D'Angelo, F. (1975) *A Conceptual Theory of Rhetoric*, Winthrop, Cambridge

Duffy, J. (1982) 'Theories of discourse and the composing process', *The English Quarterly*, 15, 23-47

Dutch, W. L. (1980) 'A comparison of student-generated heuristics with the use of Larson-generated heuristics in a college classroom', *Dissertation Abstracts International*, 40, 6177A

Ebbert, D. M. (1980) *A Comparison of Three Instructional Approaches for Teaching Written Composition: Pentadic, Tagmemic and Control Treatment*, Ph.D. Thesis, Boston University, Massachusetts

Elbow, P. (1973) *Writing without Teachers*, Oxford University Press, New York

———— (1981) *Writing with Power*, Oxford University Press, New York

Ennis, R. H. (1976) 'An alternative to Piaget's conceptualisation of logical competence', *Child Development*, 47, 903-19

Flower, L. (1979) 'Writer-based prose: a cognitive basis for problems in writing', *College English*, 41, 19-37

———— and Hayes, J. R. (1981a) 'The pregnant pause: an inquiry into the nature of planning', *Research in the Teaching of English*, 15, 229-43

———— and ———— (1981b) 'A cognitive process theory of writing', *College Composition and Communication*, 32, 365-87

———— et al. (1986) 'Detection, diagnosis and revision', *College Composition and Communication*, 37, 16-53

Gardner, H., Kircher, M., Winner, E. and Perkins, D. (1975) 'Children's metaphoric productions and preferences', *Journal of Child Language*, 2, 125-41

Garner, R. (1985) 'Text summarisation deficiencies among older students', *American Education Research Journal*, 22, 549-60

Greenfield, D. M. (1972) 'Oral or written language: The consequences for cognitive development in Africa, the United States and England', *Language and Speech*, 15, 169-78

Hirsch, E. D. (1977) *The Philosophy of Composition*, University of Chicago Press, Chicago

Kroll, B. M. (1978) 'Cognitive egocentrism and the problem of audience awareness in written English', *Research in the Teaching of English*, 12, 269-71

———— (1985) 'Rewriting a complex story for a young reader', *Research in the Teaching of English*, 19, 120-39

Larson, R. L. (1968) 'Discovery through questioning: a plan for teaching rhetorical invention', *College English*, 30, 126-34

Manzo, A. V. (1969) 'The ReQuest procedure', *Journal of Reading*, 13, 123-6

Moffatt, J. (1968) *Teaching in the Universe of Discourse*, Houghton Mifflin, Boston

Monahan, B. D. (1984) 'Revision strategies of basic and competent writers as they write for different audiences', *Research in the Teaching of English*, 18, 288-303

Murray, D. M. (1978) 'Internal revision; a process of discovery', in C. R. Cooper and L. Odell (eds), *Research on Composing: Points of Departure*, National Council of Teachers of English, Urbana

Odell, C. L. (1974) 'Measuring the effect of instruction in pre-writing', *Research in the Teaching of English*, 8, 230

Olson, D. R. (1977) 'From utterance to text: the bias of language in speech and writing', *Harvard Educational Review*, 47, 257-81

Ortony, A. (1984) 'Understanding figurative language', in P. D. Pearson (ed.), *Handbook of Reading Research*, Longman, New York

Peel, E. A. (1966) 'A study of differences in judgments of adolescent pupils', *British Journal of Educational Psychology*, 36, 77-86

———— (1971) *The Nature of Adolescent Judgement*, Wiley, New York

Piaget, J. (1926) *The Language and Thought of the Child*, Routledge, London

Pollio, M. R. (1973) *The Development and Augmentation of figurative Language*, Ph.D. Thesis, University of Tennessee, Tennessee

———— and Pollio, H. R. (1974) 'Development of figurative language in school children', *Journal of Psycholinguistic Research*, 3, 185-201

———— and ———— (1979) 'A test of metaphoric comprehension and some preliminary developmental data', *Journal of Child Language*, 6, 111-20

———— and Pickens, J. D. (1980) 'The development of figurative competence', in R. P. Honeck and R. R. Hoffman (eds), *Cognition and Figurative Language*, Erlbaum, Hillsdale

Robinson, F. P. (1961) *Effective Study*, Harper and Row, New York

Schonberg, R. B. (1974) *Adolescent Thought and Figurative Language*, Ph.D., University of Tennessee, Tennessee

Shaughnessey, M. (1977) *Errors and Expectations*, Oxford University Press, New York

Smith, F. (1977) 'Making sense of reading—and of reading instruction', *Harvard Educational Review*, 47, 386-95

Smith, J. W. (1976) 'Children's comprehension of metaphor', *Language and Speech*, 19, 236-43

Sommers, N. (1980) 'Revision strategies of student writers', *College Composition and Communication*, 31, 378-88

Stauffer, R. G. (1975) *Directing the Reading-Thinking Process*, Harper and Row, New York

Tamburrini, J. *et al.* (1984) 'Children's conceptions of writing', in H. Cowie (ed.), *The Development of Children's Imaginative Writing*, Croom Helm, London

Tierney, R. J. and Cunningham, J. W. (1984) 'Research on teaching reading comprehension', in P. D. Pearson (ed.), *Handbook of Reading Research*, Longman, New York

Toulmin, S. (1958) *The Uses of Argument*, Cambridge University Press, Cambridge

Wason, P. C. (1970) 'On writing scientific papers', *Physics Bulletin*, 21, 407-8

Winner, E., Rosentiel, A. K. and Gardner, H. (1976) 'The development of metaphoric understanding', *Developmental Psychology*, 12, 289-97

Young, R. L. and Koen, F. (1973) *The Tagmemic Discovery Procedure: An Evaluation of its Uses in the Teaching of Rhetoric*, University of Michigan Press, Ann Arbor

————, Becker, A. L. and Pike, K. L. (1970) *Rhetoric: Discovery and Change*, Harcourt Brace Jovanovich, New York

Chapter 3

Ackerman, A. M. *et al.* (1984) 'Mock trial jury decisions as a function of adolescent juror guilt and hostility', *Journal of Genetic Psychology*, 144, 195-201

Adelson, J. *et al.* (1969) 'The growth of the idea of law in adolescence', *Developmental Psychology*, 1, 333-39

Almond, G. and Verba, S. (1963) *The Civic Culture*, Princeton University Press, Princeton

Armsby, R. E. (1971) 'A re-examination of the development of moral judgement in children', *Child Development*, 42, 1241-48

Arsenio, W. F. and Ford, M. E. (1985) 'The role of affective information in social-cognitive development', *Merrill-Palmer Quarterly*, 31, 1-17

Berti, A. E. and Bombi, A. S. (1981) 'The development of the concept of money and its value', *Child Development*, 52, 1179-82

———— *et al.* (1986) 'Acquiring economic notions: profit', *International Journal of Behavioural Development*, 9, 15-29

Black, A. E. (1976) *Co-ordination of Logical and Moral Reasoning in Adolescence*, Ph.D. Thesis, University of California

Buck-Morss, S. (1975) 'Socio-economic bias in Piaget's theory and its implications for cross-culture studies', *Human Development*, 18, 34-49

Burris, V. I. (1976) *The Child's Conception of Economic Relations: A Genetic Approach to the Sociology of Knowledge*, Ph.D. Thesis, Princeton University, Princeton

Byrne, D. F. (1974) 'The development of role-taking in adolescence', *Dissertation Abstracts*, 34, 11, 56747B

Connell, R. W. (1971) *The Child's Construction of Politics*, Melbourne University Press, Melbourne

Costanzo, P. R. *et al.* (1973) 'A re-examination of the effects of intent and consequences on children's moral judgements', *Child Development*, 44, 154-61

Cox, C. B. and Cousins, J. E. (1965) 'Teaching Social Studies in Secondary Schools and Colleges', in B. Massialas and F. R. Smith (eds), *New Challenges in the Social Studies*, Wadsworth, Belmont

Crittenden, B. S. (1978) *Bearings in Moral Education*, ACER, Melbourne

Cummings, S. and Taebel, D. (1978) 'The economic socialization of children: a NeoMarxist analysis', *Social Problems*, 26, 198-210

Danziger, K. (1958) 'Children's earliest conceptions of economic relationships', *Journal of Social Psychology*, 47, 231-40

Darley, J. M. *et al.* (1978) 'Intentions and their contexts in the moral judgement of children and adults', *Child Development*, 49, 56-74

Davies, A. F. (1980) 'Political socialisation', in F. J. Hunt (ed.), *Socialisation in Australia*, Australia International Press, Melbourne

Davison, M. L. *et al.* (1980) 'The stage sequence concept in cognitive and social development', *Developmental Psychology*, 16, 121-31

Durio, H. F. (1976) 'A taxonomy of democratic development: a theoretical interpretation of the internalizing of democratic principles', *Human Development*, 19, 197-219

Edwards, C. P. (1975) 'Societal complexity and moral development', *Ethos*, 3, 505-27

Elkind, D. (1967) 'Egocentrism in adolescence', *Child Development*, 38, 1025-34

———— (1968) 'Adolescent cognitive development', in J. F. Adams (ed.),*Understanding Adolescence*, Alyn and Bacon, Boston

———— and Bowen, R. (1979) 'Imaginary audience behaviour in children and adolescents', *Developmental Psychology*, 15, 38-44

———— and Dabek, R. F. (1977) 'Personal injury and property damage in the moral judgements of children', *Child Development*, 48, 518-22

Enright, R. D. *et al.* (1979) 'Adolescent egocentrism in early and late adolescence', *Adolescence*, 14, 687-95

———— *et al.* (1980) 'Adolescent egocentrism, sociocentrism and self-consciousness', *Journal of Youth and Adolescence*, 9, 101-16

———— *et al.* (1983) 'Moral education strategies', in M. Pressley and J. R. Levin (eds), *Cognitive Strategy Research*, Springer-Verlag, New York

Erlanger, H. S. and Klegon D. A. (1978) 'Socialization effects of professional school', *Law and Society Review*, 13, 11-35

Fox, K. F. A. (1978) 'What children bring to school: the beginnings of economic education', *Social Education*, 5, 478-81

Furth, H. G. (1980) *The World of Grown-ups*, Elsevier, New York

———, Baur, M. and Smith, J. E. (1976) 'Children's conceptions of social institutions: a Piagetian framework', *Human Development*, 19, 351-74

Gallatin, J. and Adelson, J. (1971) 'Legal guarantees of individual freedom: a cross-national study of the development of political thought', *Journal of Social Issues*, 27, 91-108

——— (1980) 'Political thinking in adolescence', in J. Adelson (ed.) *Handbook of Adolescent Psychology*, Wiley, New York

Gibbs, J. C. *et al.* (1984) 'Construction and validation of a multiple-choice measure of moral reasoning', *Child Development*, 55, 527-36

Graham, D. (1972) *Moral Learning and Development: Theory and Research*, Batsford, London

Gray, W. M. and Hudson, L. M. (1984) 'Formal operations and the imaginary audience', *Developmental Psychology*, 20, 619-27

Greenstein, F. I. and Tarrow, S. (1970) *Political Orientations in Children*, Sage, Beverley Hills

Haan, N. (1985) 'Processes of moral development', *Developmental Psychology*, 21, 996-1006

Hansen, W. L. *et al.* (1977) *Master Curriculum Guide for the Nation's Schools: A Framework for Teaching Economic Concepts*, Joint Council on Economic Education, New York

Hess, R. D. and Torney, J. V. (1967) *The Development of Political Attitudes in Children*, Aldine, Chicago

Hewitt, L. S. (1975) 'The effects of provocation, intentions and consequences on children's moral judgements', *Child Development*, 46, 540-44

Hoffman, M. and Saltzstein, H. (1967) 'Parent discipline and the child's moral development', *Journal of Personality and Social Psychology*, 5, 45-57

Holstein, C. (1968) *Parental Determinants of the Development of Moral Judgement*, Ph.D. Thesis, University of California

Jahoda, G. (1979) 'The construction of economic reality by some Glaswegian children', *European Journal of Social Psychology*, 9, 115-27

——— (1981) 'The development of thinking about economic institutions: the bank', *Cahiers de Psychologie Cognitive*, 1, 55-73

Jennings, M. K., Ehman, L. H. and Niemi, R. G. (1974) 'Social studies teachers and their pupils', in M. K. Jennings and R. G. Niemi (eds), *The Political Character of Adolescence*, Princeton University Press, Princeton

———, Langton, K. P. and Niemi, R. G. (1974) 'Effects of the High School Civics Curriculum', in M. K. Jennings and R. G. Niemi (eds),

The Political Character of Adolescence, Princeton University Press, Princeton
————— and Niemi, R. G. (1974) *The Political Character of Adolescence*, Princeton University Press, Princeton
————— and ————— (1981) *Generations and Politics*, Princeton University Press, Princeton
Keasey, C. B. (1975) 'Implications of cognitive development', in D. J. De Palma and J. M. Foley (eds), *Moral Development: Current Theory and Research*, Erlbaum, Hillsdale
Kohlberg, L. (1963) 'The development of children's orientations towards a moral order', *Vita Humana*, 6, 11-33
————— (1967) 'Moral and religious education and the public schools: a developmental view', in T. Sizer (ed), *Religion and Public Education*, Houghton-Mifflin, Boston
————— (1969) 'Stage and sequence: the cognitive-developmental approach to socialization', in D. A. Goslin (ed.), *Handbook of Socialization Theory and Research*, Rand McNally, Chicago
————— (1974) 'Continuities in childhood and adult moral development revisited', in P. B. Baltes and Schaie, H. W. (eds), *Lifespan Developmental Psychology: Personality and Socialisation*, Academic Press, New York
————— (1976) 'Moral stages and moralization: the cognitive-developmental approach', in T. Lickona (ed.), *Moral Development and Behaviour: Theory, Research and Social Issues*, Holt, Rinehart and Winston, New York
————— *et al.* (1977) *Assessing Moral Stages: a Manual* (unpublished manuscript, Harvard University)
————— (1981) *The Meaning and Measurement of Moral Development*, Clark University Press, Worcester
————— (1984) *The Psychology of Moral Development*, Harper and Row, New York
————— and Kramer, R. (1969) 'Continuities and discontinuities in childhood and adult moral development', *Human Development*, 12, 93-120
Kramer, D. and Kramer, H. (1975) 'Jugend und Gesellschaft in Östereich in 1973', in H. Fischer (ed.), *Das Politische System Österreichs*, Europaverlag, Sonderdruck
Kubey, H. (1976) 'Three years of adjustment: where your ideals go', *Juris Doctor*, 6, 34-43
Kuhn, D. *et al.* (1977) 'The development of formal operations in logical and moral judgement', *Genetic Psychology Monographs*, 95, 97-188
Langford, P. E. (1975) 'The development of the concept of development', *Human Development*, 18, 321-32
————— and George, S. (1975) 'Intellectual and moral development in adolescence', *British Journal of Educational Psychology*, 45, 330-32

Langton, K. P. (1969) *Political Socialization*, Oxford University Press, New York

Lapsey, D. K. and Murphy, M. N. (1985) 'Another look at the theoretical assumptions of adolescent egocentrism', *Developmental Review*, 5, 201-7

Lasswell, H. D. (1960) *Psychopathology and Politics*, Viking, New York

Leahy, R. L. (1983a) 'Development of the conception of economic inequality: 1. Explanations, justifications and concepts of social mobility and change', *Developmental Psychology*, 19, 111-25

—————— (1983b) 'The development of the conception of social class', in R. L. Leahy (ed.), *The Child's Construction of Social Inequality*, Academic Press, New York

Lee, L. C. (1971) 'The concomitant development of cognitive and moral modes of thought', *Genetic Psychology Monographs*, 83, 93-146

Lenin, V. I. (1961) *Collected Works*, Vol. 38, Foreign Languages Publishing, Moscow

Levine, C. *et al.* (1985) 'The current formulation of Kohlberg's theory and a response to critics', *Human Development*, 28, 94-100

Litt, E. (1963) 'Civic education norms and political indoctrination', *American Sociological Review*, 28, 69-75

Moessinger, P. (1981) 'The development of the concept of majority decision: a pilot study', *Canadian Journal of Behavioural Science*, 13, 359-62

Murray, H. A. (1945) 'A clinical study of sentiments', *Genetic Psychology Monographs*, 26, 56-82

Muuss, R. E. (1979) 'Eine taxonomie der psychologie der adoleszenz', *Der Kinderarzt*, 10, 1471-75; 11, 1637-42; 12, 1801-9

Osterweil, Z. O. (1982) 'The development of political concepts in Israeli schoolboys', *International Journal of Political Education*, 5, 141-58

Parikh, B. S. (1975) *Moral Judgement and its Relation to Family Environment Factors in Indian and American Urban Upper Middle Class Families*, Ph.D. Thesis, Boston University, Massachusetts

Peck, R. F. and Havighurst, R. J. (1960) *The Psychology of Character Development*, Wiley, New York

Pellegrini, D. S. (1985) 'Social cognition and competence in middle childhood', *Child Development*, 56, 253-64

Peters, R. S. (1975) 'A reply to Kohlberg', *Phi Delta Kappan*, 56, 678

Piaget, J. (1965) *The Moral Judgement of the Child*, The Free Press of Glencoe, New York

—————— (1967) *Six Psychological Studies*, Random House, New York

—————— (1972) 'Intellectual evolution from adolescence to adulthood', *Human Development*, 15, 1-12

Radosevich, M. J. and Krohn, M. (1981) 'Cognitive moral development and legal socialization', *Criminal Justice and Behaviour*, 8, 401-24

Remmers, H. H. and Radler, D. H. (1962) *The American Teenager*, Charter, New York

Rest, J. R. (1974) 'The cognitive-developmental approach to morality: the state of the art', *Counselling and Values*, 18, 64-78

———— (1979) *Development in Judging Moral Issues*, University of Minnesota Press, Minneapolis

————, Turiel, E. and Kohlberg, L. A. (1969) 'Level of moral development as a determinant of preference and comprehension of moral judgements made by others', *Journal of Personality*, 37, 225-52

———— and Thoma, S. J. (1985) 'Relation of moral development to formal education', *Developmental Psychology*, 21, 709-14

Riegel, K. F. (1973) 'Dialectical operations, the final period in cognitive development', *Human Development*, 16, 346-80

Rogers, D. W. (1976) 'Protest: development of a concept', *Social Studies*, 67, 160-3

Rule, B. G. *et al.* (1974) 'Children's reactions to information about the intentions underlying an aggressive act', *Child Development*, 45, 794-98

———— and Duker, P. (1973) 'The effect of intentions and consequences of children's evaluations of aggressors', *Journal of Personality and Social Psychology*, 27, 184-89

Schlaefli, A. *et al.* (1985) 'Does moral education improve moral judgement?', *Review of Educational Research*, 55, 319-52

Schug, M. (1980) 'The development of economic reasoning in children and adolescents', Paper given to the American Economic Association, Denver, Colorado

———— (1983) 'The development of economic thinking in children and adolescents', *Social Education*, 12, 141-45

Schwartz, D. C. and Schwartz, S. K. (1975) *New Directions in Political Socialization*, Free Press, New York

Selman, R. L. (1971) 'The relation of role-taking to the development of moral judgement in children', *Child Development*, 42, 79-91

———— (1976a) 'Social-cognition understanding: a guide to educational and clinical practice', in T. Lickona (ed.), *Moral Development and Behaviour: Theory, Research and Social Issues*, Holt, Rinehart and Winston, New York

———— (1976b) 'Toward a structural analysis of developing interpersonal relations concepts: research with normal and disturbed preadolescent boys', in A. D. Pick (ed.), *Minnesota Symposia on Child Psychology*, University of Minneapolis Press, Minneapolis

———— (1977) 'A structural-developmental model of social cognition: implications for intervention research', *The Counselling Psychologist*, 6, 3-6

———— (1984) *The Growth of Interpersonal Understanding: Development and Clinical Analysis*, Academic Press, New York

————— and Byrne, D. F. (1974) 'A structural-developmental analysis of levels of role-taking in middle childhood', *Child Development*, 45, 803-6

————— *et al.* (1983) 'A naturalistic study of children's social understanding', *Developmental Psychology*, 19, 82-102

Sigel, R. A. (1979) 'Students' comprehension of democracy and its application to conflict situations', *International Journal of Political Education*, 2, 47-65

Simpson, E. L. (1974) 'Moral development research: A case study of scientific cultural bias', *Human Development*, 17, 81-106

Smetana, J. G. (1983) 'Social-cognitive development: domain distinctions and coordinations', *Developmental Review*, 3, 131-47

————— (1985a) 'Preschool children's conceptions of transgressions', *Developmental Psychology*, 21, 18-29

————— (1985b) 'Children's impressions of moral and conventional transgressors', *Developmental Psychology*, 21, 715-24

Snarey, J. R. (1985) 'Cross-cultural universality of social-moral development', *Psychological Bulletin*, 97, 202-32

————— *et al.* (1985) 'Development of social-moral reasoning among Kibbutz adolescents', *Developmental Psychology*, 21, 3-17

Sosin, K. and McConnell, C. R. (1979) 'The impact of introductory economics on students' perceptions of income distribution', *Journal of Economics Education*, 11, 13-19

Stacey, B. (1978) *Political socialization in Western Society*, Edward Arnold, London

Strauss, A. (1952) 'The development and transformation of monetary meaning in the child', *American Sociological Review*, 17, 275-86

Steele, W. W. (1970) 'A comparison of attitudes of freshmen and senior law students', *Journal of Legal Education*, 23, 56-79

Suls, J. and Kalle, R. J. (1979) 'Children's moral judgements as a function of intention, damage and actor's physical harm', *Developmental Psychology*, 15, 93-4

Surber, C. F. (1977) 'Developmental processes in social inference: averaging of intentions and consequences in moral judgement', *Developmental Psychology*, 13, 654-55

Sutton, R. S. (1962) 'Behaviour in the attainment of economic concepts', *Journal of Psychology*, 53, 37-46

Tapp, J. L. and Kohlberg, L. (1971) 'Developing senses of law and legal justice', *Journal of Social Issues*, 27, 65-91

————— and Levine, S. (1974) Legal socialization: strategies for an ethical legality', *Stanford Law Review*, 27, 16-30

Thomas, D. *et al.* (1984) 'Moral reasoning and political obligation: cognitive-developmental correlates of orientations toward law and civil disobedience', *International Journal of Political Education*, 6, 223-44

Tomlinson, (1980) 'Moral judgement and moral psychology: Piaget, Kohlberg and beyond', in S. and C. Modgil (eds), *Towards a Theory of Psychological Development*, NFER, Slough

Torney, J. *et al.* (1975) *Civic Education in Ten Nations: An Empirical Study*, Wiley, New York

Trotsky, L. (1966) *In Defence of Marxism*, New Park, London

Turiel, E. (1977) 'Social convention and the development of societal concepts', Unpublished manuscript, University of California

———— (1978) 'The development of concepts of social structure: Social convention', in J. Glick and A. Clarke-Stuart (eds), *Personality and Social Development*, Gardner Press, New York

———— (1983) *The Development of Social Knowledge*, Cambridge University Press, Cambridge

Walker, L. J. (1984) 'The hierarchical nature of stages of moral development', *Developmental Psychology*, 20, 960-66

Ward, S. *et al.* (1977) *How Children Learn to Buy*, Sage, Beverly Hills

Weinreich, H. E. (1977) 'Some consequences of replicating Kohlberg's original moral development study on a British sample', *Journal of Moral Education*, 7, 32-39

Weinreich, H. (1983) 'Kohlberg's theory of moral development', in H. Weinreich-Haste (ed.), *Morality in the Making*, Wiley, New York

White, C. B. (1975) 'Moral development in Bahamian schoolchildren: cross-cultural examination of Kohlberg's stages of moral reasoning', *Developmental Psychology*, 11, 535-56

Wilging, T. E. and Dunn, T. G. (1981) 'The moral development of the law student: theory and data on legal education', *Journal of Legal Education*, 31, 306-58

Zeidler, D. L. (1985) 'Hierarchical relationships among formal cognitive structures and their relationship to principled moral reasoning', *Journal of Research in Science Teaching*, 22, 461-71

Zellman, G. L. and Sears, D. O. (1978) 'Childhood origins of tolerance for dissent', in J. L. Tapp (ed.), *The Pattern of Legal Development*, Freeman, San Francisco

Chapter 4

Alilunas, L. J. (1967) 'The problem of children's historical mindedness', in J. S. Roucek (ed.), *The Teaching of History*, Philosophical Library, New York

Anastasi, A. (1958) *Differential Psychology*, Macmillan, New York

Asch, S. E. (1936) 'A study of change of mental organisation', *Archives of Psychology*, 195

Ault, C. R. (1982) 'Time in geological explanations as perceived by elementary school children', *Journal of Geological Education*, 30, 304-9

Bartz, B. S. (1970) 'Maps in the classroom', in J. M. Ball *et al.* (eds), *The Social Sciences and Geographic Education*, Wiley, New York

Booth, M. B. (1978) 'Children's inductive historical thought', *Teaching History*, 6, 3-9

——— (1980) 'A modern world history course and the thinking of adolescent pupils', *Educational Review*, 32, 245-57

Brainerd, C. J. (1978) 'The stage question in cognitive-developmental theory', *Behavioural and Brain Sciences*, 2, 173- 213

Case, D. and Collinson, J. M. (1962) 'The development of formal thinking and verbal comprehension', *British Journal of Educational Psychology*, 32, 103-12

Cohen, J., Hansel, C. E. and Sylvester, J. (1954) 'An experimental study of comparative judgements of time', *British Journal of Psychology*, 45, 108-14

Cohen, R. *et al.* (1982) *Children's Conceptions of Spatial Relationships*, Jossey-Bass, San Francisco

Coltham, J. B. (1960) *Junior School Children's Understanding of some Terms Commonly used in the Teaching of History*, Manchester University, Ph. D. Thesis

Cousins, J. H. *et al.* (1983) 'Way finding and cognitive mapping in large scale environments', *Journal of Experimental Child Psychology*, 35, 1-20

Dickinson, A. K. and Lee, P. J. (1978) 'Understanding and research', in A. K. Dickinson and P. J. Lee (eds), *History Teaching and Historical Understanding*, Heinemann, London

——— and ——— (1984) 'Making sense of history' in A. K. Dickinson (ed.), *Learning History*, Heinemann, London

Downs, R. M. and Stea, D. (1977) *Maps in Minds*, Harper and Row, New York

Dray, W. H. (1957) *Laws and Explanation in History*, OUP, Oxford

——— (1964) *Philosophy of History*, Prentice Hall, New York

Gagné, R. M. and White, R. T. (1978) 'Memory structures and learning outcomes', *Review of Educational Research*, 48, 187- 222

Ghuman, P. S. and Davis, R. (1981) 'An assessment of adolescent comprehension of some geographical concepts using Peel's theoretical framework', *Educational Review*, 33, 231-40

Gladwin, T. (1970) *East is a Big Bird*, Harvard University Press, Cambridge

Hall, D. (1975) *Geography and the Geography Teacher*, Allen and Unwin, London

Hallam, R. N. (1967) 'Logical thinking in history', *Educational Review*, 119, 182-202
———— (1975) *A Study of the Effect of Teaching Method on the Growth of Logical Thought*, Leeds University, Ph. D. Thesis
———— (1978) 'An approach to learning history in primary schools', *Teaching History*, 6, 9-14
Hempel, C. G. (1959) 'The function of general laws in history', in P. Gardiner (ed.), *Theories of History*, The Free Press, Glencoe
———— (1963) 'Reasons and covering laws in historical explanation', in S. Hook (ed.), *Philosophy and History*,New York University Press, New York
———— (1966) 'Explanation in science and history', in W. H. Dray (ed.), *Philosophical Analysis and History*,Harper and Row, New York
Inhelder, B. and Piaget, J. (1955) *The Growth of Logical Thinking from Childhood to Adolescence*, Humanities Press, New York
Ives, S. W. and Rakow, J. (1983) 'Children's use of feature descriptions to solve spatial perspective and rotation problems', *British Journal of Educational Psychology*, 53, 143-51
Jahoda, G. (1963) 'Children's concept of time and history', *Educational Review*, 15, 87-104
Jurd, M. F. (1978) 'An empirical study of operational thinking in history-type material', in J. A. Keats *et al.* (eds), *Cognitive Development*, Wiley, Chichester
Langford, P. E. (1979) *Beyond Piaget: Recent Theories of Concept Development and their Significance for Teaching*, School of Education, La Trobe University, Melbourne
Lee, P. J. (1978) 'Explanation and understanding in history', in A. K. Dickinson and P. J. Lee (eds), *History Teaching and Historical Understanding*, Heinemann, London
Lello, J. (1980) 'The concept of time, the teaching of history and school organization', *History Teaching*, 13, 341-50
Liben, L. S., Patterson, A. H. and Newcombe, N. (1981) *Spatial Representation and Behaviour Across the Life Span*, Academic Press, New York
Lodwick, A. R. (1959) 'Experimental examination of some of Piaget's schemata concerning children's perception and thinking and a discussion of their educational significance', *British Journal of Educational Psychology*, 29, 89-103
Mackenzie, A. A. and White, R. T. (1982) 'Fieldwork in geography and long term memory structures', *American Educational Research Journal*, 19, 623-32
Naish, M. C. (1982) 'Mental development and the learning of geography', in N. J. Graves (ed.), *New UNESCO Source Book for Geography Teaching*, Longman, Harlow

Paivio, A. (1969) 'Mental imagery in associative learning and memory', *Psychological Review*, 76, 241-63

Peel, E. A. (1966) 'A study of differences in judgments of adolescent pupils', *British Journal of Educational Psychology*, 36, 77-86

———— (1967a) 'Some problems in the psychology of history teaching: 1. Historical ideas and concepts', in W. H. Burston and D. Thompson (eds), *Studies in the Nature and Teaching of History*, Routledge, London

———— (1967b) 'Some problems in the psychology of history teaching: 2. The pupil's thinking and inference', in W. H. Burston and D. Thompson (eds) *Studies in the Nature and Teaching of History*, Routledge, London

———— (1971) *The Nature of Adolescent Judgement*, Wiley, New York

Piaget, J. (1926) *The Language and Thought of the Child*, Harcourt Brace, New York

———— (1952) *The Child's Conception of Number*, Humanities Press, New York

————, Inhelder, B. and Szeminska, A. (1960) *The Child's Conception of Geometry*, Basic Books, New York

———— and ———— (1967) *The Child's Conception of Space*, Norton, New York

Rhys, W. T. (1966) *The Development of Logical Thought in the Adolescent with Reference to the Teaching of Geography in the Secondary School*, University of Birmingham, M. Ed. Thesis

———— (1972) 'The development of logical thinking', in N. Graves (ed.) *New Movements in the Study and Teaching of Geography*, Temple Smith, London

Rushdoony, H. A. (1968) 'A child's ability to read maps: summary of the research', *Journal of Geography*, 67, 213-22

Salt, C. D. (1971) *An Investigation into the Ability of 11 to 12 Year Old Pupils to Read and Understand Maps*, University of Sheffield, M. A. Thesis

Shemilt, D. (1976) 'Formal operations thought in history', *Teaching History*, 4, 245-51

———— (1980) *History 13-16 Evaluation Study*, Holmes McDougall, Edinburgh

———— (1984) 'Beauty and the philosopher: empathy in history and the classroom', in A. K. Dickinson *et al.* (eds) *Learning History*, Heinemann, London

Siegel, A. W. (1981) 'The externalisation of cognitive maps by children and adults', in L. S. Liben *et al.* (eds), *Spatial Representation and Behaviour Across the Life Span*, Academic Press, New York

———— (1982) 'Towards a social ecology of cognitive mapping', in R. Cohen (ed), *Children's Conceptions of Spatial Relationships*, Jossey-Bass, San Francisco

Siegel, A. W. and White, S. H. (1975) 'The development of spatial representations of large-scale environments', in H. W. Reese (ed.), *Advances in Child Development and Behaviour*, 10, Academic Press, New York

Siegel, A.W., Herman, J. F., Allen, G. L. and Kirasic, K. C. (1979) 'The development of cognitive maps of large- and small-scale space', *Child Development*, 50, 582-5

Slack, J. P and Larkins, A. G. (1982) 'The effect of two instructional treatments on college students' topographical map skills achievement', *Journal of Social Studies Research*, 6, 13-16

Watts, D. G. (1972) *The Learning of History*, Routledge, London

Wood, D. M. (1964) *Some Concepts of Social Relations in Childhood and Adolescence Investigated by Means of the Analysis of the Definitions*, Nottingham University, M. Ed. Thesis

Wright, G. H. von (1971) *Explanation and Understanding*, Routledge, London

Chapter 5

Aguirre, J. and Erickson, G. (1984) 'Students' conceptions about the vector characteristics of three physics concepts', *Journal of Research in Science Teaching*, 21, 439-57

Anderson, N. H. (1983) 'Intuitive physics: understanding and learning of physical relations', in T. J. Tighe and B. E. Shepp (eds), *Perception, Cognition and Development*, Erlbaum, Hillsdale

Archenhold, F. (1979) 'An empirical study of the understanding by 16-19 year old students of the concepts of work and potential in physics', in F. Archenhold et al. (eds), *Cognitive Development Research in Science and Mathematics*, University of Leeds, Leeds

Arlin, P. K. (1974) *Problem Finding: The Relation Between Selected Cognitive Process Variables and Problem Finding Performance*, University of Chicago, Ph.D. Thesis

———— (1975) 'Cognitive development in adulthood: a fifth stage?', *Developmental Psychology*, 11, 602-6

———— (1977) 'Piagetian operations in problem finding', *Developmental Psychology*, 13, 297-8

Blake, A. J. D. and Nordland, F. H. (1978) 'Science instruction and cognitive growth in college students', *Journal of Research in Science Teaching*, 15, 413-9

Brainerd, C. J. (1978) 'The stage question in cognitive-developmental theory', *Behavioural and Brain Sciences*, 2, 245-57

Bredderman, T. A. (1973) 'The effects of training on the development of the ability to control variables', *Journal of Research in Science Teaching*, 10, 189-200

Brehmer, B. (1973) 'Hypotheses about relations between scaled variables in the learning of probabilistic inference tasks', *Organizational Behaviour and Human Performance*, 197, 482-91

Brumby, M. (1979) 'Problems in learning the concept of natural selection', *Journal of Biological Education*, 13, 119-22

Brumby, M. N. (1984) 'Misconceptions about the concept of natural selection by medical biology students', *Science Education*, 68, 493-503

Bruner, J. S., Goodnow, J. J. and Austin, G. A. (1956) *A Study of Thinking*, Wiley, New York

Burnett, A. L. and Eisner, T. (1964) *Animal Adaptation*, Holt, Rinehart and Winston, New York

Cantu, L. L. and Herron, J. D. (1978) 'Concrete and formal Piagetian stages and science concept attainment', *Journal of Research in Science Teaching*, 15, 135-43

Caramazza, A., McCloskey, M. and Green, B. (1981) 'Naive beliefs in sophisticated subjects', *Cognition*, 9, 117-23

Chiappetta, E. L. (1976) 'A review of Piagetian studies relevant to science instruction at the secondary and college level', *Science Education*, 60, 253-61

Clough, F. and Wood-Robinson, C. (1985a) 'How secondary students interpret instances of biological adaptation', *Journal of Biological Education*, 19, 125-30

————— and ————— (1985b) 'Children's understanding of inheritance', *Journal of Biological Education*, 19, 304-10

Coulter, D. *et al.* (1978) 'Formal operational ability and the teaching of science processes', *School Science and Mathematics*, 78, 131-8

Cropper, D. A. *et al.* (1977) 'The relation between formal operations and a possible fifth stage of cognitive development', *Developmental Psychology*, 13, 517-8

Day, M. C. and Stone, C. A. (1982) 'Developmental and individual differences in the use of control-of-variables strategy', *Journal of Educational Psychology*, 74, 749-60

Deadman, J. A. and Kelly, P.J. (1978) 'What do secondary school boys understand about evolution and heredity before they are taught the topics', *Journal of Biological Education*, 12, 7-15

Disessa, A. A. (1982) 'Unlearning Aristotelian physics: a study of knowledge-based learning', *Cognitive Science*, 6, 37-75

Dulit, E. (1972) Adolescent thinking *à la* Piaget: the formal stage', *Journal of Youth and Adolescence*, 1, 281-301

Erickson, G. L. (1979) 'Children's conceptions of heat and temperature', *Science Education*, 63, 221-30

————— (1980) 'Children's viewpoints of heat: a second look', *Science Education*, 64, 323-36

153

Fakouri, M. E. (1976) 'Cognitive development in adulthood: a fifth stage?: a critique', *Developmental Psychology*, 12, 472

Ferretti, R. P. and Butterfield, E. C. (1985) 'The classification of children's knowledge development on the balance-scales and inclined-plane tasks', *Journal of Experimental Child Psychology*, 39, 131-60

Feyerabend, P. K. (1975) *Against Method: Outline of an Anarchist Theory of Knowledge*, NLB, London

Gabel, D. and Sherwood R. (1980) 'The effect of student manipulation of molecular models on chemistry achievement according to Piagetian level', *Journal of Research in Science Teaching*, 17, 75-81

Gabel, D. L. and Sherwood, R. D. (1981) 'High school science courses do make a difference', *School Science and Mathematics*, 81, 502-6

Gardner, P. L. (1984) 'Circular motion', *Research in Science Education*, 14, 26-31

————— (1985) 'Physics students' comprehension of motion with a constant velocity', *Australian Science Teachers Journal*, 31, 26-31

Gentner, D. and Gentner D. R. (1983) 'Flowing waters or teeming crowds: mental models of electricity', in D. Gentner and A. L. Stevens (eds), *Mental Models*, Hillsdale, Erlbaum

Goodstein, M. P. and Howe, A. C. (1978a) 'Application of Piagetian theory to introductory college chemistry', *Journal of Chemical Education*, 55, 171-3

————— and ————— (1978b) 'The use of concrete methods in secondary chemistry instruction', *Journal of Research in Science Teaching*, 15, 361-6

Greeno, J. G. *et al.* (1979) 'Theory of constructions and set in problem solving', *Memory and Cognition*, 7, 445-61

Hackling, M. W. and Garnett, P. J. (1985) 'Misconceptions of chemical equilibrium', *European Journal of Science Education*, 7, 205-14

————— and Treagust, D. (1984) 'Research data necessary for meaningful review of grade 10 high school genetics curricula', *Journal of Research in Science Teaching*, 20, 197-209

Hartford, F. and Good, R. (1982) 'Training chemistry students to ask research questions', *Journal of Research in Science Teaching*, 19, 559-70

Haupt, G. (1952) 'Concepts of magnetism held by school children', *Science Education*, 36, 162-8

Hensley, J. H. (1974) *An Investigation of Proportional Thinking in Children from Grades Six through Twelve*, University of Iowa, Ph.D. Thesis

Hewson, M. G. A'B. (1984) 'The influence of intellectual environment on conceptions of heat', *European Journal of Science Education*, 6, 245-62

Howe, A. C. and Mierzwa, J. (1977) 'Promoting the development of logical thinking in the classroom', *Journal of Research in Science Teaching*, 14, 467-72

Inhelder, B. and Piaget, J. (1955) *The Growth of Logical Thinking from Childhood to Adolescence*, Humanities Press, New York

Johnstone, A. H. and Mahmoud, N. A. (1980) 'Isolating topics of high perceived difficulty in school biology', *Journal of Biological Education*, 14, 163-6

Joshua, S. (1984) 'Students' interpretation of simple electrical diagrams', *European Journal of Science Education*, 6, 271-5

Jungwirth, E. (1975) 'Preconceived adaptation and inverted evolution', *Australian Science Teachers' Journal*, 21, 105-13

Juraschek, W. A. and Grady, M. T. (1981) 'Format variations on equilibrium in the balance', *Journal of Research in Science Teaching*, 18, 47-9

Kaiser, M. K. *et al.* (1986) 'Development of intuitive theories of motion'. *Developmental Psychology*, 22, 67-71

Kargbo, D. R. *et al.* (1980) 'Children's beliefs about inherited characteristics', *Journal of Biological Education*, 14, 137-46

Kishter, M. A. (1979) 'Proportional and combinatorial reasoning in two cultures', *Journal of Research in Science Teaching*, 16, 439-43

Kuhn, D. and Angelev, J. (1976) 'An experimental study of the development of formal operational thought', *Child Development*, 47, 697-706

———— *et al.* (1979) 'Formal reasoning among pre and late adolescents', *Child Development*, 50, 1128-35

Kuhn, T. S. (1970) *The Structure of Scientific Revolutions*, 2nd edn, University of Chicago Press, Chicago

Lawson, A. E. (1977) 'Relationships among performances on three formal operations tasks', *Journal of Psychology*, 96, 235-41

———— (1979) 'Relationships among performances on group administered items of formal reasoning', *Perceptual and Motor Skills*, 48, 71-8

———— (1982) 'The nature of advanced reasoning and science instruction', *Journal of Research in Science Teaching*, 19, 743-60

———— (1983a) 'The acquisition of formal operational schemata during adolescence', *Journal of Research in Science Teaching*, 20, 347-56

———— (1983b) 'The effects of causality, response alternatives and context continuity on hypothesis testing reasoning', *Journal of Research in Science Teaching*, 20, 297-310

———— (1985) 'A review of research on formal reasoning and science teaching', *Journal of Research in Science Teaching*, 22, 569-618

———— *et al.* (1974) 'Piaget and formal operational tasks', *Science Education*, 58, 267-76

———— and Bealer, J. M. (1984) 'Cultural diversity and differences in formal reasoning ability', *Journal of Research in Science Teaching*, 21, 735-43

————, Blake, A. J. D. and Nordland, F. H. (1975) 'Training effects and generalization of the ability to control variables in high school biology students', *Science Education*, 59, 387-96

———— and Renner, J. W. (1974) 'A quantitative analysis of responses to Piagetian tasks', *Science Education*, 58, 545-59

Linn, M. C. (1978) 'Influence of cognitive style and training on tasks requiring the separation of variables schema', *Child Development*, 49, 874-77

————, Pulos, S. and Gans, A. (1981) 'Correlates of formal reasoning: content and problem effects', *Journal of Research in Science Teaching*, 18, 435-47

McCloskey, M. (1983) 'Naive theories about motion', in D. Gentner and A. L. Stevens (eds), *Mental Models*, Hillsdale, Erlbaum

————, Caramazza, A. and Green, B. (1980) 'Curvilinear motion in the absence of external forces: naive beliefs about the motion of objects', *Science*, 210, 1139-41

———— and Kohl, D. (1983) 'Naive physics: the curvilinear impetus principle and its role in interactions with moving objects', *Journal of Experimental Psychology*, 9, 146-56

Maloney, D. P. (1983) 'Proportional reasoning and rule-governed behaviour with the balance beam', *Science Education*, 67, 245-54

———— (1985) 'Rule-governed approaches to physics: conservation of mechanical energy', *Journal of Research in Science Teaching*, 22, 261-78

Moshman, D. and Thompson, P. A. (1981) 'Hypothesis testing in students: sequences, stages and instructional strategies', *Journal of Research in Science Teaching*, 18, 341-52

Novick, S. and Nussbaum, J. (1978) 'Junior high school students' understanding of the particulate theory of matter', *Science Education*, 62, 273-81

———— and ———— (1981) 'Pupils' understanding of the particulate nature of matter', *Science Education*, 65, 187-96

Piaget, J. (1929) *The Child's Conception of the World*, RKP, London

———— (1930) *The Child's Conception of Physical Causality*, RKP, London

———— (1974) *Understanding Causality*, Norton, New York

———— and Inhelder, B. (1941) *Le Developpement des Quantités chez l'Enfant*, Delachaux et Niestlé, Neûchatel and Paris

Popper, K. R. (1959) *The Logic of Scientific Discovery*, Hutchinson, London

Pouler, C. A. and Wright, E. L. (1980) 'An analysis of the influence of reinforcement and knowledge of criteria on the ability of students to generate hypotheses', *Journal of Research in Science Teaching*, 17, 31-7

Pulos, S. and Linn, M. C. (1981) 'Generality of the controlling variables schema in early adolescence', *Journal of Early Adolescence*, 1, 29-36

Pumfrey, P. (1968) 'The growth of the schema of proportionality', *British Journal of Educational Psychology*, 38, 202-4

Rodrigues, D. M. A. P. (1980) 'Notions of physical laws in childhood', *Science Education*, 64, 59-84

Ross, J. A. and Maynes, F. J. (1983) 'Experimental problem solving: an instructional improvement field experiment', *Journal of Research in Science Teaching*, 20, 543-56

Rowell, J. A. and Dawson, C. J. (1977a) 'Teaching about floating and sinking: an attempt to link cognitive psychology with classroom practice', *Science Education*, 61, 243-51

———— and ———— (1977b) 'Teaching about floating and sinking: further studies toward closing the gap between cognitive psychology and classroom practice', *Science Education*, 527-40

———— and ———— (1984) 'Controlling variables: testing a programme for teaching a general solution strategy', *Research in Science and Technological Education*, 2, 37-46

Sayre, S. and Ball, D. W. (1975) 'Piagetian cognitive development and achievement in science', *Journal for Research in Science Teaching*, 12, 165-74

Scardamalia, M. and Bereiter, C. (1984) 'Development of strategies in text processing', in H. Mandl (ed.), *Learning and the Comprehension of Text*, Hillsdale, Erlbaum

Seddon, G. M. and Moore, R. G. (1986) 'An unexpected effect of the use of models for teaching the visualisation of rotation in molecular structure', *European Journal of Science Education*, 8, 79-86

Selman, R. L. *et al.* (1982) 'Concrete operational thought and the emergence of the concept of unseen force in children's theories of electromagnetism and gravity', *Science Education*, 66, 181-94

Shayer, M. (1979) 'Has Piaget's construct of formal operations any utility?', *British Journal of Educational Psychology*, 49, 265-76

———— (1980) 'Piaget and science education', in S. and C. Modgil (eds), *Toward a Theory of Psychological Development*, NFER, Slough

———— and Wylam, H. (1978) 'The distribution of Piagetian stages of thinking in British middle and secondary school children', *British Journal of Educational Psychology*, 48, 62-70

———— and ———— (1981) 'The development of the concepts of heat and temperature in 10-13 year olds', *Journal for Research in Science Teaching*, 18, 419-34

Shipstone, D. M. (1984) 'A study of children's understanding of electricity in simple D.C. circuits', *European Journal of Science Education*, 6, 185-98

Shultz, T. R. and Coddington, M. (1981) 'Development of the concepts of energy conservation and entropy', *Journal of Experimental Child Psychology*, 31, 131-53

Siegler, R. S. and Liebert, R. M. (1975) 'Acquisition of formal scientific reasoning by 10 and 13 year olds', *Developmental Psychology*, 11, 401-2

Slovik, P. (1974) 'Hypothesis testing in the learning of positive and negative linear functions', *Organizational Behaviour and Human Performance*, 11, 368-76

Smith, M. U. and Good, R. (1984) 'Problem solving and classical genetics', *Journal of Research in Science Teaching*, 21, 896-912

Staver, J. R. and Halsted, D. A. (1985) 'The effects of reasoning, use of models, sex type, and their interactions on post-test achievement in chemical bonding after constant instruction', *Journal of Research in Science Teaching*, 22, 437-47

Stavy, R. and Berkowitz, B. (1980) 'Cognitive conflict as a basis for teaching quantitative aspects of the concept of temperature', *Science Education*, 64, 679-92

Stewart, J. H. (1982) 'Difficulties experienced by high school students when learning basic Mendelian genetics', *The American Biology Teacher*, 44, 80-4, 89

———— (1983) 'Student problem-solving in high school genetics', *Science Education*, 67, 523-40

Stone, C. A. and Day, M. C. (1978) 'Levels of availability of a formal operational strategy', *Child Development*, 49, 1054-65

Strawitz, B. M. (1984a) 'Cognitive style and the acquisition and transfer of the ability to control variables', *Journal of Research in Science Teaching*, 21, 133-41

———— (1984b) 'Cognitive style and the effects of two instructional treatments on the acquisition and transfer of the ability to control variables', *Journal of Research in Science Teaching*, 21, 833-41

Tamir, P. (1985) 'Causality and teleology in high school biology', *Research in Science and Technological Education*, 3, 19-27

Thomson, N. and Stewart, J. (1985) 'Secondary school genetics instruction', *Journal of Biological Education*, 19, 53-62

Tomlinson-Keasey, C. (1972) 'Formal operations in females from eleven to fifty-four years of age', *Developmental Psychology*, 6, 364

Tschirgi, J. E. (1980) 'Sensible reasoning: a hypothesis about hypotheses', *Child Development*, 51, 1-10

Viennot, L. (1978) *Le Raisonnement Spontané en Dynamique Elémentaire*, Université de Paris VII, Ph.D. thesis

———— (1979) 'Spontaneous reasoning in elementary dynamics', *European Journal of Science Education*, 1, 205-21

———— (1985) 'Analysing students' reasoning in science: a pragmatic view of theoretical problems', *European Journal of Science Education*, 7, 151-62

Violino, P. and di Giagomo, B. S. (1981) 'An investigation of Piagetian stages in secondary school children', *Journal of Chemical Education*, 58, 639-421

Volk, T. L. and Hungerford, H. R. (1984) 'The effects of process instruction on problem identification skills in environmental education', *Journal of Environmental Education*, 6, 36-40

Wollman, W. (1977a) 'Controlling variables: assessing levels of understanding', *Science Education*, 61, 371-83

———— (1977b) 'Controlling variables: a neo-Piagetian developmental sequence', *Science Education*, 61, 385-91

———— (1982) 'Form versus content in Piagetian testing', *Science Education*, 66, 751-61

———— (1983) 'Models and procedures: a classroom study of teaching for transfer', *School Science and Mathematics*, 83, 419-29

———— and Chen, B. (1982) 'Effects of structured social interaction on learning to control variables: a classroom training study', *Science Education*, 66, 717-30

———— and Lawson, A. E. (1977) 'Teaching the procedure of controlled experimentation', *Science Education*, 61, 57-70

———— *et al.* (1979) 'Acceptance of lack of closure: is it an index of advanced reasoning?', *Child Development*, 50, 656-65

Wright, E. L. (1979) 'Effect of intensive instruction in cue attendance on solving formal operational tasks', *Science Education*, 63, 381-93

Yarroch, W. L. (1985) 'Student understanding of chemical equation balancing', *Journal of Research in Science Teaching*, 22, 449-59

Zeitoun, H. H. (1984) 'Teaching scientific analogies: a proposed model', *Research in Science and Technological Education*, 2, 107-25

Chapter 6

Anderson, J. R. *et al.* (1981) 'Acquisition of problem-solving skill', in J. R. Anderson (ed.), *Cognitive Skills and Their Acquisition*, Hillsdale, Erlbaum

Behr, M. *et al.* (1976) 'How children view equality sentences', ERIC Doct. Repro. Service No. 144802

Bell, A. W. (1976a) 'Stages in generalisation and proof', in *Proceedings of the CIMI Conference*, Nyireghaza, Hungary

———— (1976b) 'A study of pupils' proof-explanations in mathematical situations', *Educational Studies in Mathematics*, 7, 23-40

Björkman, M. (1965) *Learning of Linear Functions*, Stockholm: Psychological Labs, University of Stockholm

Boyer, C. B. (1939) *The Concepts of the Calculus*, Columbia University Press, New York

Brainerd, C. J. (1973) 'Judgments and explanations as criteria for the presence of cognitive structures', *Psychological Bulletin*, 79, 172-9

────── (1981) 'Working memory and the developmental analysis of probability judgment', *Psychological Review*, 6, 463-502

Brehmer, B. (1973) 'Effects of cue validity on interpersonal learning of inference tasks with linear and nonlinear cues', *American Journal of Psychology*, 86, 29-48

Case, R. (1979) 'Intellectual development and instruction: a neo-Piagetian view', in A. E. Lawson (ed.), *The 1980 AETS Yearbook*, ERIC/SMEAT, Columbus

Chapman, R. H. (1975) 'The development of children's understanding of proportion', *Child Development*, 46, 141-8

Cohen, L. J. (1970) *The Implications of Induction*, Methuen, London

────── (1979) 'On the psychology of prediction: whose is the fallacy?', *Cognition*, 7, 385-407

Collis, K. F. (1975) *A Study of Concrete and Formal Operations in School Mathematics*, ACER, Melbourne

Copeland, R. W. (1979) *How Children Learn Mathematics*, 3rd edn, Macmillan, New York

Crépault, J. (1978a) 'Le raisonnement cinématique chez le préadolescent et l'adolescent, 1', *Archives de Psychologie*, 178, 133-83

────── (1978b) 'Le raisonnement cinématique chez le préadolescent et l'adolescent, 2', *Archives de Psychologie*, 179, 185-203

────── (1979) 'Influence de repérage sur la durée, étude génétique des inférences cinématiques', *L'Année Psychologique*, 80, 43-64

────── (1980) 'Compatibilité et symétrie, étude génétique des inférences cinématiques chez des sujets de 11 et 13 ans', *L'Année Psychologique*, 80, 81-97

Darke, J. (1982) 'A review of research related to the topological primacy thesis', *Educational Studies in mathematics*, 13, 119-42

Davies, C. (1965) 'The development of the probability concept in children', *Child Development*, 36, 779-88

De Bono, E. (1967) *The Use of Lateral Thinking*, Jonathan Cape, London

Denmark, T. *et al.* (1976) 'Final report: a teaching experiment on e-quality', ERIC Doct. Repr. Service No. ED144805

Dreyfus, T. and Eisenberg, T. (1982) 'Intuitive functional concepts: a baseline study on intuitions', *Journal for Research in Mathematics Education*, 13, 360-80

Dubois, J.-G. (1984) 'Un systematique des configurations combinatoires simples', *Educational Studies in Mathematics*, 15, 37-57

Duncker, K. (1945) 'On problem solving', *Psychological Monographs*, 58(5), 1-63

Eade, S. K. (1967) 'The Effect of Magnitude of Criterion Availability and Positive Validity on Human Inference Behaviour', Ohio State University, M.Sc. thesis

Eastman, P. M. and Salhab, M. (1978) 'The interaction of specific and general reasoning abilities with instructional treatment on absolute value equations', *Journal for Research in Mathematics Education*, 9, 152-4

Falk, R. et al. (1980) 'A potential for learning probability in young children', *Educational Studies in Mathematics*, 11, 181-204

Ferretti, R. P. et al. (1985) 'The classification of children's knowledge development on the balance scale and inclined plane tasks', *Journal of Experimental Child Psychology*, 39, 131-60

Fischbein, E. (1975) *The Intuitive Sources of Probabilistic Thinking in Children*, Reidel, Dordrecht

——— et al. (1970) 'Comparison of ratios and chance concept in children', *Child Development*, 41, 365-76

——— et al. (1971) 'Intuitions primaires et intuitions secondaires dans l'initiation aux probabilités', *Educational Studies in Mathematics*, 4, 264-80

——— et al. (1979) 'The intuition of infinity', *Educational Studies in Mathematics*, 10, 3-40

——— et al. (1981) 'Is it possible to measure the intuitive acceptance of a mathematical statement?', *Educational Studies in Mathematics*, 12, 491-512

——— and Gazit, A. (1984) 'Does the teaching of probability improve probabilistic intuitions?', *Educational Studies in Mathematics*, 15, 1-24

Freeman, N. (1980) *Strategies of Representation in Young Children*, Academic Press, London

Ginsburg, H. (1977) *Children's Arithmetic*, Van Nostrand, New York

Goldberg, S. (1966) 'Probability judgments by preschool children: task conditions and performance', *Child Development*, 37, 157-68

Green, D. (1983) 'From thumbtacks to inference', *School Science and Mathematics*, 83, 541-51

Green, M. G. (1978) 'Structure and sequence in children's concepts of chance and probability: a replication study of Piaget and Inhelder', *Child Development*, 49, 1045-53

Greeno, J. G. (1983) 'Forms of understanding in mathematical problem solving', in S. G. Paris (ed.), *Learning and Motivation in the Classroom*, Hillsdale, Erlbaum

Hadar, N. and Hadass, R. (1981) 'The road to solving a combinatorial problem is strewn with pitfalls', *Educational Studies in Mathematics*, 12, 435-43

Hart, K. M. (1981a) 'Measurement', in K. M. Hart (ed.), *Children's Understanding of Mathematics 11-16*, John Murray, London

————— (1981b) 'Fractions', in K. M. Hart (ed.), *Children's Understanding of Mathematics 11-16*, John Murray, London

Häussler, P. (1977) *Denkoperationen und kernprozesse 12-bis 16 Jähriger Schüler beim erkennen einfacher funktionaler Beziehungen im Physikunterricht*, IPN, Kiel

Hawkins, A. S. and Kapadia, R. (1984) 'Children's conceptions of probability — a psychological and pedagogical review', *Educational Studies in Mathematics*, 15, 349-77

Hayes, J. R. (1980) 'Teaching problem solving mechanisms', in D. T. Tuma and F. Reif (eds), *Problem Solving and Education*, Hillsdale, Erlbaum

Hensley, J. H. (1974) *An Investigation of Proportional Thinking in Children from Grades Six through Twelve*, University of Iowa, Ph.D. thesis

Herscovics, N. and Kieran, C. (1980) 'Constructing meaning for the concept of equation', *The Mathematics Teacher*, 73, 572-80

Hoemann, H. and Ross, B. M. (1971) 'Children's understanding of probability concepts', *Child Development*, 42, 221-36

Hoffer, A. (1983) 'Van Hiele-based research', in R. Lesh and M. Landau (eds), *Acquisition of Mathematics Concepts and Processes*, Academic Press, New York

Hoz, R. (1981) 'The effects of rigidity on school problem solving', *Educational Studies in Mathematics*, 12, 191-204

Inhelder, B. and Piaget, J. (1955) *The Growth of Logical Thinking from Childhood to Adolescence*, Humanities Press, New York

Juraschek, W. A. and Grady, M.T. (1981) 'Format variations on equilibrium in the balance', *Journal of Research in Science Teaching*, 18, 47-9

Kantowski, M. G. (1977) 'Processes involved in mathematical problem solving', *Journal for Research in Mathematics Education*, 8, 163-80

Karplus, R. (1979) 'Continuous functions: students' viewpoints', *European Journal of Science Education*, 1, 397-415

————— and Karplus, E. F. (1972) 'Intellectual development beyond elementary school 111: Ratio, a longitudinal survey', unpublished paper, University of California

————— and Peterson, R. W. (1970) 'Intellectual development beyond elementary school 11: Ratio, a survey', *School Science and Mathematics*, 70, 813-20

————— et al. (1983) 'Proportional reasoning in early adolescents', in R. Lesh and M. Landau (eds), *Acquisition of Mathematics Concepts and Processes*, Academic Press, New York

Kidder, F. R. (1976) 'Elementary and middle school children's comprehension of Euclidean transformations', *Journal for Research in*

Mathematics Education, 6, 40-52

Kieran, C. (1979) 'Children's operational thinking within the concept of bracketing and the order of operations' in D. Tall (ed.), *Proceedings of the Third International Conference for the Psychology of Mathematics Education*, Warwick University, Coventry

———— (1980) 'Constructing meaning for non-trivial equations', ERIC Doct. Repro. Service No. 184899

Kishta, M. A. (1979) 'Proportional and combinatorial reasoning in two cultures', *Journal of Research in Science Teaching*, 16, 439-43

Klein, F. (1872) *Elementary Mathematics from an Advanced Standpoint: Geometry*, (English edn, 1939), Dover, New York

Kuchemann, D. (1978) 'Children's understanding of numerical variables', *Mathematics in School*, 7, 23-6

———— (1980) 'The meanings children give to the letters in generalised arithmetic', in W. F. Archenhold *et al.* (eds), *Cognitive Development Research in Science and Mathematics*, University of Leeds Press, Leeds

Kulm, G. and Bussman, H. (1980) 'Mathematics problem solving', *Journal for Research in Mathematics Education*, 11, 179-89

Lang, D. and Ruane, P. (1981) 'Geometry in English secondary schools', *Educational Studies in Mathematics*, 12, 123-32

Langford, P. E. (1974) 'Development of concepts of infinity and limit in mathematics', *Archives de Psychologie*, 42, 458-72. Reprinted in S. and C. Modgil (eds) (1976), *Piagetian Research: Compilation and Summary*, Vol. 4, NFER, Slough

Langley, P. and Simon, H. A. (1981) 'The central role of learning in cognition', in J. R. Anderson (ed.) *Cognitive Skills and their Acquisition*, Erlbaum, Hillsdale

Lawson, A. E. (1984) 'Proportional reasoning and the linguistic abilities required for hypothetico-deductive reasoning', *Journal of Research in Science Teaching*, 21, 119-31

Le Halle, H. and Savois, C. (1985) 'Signification et ancrage significatif dans une situation dite de proportionnalité', *Archives de Psychologie*, 53, 345-64

Lester, F. (1980) 'Mathematical problem-solving research', in R. Shumway (ed.) *Research in Mathematics Education*, National Council of Teachers of Mathematics, Reston, Virginia

Levin, I. (1979) 'Interference of time-related and unrelated cues with duration comparisons of young children', *Child Development*, 50, 469-77

Lewis, C. (1981) 'Skill in algebra', in J. R. Anderson (ed.) *Cognitive Skills and their Acquisition*, Hillsdale, Erlbaum

Lovell, K. and Butterworth, T. (1966) 'Abilities underlying the understanding of proportionality', *Mathematics Teaching*, 37, 5-9

———— (1971) 'Some aspects of the growth of the concept of a function', in M. F. Rosskopf *et al.* (eds), *Piagetian Cognitive Developmental Research and Mathematical Education*, National Council of Teachers of Mathematics, Washington

Luchins, A. S. and Luchins, E. H. (1959) *Rigidity and Behaviour*, University of Oregon Press, Oregon

Lunzer, E. A. and Pumphrey, W. (1966) 'Understanding proportionality', *Mathematics Teaching*, 34, 7-12

Malin, J. T. (1979) 'Strategies in mathematical problem solving', *Journal of Educational Research*, 73, 101-8

Maury, S. (1985) 'Influence de la question dans un epreuve relative à la notion d'indépendance', *Educational Studies in Mathematics*, 16, 283-301

Mayer, R. E. (1977) *Thinking and Problem Solving*, Scott, Foresman, Glenview

———— (1982) 'Different problem-solving strategies for algebra word and equation problems', *Journal of Experimental Psychology*, 8, 448-62

———— (1983) *Thinking, Problem Solving, Cognition*, Freeman, New York

Mayer, S. E. (1967) *The Effect of Magnitude of Criterion Availability and Negative Validity upon Human Inference Behaviour*, Ohio State University, M.Sc. thesis

Mendelsohn, P. (1981) 'Analyse procedurale et analyse structurale des activités de permutation d'objets', *Archives de Psychologie*, 49, 171-98

Modgil, S. and Modgil, C. (1976) *Piagetian Research: Compilation and Commentary*, NFER, Slough

Moyer, J. C. (1978) 'The relation between the mathematical structure of Euclidean transformations and the spontaneously developed cognitive structures of young children', *Journal for Research in Mathematics Education*, 8, 83-92

Myers, J. L. *et al.* (1983) 'The role of explanation in learning elementary probability', *Journal of Educational Psychology*, 75, 374-81

Naylor, J. C. and Clark, R. D. (1968) 'Intuitive inference strategies in interval learning tasks as a function of validity magnitude and sign', *Organizational Behaviour and Human Performance*, 3, 378-99

Newell, A. and Simon, H. A. (1972) *Human Problem Solving*, Prentice-Hall, Englewood Cliffs

Noelting, G. (1980a) 'The development of proportional reasoning and the ratio concept, Part 1', *Educational Studies in Mathematics*, 11, 217-53

———— (1980b) 'The development of proportional reasoning and the ratio concept, Part 2', *Educational Studies in Mathematics*, 11, 331-63

Orton, A. (1970) *A Cross Sectional Study of the Development of the Mathematical Concept of Function in Secondary School Children of Average and Above Average Ability*, Leeds University, M.Ed. thesis

————— (1983a) 'Students' understanding of integration', *Educational Studies in Mathematics*, 14, 1-18

————— (1983b) 'Students' understanding of differentiation', *Educational Studies in Mathematics*, 14, 235-50

Perner, J. (1979) 'Discrepant results in experimental studies of young children's understanding of probability', *Child Development*, 50, 1121-7

Piaget, J. (1952) *The Child's Conception of Number*, Routledge, London

————— (1971) *The Child's Conception of Movement and Speed*, Routledge, London

————— and Inhelder, B. (1951) *La Genèse de l'Idée de Hazard chez d'Enfant*, PUF, Paris

————— and ————— (1956) *The Child's Conception of Space*, Routledge, London

————— *et al.* (1960) *The Child's Conception of Geometry*, Basic Books, New York

————— *et al.* (1968) *Epistémologie et Psychologie de la Fonction*, PUF, Paris

Polya, G. (1965) *Mathematical Discovery: On Understanding Learning and Teaching Problem Solving*, Vol. 2, Wiley, New York

Quintero, A. H. (1980) *The Role of Semantic Understanding in Solving Multiplication Word Problems*, Massachusetts Institute of Technology, Boston, Ph.D. thesis

————— (1981) 'Conceptual understanding in solving multiplication word problems', ERIC Doct. Repro. Service No. ED201497

————— (1983) 'Conceptual understanding in solving two-step word problems with a ratio', *Journal for Research in Mathematics Education*, 14, 102-12

Ricco, G. (1982) 'Les premières acquisitions de la notion de fonction linéaire chez l'enfant de 7 a 11 ans', *Educational Studies in Mathematics*, 13, 289-327

Roberge, J. J. (1976) 'Developmental analyses of two formal operational structures: combinatorial thinking and conditional reasoning', *Developmental Psychology*, 12, 563-4

————— and Flexer, B. K. (1979) 'Further examination of formal operations reasoning ability', *Child Development*, 50, 478-84

Rosnick, P. and Clement, J. (1980) 'Learning without understanding: the effect of tutoring strategies on algebra misconceptions', *Journal of Mathematical Behaviour*, 3, 3-27

Ross, B. M. and DeGroot, J. F. (1982) 'How adolescents combine probabilities', *Journal of Psychology*, 110, 75-90

Scardamalia, M. (1977) 'Information-processing capacity and the problem of horizontal decalage', *Child Development*, 48, 28-37

Schoenfeld, A. H. (1979) 'Explicit heuristic training as a variable in

problem-solving performance', *Journal for Research in Mathematics Education*, 10, 173-87
———— (1982) 'Measures of problem-solving performance and of problem-solving instruction', *Journal for Research in Mathematics Education*, 13, 31-49

Schultz, K. A. and Austin, J. D. (1983) 'Directional effects in transformation tasks', *Journal for Research in Mathematics Education*, 14, 95-101

Sellwood, R. (1973) 'Understanding of Infinitistic Reasoning Among Adults with and without Mathematical Training', B.Sc. project, Psychology Department, Birkbeck College, University of London

Siegel, S. and Andrews, J. (1962) 'Magnitude of reinforcement and choice behaviour in children', *Journal of Experimental Psychology*, 63, 337-41

Siegler, R. S. (1976) 'Three aspects of cognitive development', *Cognitive Psychology*, 8, 481-520
———— (1984) 'Mechanisms of cognitive growth', in R. J. Sternberg (ed.) *Mechanisms of Cognitive Development*, Freeman, New York

Sims-Knight, J. E. and Kaput, J. J. (1983) 'Exploring difficulties in transforming between natural language and image-based representations and abstract symbol systems in mathematics', in D. Rogers and J. A. Sloboda (eds), *The Acquisition of Symbolic Skills*, Plenum, New York

Slovik, P. (1974) 'Hypothesis testing in the learning of positive and negative linear functions', *Organizational Behaviour and Human Performance*, 11, 368-76

Sommerville, S. C. and Bryant, P. E. (1985) 'Young children's use of spatial co-ordinates', *Child Development*, 56, 604-13

Strauss, S. (1977) 'Curvilinear development in proportional reasoning', unpublished paper, University of Tel Aviv

Suarez, A. (1977) *Formales Denken und Funktionsbegriff bei Jugendlichen*, Hubes, Bern

Suydam, M. (1980) 'Untangling clues from research on problem solving', in S. Krulik (ed.), *Problem Solving in School Mathematics*, National Council of Teachers of Mathematics, Reston, Va.

Taback, S. F. (1969) *The Child's Concept of Limit*, Teachers College, Columbia University, New York, Ph.D. thesis

Tall, D. and Vinner, S. (1981) 'Concept image and concept definition in mathematics with particular reference to limits and continuity', *Educational Studies in Mathematics*, 12, 151-69

Thomas, H. L. (1975) 'The concept of function', in M. F. Rosskopf (ed.), *Children's Mathematical Concepts*, Teachers College Press, New York

Tourniaire, F. and Pulos, S. (1985) 'Proportional reasoning: a review of the literature,' *Educational Studies in Mathematics*, 16, 181-204

Tversky, A. and Kahnemann, D. (1974) 'Judgment under uncertainty:

heuristics and biases', *Science*, 125, 1124-31

————— and ————— (1979) 'Reply to Cohen', *Cognition*, 7, 408-22

Van Hiele, P. M. (1973) *Begrip en Insicht*, Muusses Purmerend, Netherlands

Vergnaud, G. *et al.* (1979) *La Coordination de l'Enseignement des Mathématiques entre le Cours moyen 2e Année et la Classe de 6e*, Institut Nationale de la Recherche Pedagogique, Paris

Wagner, S. (1981) 'Conservation of equation and function under transformations of variable', *Journal for Research in Mathematics Education*, 12, 107-18

Wallace, J. R. and Fonte, M. E. (1984) 'Piagetian and information processing approaches to chance and probability', *Journal of Genetic Psychology*, 144, 185-94

White, H. (1985) 'The development of combinatorial reasoning', *Journal of Genetic Psychology*, 145, 185-94

Wilkening, F. (1982) 'Children's knowledge about time, distance and velocity interrelations', in W. J. Friedman (ed.), *The Developmental Psychology of Time*, Academic Press, New York

Williams, A. (1980) 'Brief reports: High school students' understanding of proof', *Journal for Research in Mathematics Education*, 11, 239-41

Wollman, W. *et al.* (1979) 'Acceptance of lack of closure: is it an index of advanced reasoning?', *Child Development*, 50, 656-65

Yost, P. A. *et al.* (1962) 'Nonverbal probability judgments by young children', *Child Development*, 33, 769-80

Young, C. D. and Becker, J. P. (1979) 'Comparison of learning with sequences of figural and symbolic treatments of mathematical inequalities', *Journal of Research in Mathematics Education*, 10, 24-36

INDEX

To locate references to an author not in the main text, consult the bibliographies at the end of the book. Then consult this index and the Further Reading and Notes sections to that chapter to find the exact location.